Further praise for The Stakeholder Balance Sheet

"My 40 years of international business experience would completely endorse this total focus on the stakeholder balance sheet. The managers who get this right will set themselves apart by getting the perfect balance for long term success."
Sir Peter Bonfield CBE FREng, Chairman of NXP Supervisory Board and formerly CEO of BT Group plc and ICL plc

"Suntook and Murphy have distilled their wealth of experience into a book which makes useful practical suggestions for action which can improve company effectiveness. The book addresses the complexity of customers' decision making and suggests a systematic approach to marketing which allows an organisation to check itself against best standards."
Andrew Wright, Managing Director, Syngas & GTL Johnson Matthey Catalysts

"This thoughtful and innovative crossover book enhances our understanding of the complex processes that link many aspects of business strategy, with a specific focus on how best organizations can understand the stakeholders in their marketplace so as to enhance long-run financial performance. Utilizing a comprehensive checklist of questions at the end of each chapter, The Stakeholder Balance Sheet *is an excellent and highly practical framework for understanding these processes, monitoring the key dimensions of market performance, identifying areas for improvement in the organization, and modifying strategy to improve performance. This book is a must-read for decision makers in any organization, regardless of level or function."*
Professor Sharan Jagpal, Professor of Marketing, Rutgers Business School, and author of *Fusion for Profit: How Marketing and Finance Can Work Together to Create Value* (Oxford University Press 2008)

"All business leaders should read this book. For too long businesses have partially focused on one or two stakeholders such as customers or employees. This book provides a refreshing insight into the complementary relevance of all *stakeholders."*
Ronan Dunne, Chief Executive, Telefónica O2 UK

"An excellent book for directors reflecting on their organisation, or managers starting out in their career and wanting to get it right. The unique measurement tool introduced in the book provides an overall enterprise balance sheet relative to each stakeholder."
Mark Adams, CEO, Virgin Healthcare

"Focusing on customer satisfaction alone is insufficient to achieve business goals in today's complex marketplace. This must-read book provides managers with an actionable methodology to manage both internal and external stakeholders to build the 21st century brand."
Professor Sandeep Krishnamurthy, Associate Director of Graduate Services, University of Washington

THE STAKEHOLDER

BALANCE SHEET

THE STAKEHOLDER BALANCE SHEET

Profiting from Really Understanding Your Market

Farrokh Suntook
and
John A. Murphy

A John Wiley & Sons, Ltd., Publication

Other Wiley Editorial Offices

John Wiley & Sons Inc., 111 River Street, Hoboken, NJ 07030, USA

Jossey-Bass, 989 Market Street, San Francisco, CA 94103-1741, USA

Wiley-VCH Verlag GmbH, Boschstr. 12, D-69469 Weinheim, Germany

John Wiley & Sons Australia Ltd, 42 McDougall Street, Milton, Queensland 4064, Australia

John Wiley & Sons (Asia) Pte Ltd, 2 Clementi Loop #02-01, Jin Xing Distripark, Singapore
129809

John Wiley & Sons Canada Ltd, 6045 Freemont Blvd. Mississauga, Ontario, L5R 4J3, Canada

Wiley also publishes its books in a variety of electronic formats. Some content that appears
in print may not be available in electronic books.

Library of Congress Cataloging-in-Publication Data
Suntook, Farrokh.
  The stakeholder balance sheet : profiting from really understanding your
market / Farrokh Suntook and John A. Murphy.
     p.   cm.
  Includes bibliographical references and index.
  ISBN 978-0-470-71216-0 (cloth : alk.paper)   1. Stockholders.
2. Corporations—Investor relations.   I. Murphy, John A.   II. Title.
  HD2744.S86   2008
  332.63′2042—dc22   2008033255

British Library Cataloguing in Publication Data
A catalogue record for this book is available from the British Library

ISBN 978-0-470-71216-0

Typeset in 11.5/15pt Bembo by SNP Best-set Typesetter Ltd., Hong Kong
Printed and bound in Great Britain by TJ International Ltd, Padstow, Cornwall, UK

To our families

CONTENTS

ACKNOWLEDGEMENTS

It is a truism to say that few books result solely from the efforts of their authors. We would, first and foremost, like to thank our families for their endless patience and support while this book was in progress.

More particularly, we wish to extend our sincere thanks to: Rosie Hayes of Allianz, Uwe Ellinghaus of BMW, Laura Asiala of Dow Corning Corporation, Patrick van Waes of E.I. du Pont de Nemours and Joan Fredericks of Harris Interactive for agreeing to let us use proprietary material relating to their companies; Robin Gleaves of Kitshoff Gleaves for his valuable comments on an earlier draft of the book; Dr Ram Raghavan for sharing the results of research conducted when he was at Manchester Business School; Jackie Fisk of Manchester Business School for her ongoing assistance; Claire Plimmer and Jo Golesworthy of John Wiley & Sons for all their support at the publication stage of the book; and all those who, although not mentioned by name, gave their support and encouragement as the book progressed.

INTRODUCTION: WHY THIS BOOK?

The purpose of this book is to show what you need to look out for if you wish to win the hearts and minds – and therefore influence the behaviour – of your stakeholders. It is intended to offer you an overview of the ways in which you can harness such insights in order to grow your business profitably.

You may well regard your customers and prospects as your most important stakeholders, since their actions have a direct impact on your revenue and profits. However, there are other stakeholders as well – your staff (the 'internal stakeholders'), and a variety of 'external stakeholders', such as end users, consultants, intermediaries, the government, pressure groups, shareholders, creditors, the local community, non-governmental organisations, and so on. Whereas in most instances these stakeholders do not buy your goods and services, their views must be taken into account. This is because their attitudes are liable to influence those of your direct purchasers and because your actions may well be of concern to them.

In addition to the stakeholders, mentioned above, who influence your customers and prospects 'from the outside', the various individuals operating from *within* the organisation you are dealing with can also be regarded as stakeholders/influencers. These may include individuals with whom you do not deal directly but whose opinions and clout may well have a major impact on your relations with your direct contacts. This point applies most obviously to your customers and prospects but even among other stakeholders (for example, intermediaries) there could be individuals whose role in influencing decisions is not fully recognised. These people form the subject of a specific chapter (Decision-making dynamics).

Later there is a chapter on the attitudes and role of staff – your internal stakeholders – and in a separate chapter, we specifically address the role of external stakeholders. Among the external stakeholders, we have also included 'pure influencers'; these are the opinion formers, such as the media or financial analysts, who may not have a stake as such in the outcome of your actions (as pressure groups, for example, may have), but whose opinions can have a significant impact on how you are regarded in your marketplace. For the purpose of this book, we have bracketed these influencers together with external stakeholders. This is because they all have a role in influencing the attitudes of your immediate target market, and it is important therefore to keep them on your radar screen.

To summarise, therefore, when we talk about stakeholders, we are referring to:

- the direct stakeholders in the marketplace – customers and prospects
- the internal stakeholders – staff
- other external stakeholders – pressure groups, the local community, government, intermediaries, banks, etc., who influence the decisions of customers and prospects
- opinion leaders/formers – such as media and financial analysts – in so far as they are influential in shaping how you are regarded in your marketplace

- all the individuals within the organisations you deal with – including both the key contacts with whom you interface *and* others who may influence the final decisions made.

Notwithstanding what we have said about the various types of internal and external stakeholders, customers and prospects represent the most direct source of your business and are the ultimate arbiters of the success of your enterprise. This is the reason why much of the discussion in this book revolves round them. Having said this, most of the chapters in the book are relevant to a range of stakeholders – not just customers and prospects – and two are specifically about staff and other external stakeholders precisely because their influence on your direct customers can have an important, albeit indirect, impact on your business.

In order to attract and grow business profitably, you need, therefore, to address the needs and attitudes not only of your direct customers but also of all the other parties influencing customer decision making. Adverse publicity in the media can, for example, do a lot of damage to the image you have sought to build through the advertising and promotion activities you have directed at your customers and prospects.

Similarly, even though many of the topics addressed are discussed in the context of customers, they are also relevant to other stakeholders: for example, when considering approaches to better understand the mind of the market (in Chapter 2), we will find that many of these approaches, although obviously applicable to customers and prospects, can be adapted to gain an understanding of what drives the views and actions of other stakeholders as well.

The book is not intended to be yet another academic treatise on marketing and sales management. Effective marketing/sales management is, of course, essential to any successful organisation operating in a competitive environment. However, an important premise for this book is that a genuine understanding of how customers and other stakeholders think, feel and behave offers the essential starting point for any general manager – not just the marketing or sales specialist – seeking to determine the direction of his organization. To develop a company strategy without understanding what makes your stakeholders tick is akin to driving into unknown territory without a road map.

The book is, therefore, designed to provide you with a means of assessing your organisation's 'stakeholder balance sheet': what are the effective ways of being a truly stakeholder-sensitive enterprise, and how well does your organisation perform on those criteria?

We are talking here about an understanding of stakeholder needs, attitudes and behaviours which digs deeper than the surface response. For example, rather than regurgitating what our contacts in the marketplace tell us, we need to develop the 'corporate emotional intelligence' – to adapt a concept from the field of psychology and psychometrics – which will enable us to interpret their statements so as to arrive at an understanding of what they really feel. It is what customers and other stakeholders *feel*, not necessarily what they say, that determines their actions and choices and, therefore, your organisation's future.

It is certainly true that organisations at board level increasingly recognise – or at least pay lip service to – the importance of customers and other stakeholders. A growing number of companies even use customer-centric metrics as being key performance indicators (KPIs), much as they do with financial metrics.

However, much of the substantial body of market-focused literature is targeted at those – typically specialist marketing practitioners – for whom an understanding of thinking and behaviour in the marketplace is directly relevant. For this reason, bookshops are populated with heavyweight volumes, each dedicated to a specific topic such as customer satisfaction, or branding, or communication. The general manager may be hard pressed to find a book which provides an overview of all the key issues to be considered if the attitudes and behaviour of customers (and other stakeholders) are to be understood and acted upon appropriately.

In a relentlessly competitive environment, the general manager – whether a director or any senior/middle manager who may not have a specific market-facing responsibility – cannot afford the luxury of leaving the business of understanding customers and other stakeholders entirely in the hands of the 'experts'. No responsible CEO will say 'As long as my CFO tells me that the revenue and profit situation is fine, I really don't need to look at my company's balance sheet and income statement.' Equally, the general manager who genuinely wishes to drive a market-centric organisation should not feel content to leave the analysis of the stakeholder balance sheet entirely in the hands of the specialists in areas like marketing, PR, investor relations or customer analysis.

At the same time, when seeking to assess the financial strength of his organisation, the general manager does not need to do the CFO's job; he needs to know enough to understand what the financial information means for the health of his organisation and what action needs to be taken on the basis of this information. Similarly, the general manager does not need to become an 'expert' on how to understand the stakeholder, but he should know enough to make judgements about whether and what action needs to be taken to strengthen his organisation's position among the key players in the marketplace.

For all these reasons, this book is addressed to anyone with a managerial responsibility who is interested in what makes customers and other stakeholders tick. You may be someone with a 'market-facing' responsibility – a marketing or sales manager, for example – but the book is intended at least as much for the director or executive who has a general management responsibility. It is intended to empower you, as a manager with decision-making responsibility, with a way of thinking about your stakeholders' attitudes and behaviour which will in turn help you to make the right decisions. It is designed to show how well you really understand those who are in a position, directly or indirectly, to influence your business. On the basis of this, you can decide what further steps you may need to take to penetrate 'the mind of the stakeholder' so as to enhance the success of your organisation.

The concept of a stakeholder balance sheet reflects the practical, rather than academic, slant of this book. It stems from the need to rate your organisation in terms of its pluses and minuses – its 'assets' and 'liabilities' – as a stakeholder-sensitive enterprise. By this we mean an enterprise which:

- truly understands its market and all the key stakeholders operating within it
- utilises the appropriate tools to enhance its understanding, and
- harnesses that understanding to maximise commercial success.

The rating is done through the checklist of questions shown at the end of each chapter from Chapter 2 onwards. How well you can answer those questions will determine whether, and in which areas, your organisation's rating is positive or negative. A review of how well your organisation has fared on the questions will tell you how healthy your balance sheet is in relation to the topic of each chapter. And it will provide you with the basis for an overall enterprise balance sheet which aggregates the scores you have achieved in each topic area.

If you are a general manager not specialising in marketing or sales, you can use the checklists to ask pertinent questions of your market-facing experts. Just as CEOs may ask their CFOs what the underlying reason is for an unforeseen cost revealed in the company's financial statements, so it is hoped that the points raised in this book will provide you, as a 'generalist', with the wherewithal to ask the right questions about how your organisation's position in the marketplace may be strengthened.

If, conversely, you are in a market-facing role, the checklists should provide you with an aide-mémoire of the actions which you may need to take.

Our purpose is, therefore, not to provide a detailed treatise on each of the concepts and issues discussed; this can be provided by your marketing expert, or, if you are so inclined, by the many excellent books which dwell in greater depth on the individual topics. The intention, instead, is to provide you with the 'holistic' view you need when you wish to ensure that your organisation is doing the best it can in understanding, reaching and influencing the behaviour of your customers and other stakeholders.

One point relating to the use of the term 'customer': although the term, strictly speaking, applies to those currently giving you their business, we will also use it, where appropriate, as a short-hand to include your prospects. This is because many of the issues relevant to the understanding and influencing of customer attitudes and behaviour are identical to those applying to prospects: today's prospect may be tomorrow's customer, and the reverse is also true since a lost customer becomes a potential 'prospect'. Additionally, the term 'customer' is not confined to the direct customers (and prospects) who use your products or services, and may be applied to other parties involved in the purchasing process – for example, wholesalers/main distributors, subdistributors and retailers.

A couple of final points about the type of organisation to which this book is targeted:

- It should be emphasised that the idea of a stakeholder balance sheet is as relevant to business-to-business organisations as it is to businesses which directly serve consumers, and indeed a number of the case studies cited in the book relate to the former.
- Equally, much of the material in the book is relevant to public as well as private sector organisations; if the term 'company' or 'enterprise' is used, it is deployed as a shorthand for any

organisation which interfaces with customers, whether or not it is strictly speaking a company. It is true that there are some fundamental differences between private and public sector organisations, not least the competitive pressures felt by the former which often do not apply to the latter. It is a fallacy, however, to assume that the public sector enterprise needs to pay less attention to understanding the mind of the stake-holder: for example, a public sector organisation which is slow to understand what really satisfies its customers is liable not only to end up with a number of disgruntled customers; it is also likely to incur avoidable costs handling complaints. Even if the enterprise is not judged by its profitability, its cost over-runs are liable to place it under the pressure of increased public scrutiny. The principles, if not the detail, of the arguments set out in this book should therefore apply to the public as well as the private sector – although public sector organisations may wish to make sensible adaptations: the goal for them may not be to 'sustain and grow the market profitably' (as mentioned in the 9 point plan in Chapter 1) but rather to 'offer the best service to their customers, optimising the resources available to them'. Even if the objective is redefined in this way, the main elements of the 9 point plan remain relevant to them.

- Finally, although many of the examples cited in the book are, for obvious reasons, about large, well-known companies, the messages discussed are generally relevant to organisations of all sizes, from SMEs (small/medium sized enterprises) to multinationals.

CHAPTER 1

THE 9 POINT PLAN FOR SUSTAINING AND GROWING YOUR MARKET PROFITABLY

An important premise of this book is that, to achieve a genuine understanding of your marketplace, it is important for you, whether you are a general manager or a marketing/sales specialist, to have a holistic view of all the areas which are liable to impinge upon the way in which your organisation is regarded in the marketplace. This is for two reasons:

- *'If it's Tuesday, it must be market segmentation and customer satisfaction and branding and . . .'*: In the real world, customers and other stakeholders are being bombarded with a multitude of stimuli which work in combination, not in isolation, to shape their motivations and their attitudes towards your organisation. To take an obvious example, your customers' attitudes towards you are influenced not only by how satisfied they are with your service but also by how highly they regard your brand, a point elaborated upon later in the book. Yet many companies, marketing gurus and authors of marketing textbooks often focus on these topics as though each operates in a vacuum, divorced from the impact of what else is swirling around in the mind of the customer. The point being made here about customers applies to other stakeholders and opinion formers as well: how the financial community or the media see you, for example, is liable to be influenced not only by your financial performance but also by the image you project through communications activity, reports on how satisfied your customers are with you and evidence of new product/service development.

- *'2 plus 2 can make 5'*: Taking a holistic view enables you to see connections and draw conclusions which may be missed if each area of examination is considered in isolation. Let us return to the customer satisfaction and brand example. Say you are doing everything necessary to improve your service performance and make your customers satisfied, yet these efforts are not rewarded by enhanced satisfaction levels, let alone improved business performance. This disconnect could be explained if it were found that the organisation's brand strength fails to match its performance levels. This is because the evidence suggests that a strong brand can have a 'halo' effect on customer perceptions of service performance and, ultimately, on the organisation's business performance. Looking at customer satisfaction and brand 'side by side' can, therefore, offer insights which would be missed if each area of investigation were examined in isolation.

So what is the 9 point plan for sustaining and growing your market profitably? It is a summary of the key areas, shown in Figure 1.1, which you should review when assessing your organisation's competence in understanding your marketplace. A professional approach in all these areas will help you not only to strengthen your organisation's standing in your marketplace but

Figure 1.1   The 9 point plan for sustaining and growing your market profitably

also to place resources where they are most likely to make an impact; it is for this reason that an important aspect of the 9 point plan is the recognition of the need to take actions which enhance your company's profitability. For example, anyone can make customers happy by throwing resources at them, but it is only by knowing what is critical in influencing customer decision making that you can make the best use of your resources, thereby increasing profits.

The rest of this book will show how each of the nine areas shown in Figure 1.1 can be tackled so as to enhance your business. Figure 1.2 illustrates the fact that these areas can also influence one another. This point should become evident as we go through the various chapters, but here are a few examples of these interlocking influences:

- Segmenting your market (point 1 in Figure 1.1) enables you to identify the key drivers of decision making (point 2) within each market segment, thereby enabling you to adopt a

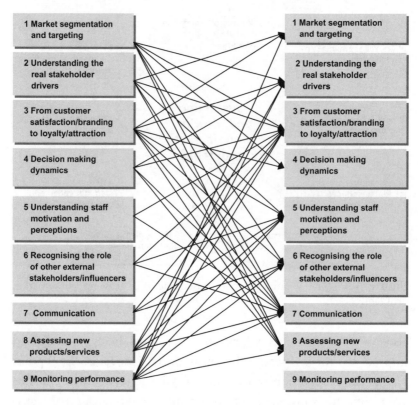

Figure 1.2 Interlocking influences

tailored, rather than a scatter gun, approach to your market;
it also reveals how customer attitudes (point 3) may vary from
one segment to the next. There can at the same time be a
reverse effect: knowing what drives your market (point 2) can
in turn form an important basis for your market segmentation
(point 1), as Chapter 2 will show.

•   Knowing the key market drivers (point 2) will help you to
better satisfy your customers (point 3), correct staff misperceptions about market needs and desires (point 5), communicate
more effectively by focusing on what really matters to your
target market (point 7) and offer new products and services
which are most likely to satisfy market requirements (point 8).

However, again there is a reverse effect: if you discover that your market is not satisfied with your performance (point 3), or that your new products/services are not as successful as planned (point 8), this may be because you are losing touch with market needs and focusing on the wrong offers, in which case you may need to revisit exactly what the key market drivers are (point 2).

The interlocking influences of the various areas of activity shown in Figure 1.2 reinforce the need, referred to earlier, for a holistic approach, which recognises that there are a number of factors, all operating in conjunction with one another, which can influence perceptions about your organisation in your marketplace.

The rest of this book will take each of the nine topics shown in Figure 1.1 one by one, starting with segmentation. For each topic, we will guide you through the factors which need to be taken into account if you are to maximise the strength of your organisation's stakeholder balance sheet. As Figure 1.1 shows, each of these topics has a bearing on your ability to sustain and grow your market profitably. And, as already mentioned, it is by considering these areas in combination, rather than in isolation, that you can make the greatest impact on your marketplace.

CHAPTER 2

IN THE BEGINNING WAS ... SEGMENTATION!

WHY IS MARKET SEGMENTATION THE FIRST STEP?

In many markets, to approach a market without attempting to segment it is to approach it blind. In one sense, we all segment our markets, even if we don't do so consciously. If you were asked to think about the market you are operating in, you would almost certainly visualise it in a way which breaks it down in some manner: you operate a retail chain, for example, in France and Germany; or you produce specialty chemicals for the domestic appliance, textiles and automotive sectors; or your strategy is to focus your management consultancy service on large, blue chip multinationals, avoiding SMEs. In the first instance, you have 'segmented' your market in terms of geography, in the second by industry sector, and in the third by company size/value.

In this respect, some form of segmentation forms part of the 'business DNA' of most organisations serving most markets. It has to be a first step at the very least because it is difficult for us to define our customers, prospects and other stakeholders without instantly thinking about the key differences between them, as we see them.

The trouble is that this form of 'visual' segmentation is not enough as the basis of a successful business and marketing strategy. The next sections explain why this is the case and summarise what makes for successful market segmentation. However, it is worth first reviewing the fundamental reasons why segmentation should, for many organisations, be the initial step in the development and harnessing of insights into the market in which you are operating:

- Segmentation, if correctly done, enables you to tailor your offerings to suit the conditions and requirements of each segment; you are, therefore, likely to create more satisfied customers who, all other things being equal, will be more loyal to you and buy more from you – thereby boosting your business.

- Segmentation enables you to adapt your marketing activity to suit the circumstances of each segment; as a result, you are avoiding the waste which would occur if you conveyed generalised, 'scatter gun' messages to your market.

- The process of segmentation enables you to prioritise those segments which are most valuable to you; this means that you can allocate your resources in favour of those segments at the expense of others which may not be so lucrative.

- Through segmentation you are able to know how customers, prospects and other stakeholders regard you within each segment and how strong the fit is between what you have to offer and what the market expects from you; you are able, therefore, to make strategic choices which you would not be able to do without this knowledge.

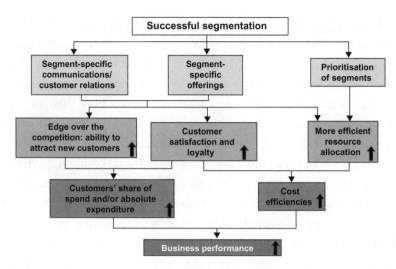

Figure 2.1 Successful segmentation → loyalty/attraction → business performance

In short, segmentation, if properly done, has a favourable impact on your business performance, a point illustrated in Figure 2.1.

The pivotal role of segmentation in a company's strategy means that much of the discussion in later chapters of this book should be viewed through a 'segmentation lens'. For example, when considering what drives your market (Chapter 3), how satisfied customers are (Chapter 4), how best to communicate with the market (Chapter 8), or what new offerings are most likely to appeal (Chapter 9), you may find it far more effective to look at these issues by segment. Whereas you need to cater for the commonalities which may exist between the various segments of your market, it is at least as important to recognise the differences between them.

Throughout this chapter, the discussion about market segmentation tends to focus on customers (current or prospect) but market segments can also be analysed in terms of the other stakeholders who may have a role to play in your market: do these stakeholders vary by market segment and do some have more influence in some segments than in others? To take a familiar example, in segments characterised by small end customers, intermediaries may have a more important role to play than in segments with higher value customers. Sometimes, the distinction between a customer and another stakeholder (like an intermediary) can become blurred and that raises questions about who should be the primary target of your activity; for example, how much of your marketing and sales effort should be focused on the end customer if he is strongly influenced by the advice given by a broker? The roles of the different types of stakeholders/influencers are discussed in greater detail in Chapter 7. In this chapter, however, for the reasons given, although we may refer to 'customers' for shorthand, it should be borne in mind that much of the discussion may be equally applicable to other stakeholders.

Before we move to the next section (on successful market segmentation), we need to highlight an exception to the rule that segmentation is an important first step. This applies to niche products and services or products and services for which the universe of customers is small. The need for segmentation is predicated on the assumption that you are serving a sufficiently broad and diverse market with a reasonably mainstream product or service which can be widely applied and sold in some volume. Clearly, if you are a provider of a niche product which is of interest to only a very narrow group of potential customers there may be no point in seeking to segment your market. Equally, if you are a manufacturer of, say, specialist mining machinery and 80% of your business comes from large customers whom you can count on the fingers of one hand, segmentation becomes meaningless.

So far so obvious. However, the number of enterprises for whom segmentation may *not* be relevant is, if anything, likely to be increasing. This is because the use of the internet as a medium for selling products and services has meant that niche products with narrow, specialist applications can increasingly be introduced relatively inexpensively without the need to find out in advance where the demand for the product is likely to lie. In the past, putative niche suppliers may have been deterred from launching their product because finding customers would have been like looking for a needle in a haystack. Now, however, any budding entrepreneur can, with relatively low risk, try introducing his offering in the hope that someone somewhere will buy it: the customer comes to him, so he does not need to look out for the customer. Among the billion or so people on line, only a tiny fraction of this number may need to find the niche product for the business to be commercially viable. This is precisely the point made so effectively by Chris Anderson in his book *The Long Tail: Why the Future of Business is Selling Less of More* (2006).

Having made this caveat, there remain a huge number of mainstream organisations for whom segmentation remains critically important, and the rest of this chapter is addressed to them.

SO WHAT IS SUCCESSFUL MARKET SEGMENTATION ALL ABOUT?

There are a number of ways in which market segmentation may be defined, and any definition will do if it encompasses all the following criteria:

- The market in which you are operating is broken down into homogeneous groups defined by similar features.
- The segmentation should enable you to reach customers, target prospects and other stakeholders in a way which caters for their requirements, attitudes, values or intentions – the 'soft' issues.

- The segmentation should be relevant and meaningful to your business.
- The segmentation should be multidimensional, not single-dimensional.

Let us look at each of these points one by one.

Breaking the market up into homogeneous groups

If you are operating internationally, you could logically break your global marketplace down by country. So France may represent a 'segment', as may Germany, Argentina, the US or Japan. Here a common feature in each instance is the nationality of the customers or prospects.

Catering for requirements, attitudes, intentions and values

The fact that the people in the US are US nationals and the people in Argentina are Argentine nationals may not be useful if the only feature which binds the members of these 'segments' is nationality. The reality of the marketplace is, in fact, almost certainly more complex: what if there are some Americans who have needs or attitudes similar to those of some Argentinians but different from those of other Americans? Then wouldn't it be more helpful to treat the Americans and Argentinians who share common views as being a single segment?

To take an example adapted from a real case study, a global manufacturer of food supplements viewed its market through a geographical lens, the market in this instance being all those who influenced the purchase of their healthy food products – for example, doctors, nutritionists and retail outlets. So there were

American doctors, nutritionists and retailers, their Singaporean counterparts, their Argentine counterparts, and so on. When the food supplements company undertook a professional investigation of its market, however, it discovered that the greatest commonality of needs and attitudes was among the functional groups (doctors, nutritionists, etc.), *irrespective of geography*, there being less homogeneity within the geographies themselves. In other words, US and Argentine doctors had more in common with one another than US doctors had with US nutritionists; and the doctors as a group, wherever they were located, were in some respects quite distinct in their attitudes and behaviours from the nutritionists. This discovery led the food supplements manufacturer to undergo a radical rethink of the way in which it viewed and segmented its global marketplace, far greater emphasis being placed on the specific concerns and intentions of the different functional groups. Now doctors, wherever they happened to be, were being targeted as a group distinct from nutritionists, which were targeted as another, separate group. Geographic differences did remain, but they were no longer treated as the primary basis for segmenting the market.

Segmentation, if it digs deeper than the superficial demographics, can, therefore, have a material impact on the way you map your marketplace and on the marketing strategy and action you pursue as a result of that mapping.

The segmentation should be relevant and meaningful to your business

To take an obvious example, if you run an international fashion business, French and German women may, in the context of your particular business, have more in common with one another than French women have with French men and, similarly, German women have with their male counterparts − in which case a segmentation based on nationality may be far less relevant than a segmentation based on gender.

Similarly, if some women prefer blue tinted contact lenses and others prefer green tinted lenses, this information is clearly relevant to a manufacturer of contact lenses but irrelevant to a couturier – unless it is found that women want the colour of their clothing to match the colour of their contact lenses!

The segmentation should be multidimensional, not single-dimensional

It should be obvious by now that the reality of any marketplace is complex: to take a single dimension, like geography, as the basis for your market segmentation is to oversimplify what is actually happening in your market. There are probably a host of other factors, operating in combination with geography, which may determine what makes one segment different from another: in the food supplements case study mentioned earlier, we found that functional group, as well as (to a lesser extent) geography, influenced the mapping of the marketplace. But the reason why functional groups were found to be relevant was that each of the groups was internally homogeneous (and externally distinct from the other groups) by virtue of its *distinctive needs and attitudes*. So, as mentioned earlier, needs, attitudes, intentions, and so on – the 'soft' issues – should be thrown into the mix when considering the most effective way of segmenting the market; simply confining oneself to one or a few dimensions based on 'hard' market features (in this case, geography or functional group) is not enough.

Why are hard market characteristics – demographics (or, in business-to-business markets, 'firmographics') – not enough? Although they are an important aspect of the segmentation process, they do not fully explain what segmentation is all about, because:

1. demographics tell you about the people or businesses you should target – *who* the targets are, but not . . .
2. what will appeal to them and make the greatest impact on them – *how* they should be reached.

To know, for example, that you need to target profitable customers is self-evidently important, but if you don't know how to target them your efforts may be wasted. It is only when you know about the requirements, attitudes and intentions of your profitable customers that you can understand what you need to do to cater for their concerns. It may well be that not all profitable customers have the same concerns, in which case the 'profitable' segment may itself need to be broken down into further subsegments defined in terms of these softer issues.

However, just as the hard issues without the soft issues only offer you part of the picture, so a knowledge of the soft issues without a knowledge of the relevant hard factors may be well-nigh useless. You may, for example, realise that some customers and prospects are highly price-sensitive, whereas others are driven more by quality considerations; if, however, you haven't been able to define the common demographic characteristics of these price-sensitive customers, it is difficult to undertake marketing activity which will effectively reach them.

So . . .

It is only by knowing *both* who the targets should be – in terms of demographics/firmographics – *and* how they should be reached – in terms of the messages you should convey and the most effective ways of communicating with them – that you can maximise the effectiveness of your segmentation.

SUCCESSFUL MARKET SEGMENTATION IS THE STARTING POINT FOR YOUR BUSINESS AND MARKETING STRATEGY

It should be clear by now that, once you have segmented your market, you are in a position to know how you stand, vis-à-vis your competitors, within each segment. You are able to form an action plan designed to maximise the potential for profitable growth offered by each segment. This is done by focusing, within each segment, on the strengths which you can capitalise on and the key areas for improvement which you need to address. The marketing and sales activity you undertake may, therefore, vary significantly from one segment to the next.

The scope to adapt your positioning according to the needs and demands of individual segments may, however, be limited. This is because an approach which is too chameleon-like can weaken the fundamental values which your organisation may stand for. Without segmentation, you are in danger of satisfying nobody by offering the same thing to everybody. Conversely, however, significant changes in the way your organisation is positioned, to suit the circumstances of individual segments, can jeopardise the equity of your brand and confuse your target market: you may be seen to stand for nothing, losing your distinctive market profile. So how do you adapt your offering without risking this danger?

Dow Corning Corporation, a specialty chemicals company, faced precisely this dilemma. As a result of market segmentation, it realised that there was a segment which desired a low cost product, with no more than a basic level of service. The company had, however, developed over the years a strong premium position. It prided itself on the quality of its product and service – second to none in its business – and charged a price which matched its premium positioning. How was it to alter its position to suit the demands of one segment – the 'no frills' segment – without seriously jeopardising the premium position which it had built over the years and which had worked well in all the other segments? Equally important, how was it to ensure that, by offering a low cost service to this segment, it would not unwittingly cannibalise its premium business?

The company answered these questions by coming up with a radical solution: in addition to its main 'Dow Corning' brand, it launched a totally new brand, with a new name (Xiameter),[1] a lower cost, no frills service which depended heavily on an e-business model. Through clever marketing and advertising, the company succeeded in conveying to the market that, although the new brand and the established parent brand were connected, they were also quite different in their positioning and in their value propositions. The company's strategy turned out to be highly successful, with the new brand doing well and the established brand's premium positioning remaining untarnished.

The experience of Dow Corning shows precisely how fundamental segmentation can be to the business and marketing strategy of an organisation – in this case resulting in a totally new brand offering.

In the case of this company, the opportunity to offer a new service was *discovered* through the segmentation process: the market segmentation was undertaken and it was then found that there was a specific no frills segment. However, segmentation can be used in a reverse way: if you are planning to introduce a new product or service which you are developing or have already developed, segmentation can help you to identify which parts of the market are going to be particularly receptive to the new offering.

In other words, you can proactively use segmentation as a way of identifying where your new product or service is most likely to be successful. Figure 2.2 illustrates the case of a company introducing an energy-related product which was designed for business

---

[1] 'Dow Corning' and 'Xiameter' are registered trademarks of the Dow Corning Corporation.

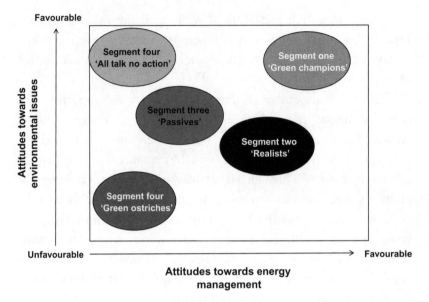

Figure 2.2   Identifying segments that offer the best opportunities for your new product/service

users. The company undertook a segmentation exercise in which attitudes towards energy management and towards environmental issues in general were two critical dimensions determining the extent to which users were likely to be interested in the new product. As a result of the segmentation, five distinct segments were established, ranging from the most enthusiastic in terms of environmental issues and energy management (the 'green champions') to those at the opposite end of the spectrum (the 'green ostriches'). Interestingly, because of the nature of the product developed by the company, the best opportunity was felt by the company to lie not with the 'green champions' but rather with the 'realists'; if the new offering had been positioned differently, the greatest opportunity may well have lain in the 'green champions' segment. This illustrates how, in this instance, the right segment was being found for a product already being developed – whereas in the previous chemicals company example it was the discovery of the segments which led to the development of the new offering.

TARGETING INDIVIDUALS AND ORGANISATIONS AS WELL AS SEGMENTING THE MARKET

Market segmentation is, by definition, about group activity; it is about the individual group whose members share characteristics which are common to them but different from those of other groups. As we have seen, segmentation, when properly done, has implications for your business strategy, your marketing activity and your overall resource allocation.

In the real world, however, you are also dealing with the specific individual or organisation (as a customer, a prospect or another stakeholder). This gives rise to two important questions:

- How do we prioritise specific individuals or organisations? – a question which is particularly pertinent to business-to-business markets in which the Pareto (80/20) rule may apply.
- How do we make the connection between market segmentation and the individual/organisation – in other words, how do we know to which segments particular individuals or organisations belong so that we know how best to approach them?

Prioritising individuals and organisations

The reference just made to Pareto makes sense if, for example, you are prioritising your customers on the basis of the amount of business they give you. In that context, it may well be that, say, 80% of your revenue comes from 20% of your customers.

Arguably, however, prioritisation of customers is more effective if it is based on the amount of profit you can gain from each customer. Here, Pareto understates the case because in reality not only are there different customers offering you different amounts of profit but also there are customers who are actually making a loss for your organisation. KPMG Consulting has found, for example, that often 25–33% of customers are unprofitable. The work done by the consultants KitshoffGleaves has revealed an even more extreme result: in their experience as much as 225% of profits can be derived from as few as 20% of customers, with the remaining 80% contributing minus 125% – in other words, their findings show that the Pareto rule can be redefined as 20% of customers make their suppliers a profit, the remaining 80% being loss-making. Whatever the exact figures, Pareto, if anything, understates the critical importance of prioritising customers.

The profit potential of individual customers may be connected with a number of factors, for example:

- *The size/overall value of the customer*: Overall value is often defined in terms of the customer's lifetime value; it stands to reason that, *all other things being equal*, a customer who gives you more business is likely to offer you more profit than one who gives you less business.
- *The cost to serve that customer*: All other things are often not equal, and, if a customer is relatively costly to serve, greater size/value may not be sufficient to compensate for such higher cost because the absolute profit derived from that customer may be less than that offered by a smaller customer. A simple illustration of this point is shown in Figure 2.3, where we see that Customer B, although more valuable than Customer A, is also far more costly to serve; if the 45 degree line represents a nil profit situation (i.e. where the absolute value of the customer, defined in terms of revenue, is equal to the cost to serve that customer), then any position above that line repre-

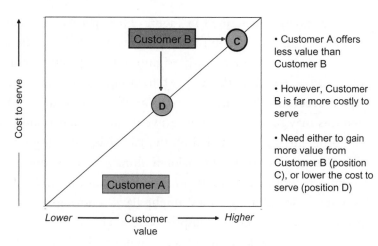

Figure 2.3 Targeting the customer

sents a loss and any position below the line represents a profit. Here Customer B is clearly making a loss for the supplier, and Customer A makes a profit, even though the former is larger than the latter. In order to reach at least a break-even situation with Customer B, you either need to draw more value out of that customer by moving it to position C or you need to reduce the cost and time spent in serving the customer so that it moves to position D.

Even if the absolute level of profit you derive from Customer B is greater than that gained from Customer A, Customer B may be less profitable in *relative* terms − that is, the cost to serve : value ratio is less favourable for Customer B than it is for Customer A. To take a simple example, Customer B may offer twice as much business as Customer A but the absolute profit gained from the former is significantly less than twice that gained from the latter. In that case, it may be advantageous for you to have two medium size Customer A-type customers than to have a single large Customer B.

The situation described in Figure 2.3 is particularly likely to apply in business-to-business markets where the cost to serve any one customer can be significant. In practice, companies often fall into the trap of focusing so hard on their largest accounts that they lose track of the fact that those accounts may be proving an excessive drain on their resources. The problem is compounded by the fact that, on many occasions, companies, including major multinationals, do not have the information enabling them to trace costs to individual accounts – so, although they might have a strong suspicion that the key accounts are disproportionately costly to serve, they have no reliable means of quantifying their view. Reducing the cost to serve such customers is made all the more difficult because of the 'relationship trap' into which the companies fall: they are too worried to do anything which may conceivably jeopardise what is often a personal relationship between the key account manager and the customer contact; the worry is often not only about putting off the customer but also about putting the account manager's nose out of joint. In addition, companies do not wish to risk losing a 'prestige' customer because of the adverse publicity such a loss may generate and the potential impact on staff morale.

Retaining key, high profile accounts, even if they are over-costly to serve, may be a justifiable course of action if the (non-financial) disadvantages of losing them are felt to outweigh the financial cost of keeping them. There is no justification, however, for focusing on potentially unprofitable customers just because there is no reliable information about the cost to serve them; however difficult it may be to trace costs accurately to individual customers, every effort should be made to do so since even indicative data can help the company to direct its efforts towards those customers who are relatively profitable.

- *The prospect of growing business with the customer*: The wise company will evaluate its customers not only in terms of the current value or profit they offer but also in terms of potential business opportunities; future prospects may be influenced by:
  - the likelihood of the customer offering a greater share of its business to the company, and/or
  - the likelihood that the absolute value of business coming from that customer will grow – for example, because the customer organisation itself is expected to grow and prosper.
- *The loyalty of the customer*: As Chapter 4 (on loyalty) discusses at some length, a genuinely loyal customer will be more attractive to you than a disloyal customer, all other things being equal, simply because that customer is likely to give you a greater share of spend, business from that customer is more predictable and such a customer may be less costly to serve. So customer attitudes and behaviour – as represented here by loyalty – as well as more 'quantifiable' factors (like value and growth) are important considerations when customers are being prioritized.

This section has tended to focus on the individual customer, but, as mentioned earlier, the points made can apply just as well to other stakeholders: returning to the earlier example of the food supplements manufacturer, the key targets for that company were not the ultimate customers – the consumers of the supplements; they were instead the doctors, the nutritionists and the retail outlets who, as specifiers and distributors of the supplements, had the main influence on what the consumers finally bought. The targeting task for the supplements manufacturer was, therefore, to identify which of these specifiers and distributors were the most valuable for the manufacturer to focus on.

Making the connection between market segmentation and the individual or organisation

In addition to the prioritisation of the individuals/organisations to be targeted, there is the question of how they can be linked to market segments. This question would be more or less irrelevant if segmentation boiled down to demographics/firmographics: if your segmentation were based purely on geography, for example, then it would be quite obvious that any French person falls into the segment called 'France'. As explained earlier, however, for segmentation to be useful, it needs to reflect the complexity of the marketplace – which means that it must be multidimensional and take into account the relevance of soft as well as hard issues.

Going back to the case of Dow Corning, which discovered a no frills segment, how was it to know, for example, whether or not a particular prospect fell into that segment? If the answer to this type of question is known, you have the opportunity to make genuine enhancements to your Customer Relationship Management (CRM) activity and thereby achieve greater effectiveness in attracting and retaining your customers. This is because knowing that a particular prospect falls within a 'needs' segment which has already been identified enables you to anticipate what his needs and wants are likely to be, so that you can tailor your approach to that prospect.

Traditionally, however, CRM has often been a term used to describe efficient, IT-driven, methods of handling customers and prospects – methods which have been developed primarily because of the drive for cost efficiencies benefiting the supplier rather than for an improved service benefiting the customer. A *Financial Times* survey quoted reports from Gartner and the META Group which estimated that the majority of CRM projects were unsuccessful. The problem, as the *FT* suggested, was that CRM was seen by many companies as a technology-based solution. The failure of many CRM initiatives is hardly surprising: if the key word in 'Customer Relationship Management' – relationship – is neglected, your CRM activity is liable to lead to dissatisfaction and alienation on the part of the very people you are targeting. If it is possible, however, to anticipate in advance what the key factors are likely to be in driving the choices made by an individual prospect, your CRM activity switches from being supplier- to customer-focused.

So how can market segmentation help us to develop a more customer-focused CRM approach? Typically, market segmentation which takes into account all the relevant soft and hard factors is done through market research and modelling approaches – which we will not go into here because a description of these would form the subject of another book. Suffice it to say for the time being that an analytical approach which research methodologists call 'Discriminant Modelling' can be utilised as a way of identifying those characteristics (whether hard or soft) which most strongly discriminate one segment from another. Thus it is possible, through information on how a relatively small number of such characteristics apply to the individual customer, to know whether a particular customer or prospect is likely to fall into one or other segment. Such information can be relatively easily gathered in the normal course of doing business – for example, by requesting the customer to complete a short questionnaire in the course of a sales call.

This process enables you, over time, to build up a powerful database of customers and prospects which contains not only the usual information – names, functions/titles, addresses, telephone numbers, email addresses, etc. – but also, for each contact on the database, the segment to which that contact is most likely to belong. The simplified diagram in Figure 2.4 illustrates the point.

Armed with such information, your direct marketing activity can be tailored to the requirements and circumstances of individual targets. Similarly, your sales team will be more confident about

Company name	Title	Initial	Surname	Function	Address	Post code	Likely segment
Abacus Limited	Mr	A	Boulder	Chief Buyer	3 Sorbonne Close	M26 4CA	3
Browings Corporation	Mr	M	Rosenburg	Technical Director	Dalston Business Park	M32 3DB	2
Consolied Metabolics dat	Mr	R	Blakeway	Production Manager	Marylebone Road	M27 2PQ	6
Doring Enterprises	Ms	S	Thornton	General Manager	Laycock	M31 6LM	1
Eagle Foods	Mr	L	Mayhew	CEO	Longmeadow	M42 5RS	4
Francis Bacon PLC	Mr	Q	Wraysbury	Design Consultant	Dillingham Road	M29 2AB	5

Figure 2.4   Targeting customers more effectively through segment allocation

conveying appropriate messages – especially to prospects who, unlike existing customers, may not be known to them. Therefore, if, for example, Segment 3 is the most price-driven, no frills segment within your marketplace, your sales people know that it is likely to be a waste of time trying to sell your latest premium-end added value offering to Abacus Limited. Later in this book (in Chapter 6 on staff motivations and perceptions) we make the point that there is often insufficient communication between front-line staff and management: sales people, for example, may fail to provide their organisations with enough feedback on their customers, but, *equally*, they are not always provided with the information they need to maximise the effectiveness of their sales approaches. Information on segment membership, as shown in Figure 2.4, is one example of how management can help their sales staff to make an impact when approaching prospects. This type of information is all the more powerful because it can help to differentiate your offering from that of your competitors by showing potential customers that your organisation really understands their specific needs and wants.

To summarise, segmentation, through the process of Discriminant Modelling, can enhance your CRM activity and enable you to use your database as a genuinely active marketing tool. All too often, databases are used as a passive source of customer/prospect information – a means of providing us with the most basic contact details and reminding you about 'who is out there'. Of course, you do need to get the basics right: however clever you have been in establishing that Abacus Limited is likely to belong to Segment 3, that will not be very helpful if the contact details for the company are wrong or out of date – as is sadly all too often the case even among the most marketing-savvy global multinationals!

THE EXECUTIVE SELF-ASSESSMENT CHECKLIST: SEGMENTATION

Here, and at the end of every chapter that follows, we have a checklist of questions for you to answer, which becomes the basis for assessing your stakeholder balance sheet. If you are a general manager, you should, where necessary, interrogate the 'experts' within your organisation to confirm whether they can answer the questions. If you are a specialist in a market-facing position, you may wish to check how confidently you can answer each question yourself.

The purpose of these checklists is three-fold:

1. To tell you how much your company does know and what is being done in the areas addressed; this will enable you to identify the gaps in knowledge which need to be filled and the activities which need to be undertaken.
2. If you are a generalist, to establish how much you are in touch with the issues raised – going back to the financial statements analogy mentioned in the Introduction to this book, how well can you read the stakeholder balance sheet even if it is not your function to be the expert on the topic? And if you are a specialist, to find out how much you are on top of all the areas that come within your remit and to identify your areas of relative strength or weakness.
3. Most important, to enable you to undertake an action plan tackling the key areas to be addressed.

A few notes on how you should score your organisation:

1. Score yourself:
    -   +3 if the answer is a confident 'yes'
    -   0 if a tentative 'yes' reflecting partial knowledge which nonetheless has some value to it
    -   −3 if a
        -   'no'
        -   a tentative 'yes' which is based more on wishful think-ing and conjecture than on partial knowledge which has genuine value
        -   'yes, but we do this badly'
        -   'don't know'.

2. For each chapter, add up your +3, 0 and −3 scores, to arrive at a net absolute score. Divide that net score by the number of questions to arrive at an average net score. That average net score should fall within the +3 to −3 spectrum. An example of how the scoring works: assume there are 30 ques-tions in a particular chapter, of which 15 result in a +3 score, 5 result in a 0 score and 10 result in a −3 score. This results in a net absolute score of +15 (+45 and −30), which, divided by the 30 questions, results in a net average score of +0.5.

3. The advantage of using the average score, rather than the absolute score, is that your balance sheet performance is not influenced by the number of questions and you can therefore make a fair comparison of your performance on the various chapter topics.

4. Where you feel that a question genuinely does not apply to your organisation, then mark the 'NA' ('not applicable') box; for example, there are a number of questions on the prioritisa-tion of individual players in your marketplace which you may feel are not so applicable to your business because there are no real reasons why one customer should be significantly more important to you than another (as may be the case in mass

consumer markets). The 'NA' box has no score attached to it, so the question which has 'NA' against it will not count in the final scoring.

Having calculated your net average score, you can assess how you have performed against the theoretical maximum score of +3 and the theoretical minimum of −3. The following is a guide to your assessment:

+3	+2	+1	0	−1	−2	−3
Excellent	Good	So-so	Watch it!	Poor	On the brink	

The score of +0.5, shown in the calculation above, would on this basis fall into the 'so-so' category.

If you feel that a particular question could be reworded to better suit your circumstances, please feel free to modify it; the checklist should be treated as a starting point in the assessment of how stakeholder-sensitive your organisation is and should be used flexibly in a way which best suits your purposes.

There is another way in which the checklist can be used flexibly: the questions here (and at the end of the other chapters) have not been prioritised, since individual questions may be more important to some organisations than to others; this should not, however, stop you from setting your own priorities to suit the specific conditions applying to your organisation.

After the checklist, there is a final, critical, question which applies to each of the earlier questions asked within the checklist: this is a question about what you are doing in practice, or, if you are not doing anything, why not. If, for example, you have answered 'yes, confident' to the question about whether you use segmentation as a starting point for your business strategy, then the follow-up question should be about what you do in practice: ask yourself (or your experts) how this has been done, how it has worked out in practice, what improvements you could initiate to make the process even more effective, etc. If your answer is 'yes, tentative' or 'no', then the line of questioning should focus on why you are not doing more and what you could do.

Question	Yes, confident +3	Yes, tentative 0	No −3	NA
Do we consciously segment our market?				
Do we use segmentation as an important starting point for our company's business and marketing strategy?				
Do we recognise that segmentation is multidimensional?				
Is our segmentation based on soft factors as well as demographics/ firmographics?				
Do we tailor our offerings to suit the requirements, attitudes and features of individual segments?				
Do we adapt our marketing activity to suit the circumstances of each segment?				
Do we prioritise our market segments?				
Do we know how we are regarded within each segment, vis-à-vis the competition?				

Question	Yes, confident +3	Yes, tentative 0	No −3	NA
Have we addressed the potential conflict which may arise between our overall corporate positioning and our segment-specific strategies?				
Have we developed action plans which take into account the segments we serve?				
Do we use segmentation to help us find out where a new product/ service offering is likely to have the greatest potential?				
Do we prioritise individual players in our market (customers, prospects or other stakeholders)?				
Do we have a reasonable idea of the cost to serve these individual players?				
If we are not confident about the cost to serve them, are we at least making active efforts to get this information?				
When prioritising the individual players, do we take into account the cost to serve them as well as the business they offer?				
Do we take active steps to increase or decrease the amount of effort and cost we invest in individual players by comparing the value they offer with the cost to serve them?				

Question	Yes, confident +3	Yes, tentative 0	No −3	NA
Do we monitor our priority customers/other stakeholders in terms of their requirements and attitudes towards us (i.e. what their expectations are, how highly they regard us, how loyal they are to us, etc.)?				
Do we monitor our priority customers/other stakeholders in terms of their own activity, growth and future prospects?				
Do we know what drives individual customers/other stakeholders in their decision making (e.g. through knowing which 'needs' segments they belong to)?				
Have we enhanced our database/ CRM activity by incorporating the needs and attitudes of the individuals/ organisations in our database?				
Do we adapt our direct marketing and sales activity to suit the needs and profile of these individuals/ organisations?				
GRAND TOTAL SCORE				
NET ABSOLUTE SCORE				
NET AVERAGE SCORE				

Now, taking each of the above questions, what in practice are we doing?

CHAPTER 3

DELVING INTO THE MIND OF THE MARKET – UNDERSTANDING THE REAL STAKEHOLDER DRIVERS

FROM MARKET DRIVERS TO BUSINESS PERFORMANCE – A STEP-BY-STEP APPROACH

Achieving a genuine understanding of what truly drives stake-holder decision making is a key challenge we all face. When seeking business from customers, it is all too easy to say 'It all boils down to price'; the evidence suggests that, whereas the perception that you are not offering a fair price is undoubtedly an important reason why customers may not buy from you, there are a host of other factors which you may be able to leverage more effectively to your advantage.

In any particular situation in which you are negotiating with a purchaser, you may be able to see the direct impact on your business of what you are offering to that purchaser: if, for example, you offer a reduced price to a price-sensitive customer you may well win a deal at the expense of your competitors. At the level of the individual customer, therefore, the impact of a particular action can often be traced to a direct outcome.

However, at a broader, more strategic level, how do you convince yourself that a policy you have adopted can be directly traceable to improved business performance? If, for example, you have decided to offer a more personalised call centre service enabling the customer or prospect to speak immediately to a real human being rather than a recorded set of instructions, how do you know that this change has materially improved your business performance in terms of, say, increased revenue? If you seek to make a direct link between the improved call centre service and your business performance, the answer will usually be 'with difficulty'. This is not least because there are a host of other factors which may at the same time be influencing the people you are targeting; how do you know, for example, that, rather than your improved call centre service, it is the customers' unhappy experience with one of your competitors which is more instrumental in moving them to give you a greater share of their business?

The answer to this sort of question is critically important because huge investments can be made in the attempt to strengthen your market position, and if you are not confident that there is a return on those investments why should you dare to embark on them? Equally, however, sitting tight and playing safe is not an option because that is a route to stagnation and paralysis.

Going back to the call centre example, the first question that needs to be answered is: 'How important is a personalised call centre service to my customers and prospects?' 'Common sense' may tell you that it is very important, but the real question is about how much *more* influence the personalised service has on customer decision making than all the other factors which the customer may consider when choosing one supplier over another. To answer this question common sense is certainly not enough, and it is necessary to find out the information directly from the customers and prospects themselves.

However, even if you were to establish that for your customers and prospects a personalised call centre service was indeed very important, this information alone would not tell you what impact its introduction would have on your overall business performance (defined in terms of increases in revenue, number of customers, purchase frequency, or whatever other measure suits your particular business). This is because it is intuitively difficult to make the leap between an action like improved call centre service and ultimate business performance. Quantifying the impact of such an improved service is even more difficult.

Rather than seeking to make a leap, we would be wiser to take a more modest, step-by-step approach, based on the logic illustrated in Figure 3.1.

The term 'market' is used in Figure 3.1 (as well as in the rest of the book, wherever appropriate) as a shorthand not only for existing and potential customers but also for other stakeholders whose attitudes and behaviour can have an impact on our business. It is clearly important for us to maintain and strengthen the loyalty of our existing customers and also to attract new customers. However, it is also important for us to maintain the loyalty of other stakeholders with whom we deal and to seek to attract key

Figure 3.1   Action → loyalty/attraction → business performance

stakeholders with whom we currently have no relationship. We need, therefore, to win over all the parties who may be involved, to a greater or lesser extent, in the purchase decisions of our customers – architects in the building industry or brokers in financial services, for example. In addition, we also need to pay attention to the loyalty of those players who influence the course of our business even though they are *not* involved in the purchasing side of our marketplace: for example, motivated and loyal staff are linked with improved market performance as well as reduced costs resulting from low employee turnover (staff motivation is discussed more fully in Chapter 6); equally, loyal suppliers are more likely to offer better terms and conditions and go the extra mile in the service they offer us.

Figure 3.1 shows that the starting point is an understanding of what the key market drivers are; if you find that a personalised call centre is indeed one of the most critical drivers influencing customer decision making then you need to take action to ensure that you offer your customers the personalised service they demand.

The next step is to measure how action taken on these market drivers has an impact on market perceptions in terms of satisfaction with your organisation or attitudes towards your brand. It is possible, through an investigation of your market, to measure the improvements in market ratings resulting from the actions you have taken – for example, how much more satisfied customers are with your call centre as a result of increased personalisation, and what impact that may have on customers' overall satisfaction with your organisation.

The step which follows is designed to trace the connection between market perceptions and market loyalty/attraction. It may seem obvious that if you improve the satisfaction of your customers or other relevant stakeholders you are bound to increase their loyalty, and in a generalised sense that point cannot be disputed: it is hardly likely that the more dissatisfied they become the more loyal they are to you! Equally, it is intuitively easy to understand why a strong brand may generate a greater feeling of attachment (among existing stakeholders) and attraction (among prospects) than a weaker one. But in any given case – as in the example of the personalised call centre service – it cannot be assumed that every perceived improvement in performance levels will automatically result in a corresponding increase in loyalty. It is possible that further performance improvements may have no impact on loyalty because the previous levels of performance were felt to be 'good enough'. The trick, therefore, is to identify whether, at what point and how much perceived improvements in specific levels of performance lead to increased market loyalty – a topic discussed in the next chapter. This can again be done through a proper investigation of the key players in your market in terms of what they want and how they feel about you.

Figure 3.1 refers to both existing customer/stakeholder loyalty and new customer/stakeholder attraction. However, as we explain later, it is generally less costly to retain existing customers and other stakeholders than to win new ones. For this reason, whereas we should not lose sight of the need to attract new players, the focus of much of the discussion here and in Chapter 4 is on loyalty. The next chapter shows how the term 'loyalty' is used to denote a feeling – in the form of advocacy, the intention to give you a greater share of wallet, the willingness to forgive the odd lapse – because the overwhelming attitude towards you is positive. Some academics and researchers have done a considerable amount of heart searching about which market attitudes are most closely correlated with business performance. For some, 'loyalty' is a passé term and they would rather refer to 'commitment' or 'advocacy', and they will engage in great debates about how precisely this should be measured: should it, for example, be based on positive word of mouth, is negative word of mouth a more telling predictor of future business performance – or should there be a combination of the two? Although there may well be merit in this kind of discussion, let us leave that in the hands of the experts; whatever the precise definition used, the bottom line is that it is the positive feeling that binds our marketplace to us which we, as general managers operating in the real world, need to be concerned about. For this practical reason we will continue to refer to 'loyalty' when we wish to describe that feeling.

Because loyalty is a feeling, it should lead to, but is not the same as, favourable market behaviour. One obvious example of such favourable behaviour is customer retention, and a common error is to equate retention with loyalty; yet we all know of cases where we stick to our existing supplier not out of a genuine feeling of loyalty but because of other factors such as high barriers to switching.

So the next task is to see how loyalty as a feeling leads to favourable market behaviour. If we have succeeded in finding the link here, then we are closer to the final step – that is, making the connection with business performance. All other things being equal, favourable market behaviour – for example, more frequent customer purchases or a retailer's decision to stock your products – *must* lead to improved business performance in the form of business expansion or increased market share. Of course, all other things are not always equal: for example, 'noise factors', like a competitor's decision to slash prices, could disrupt the process – but the disruption should be temporary, and such noise factors should not normally halt the longer-term progress towards improvements in business performance.

There is, however, one critically important reason why all other things are usually not equal: the process described in Figure 3.1 is valuable in showing how the actions you take can ultimately be traced to business expansion, but it does not take into account the costs of the alternative courses of action you can take. Whereas, for example, making product improvements may well have a beneficial impact on your performance in terms of increased business, if the cost of making those improvements is relatively high, it may be better for you to focus your energies on a second best but less costly option which may in fact have a more favourable impact on your bottom line. The next chapter tackles in greater detail (in the section on 'input–impact analysis') the issue of how cost – together with the related aspects of time and effort – should be brought into the equation when you have to choose between different courses of action.

The rest of this chapter provides some examples of the ways in which we can better understand the real drivers influencing how our key stakeholders think and behave. From now on, we will mainly refer to customers, even though many of the points made apply to other stakeholders as well – our staff, intermediaries, advisers, and so on. So, for example, when we make a point about 'customer' drivers, that point could apply equally to the factors driving our staff or other stakeholders operating in our market. The focus on customers is partly to avoid repetition and partly because in the end it is our customers who determine what finally happens to our business.

IDENTIFYING THE BUSINESS WINNERS

When considering customer drivers, it is clearly essential to know what is important to customers. But it is equally necessary to recognise that acting on what is important to customers may not win you business.

How can this be, you may well ask? Surely the very reason for identifying the issues which are most important to customers is that, by focusing on them, you will maximise customer satisfaction, loyalty and, ultimately, business performance (as summarised in Figure 3.1)?

Well, it is certainly true that it would be extremely foolish not to pay attention to what is important to customers. So how can we at the same time say that acting on the important factors won't necessarily win you business?

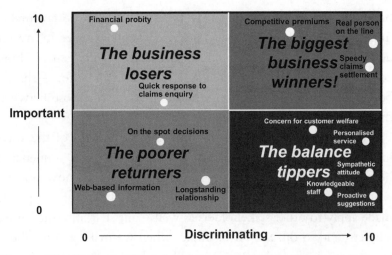

Figure 3.2 Understanding what drives customer decision making

The answer lies in the distinction to be made between what is *important* to customers and what, in the customers' view, will most strongly *distinguish* one supplier from another. Figure 3.2, a hypothetical adaptation of some work done in the insurance industry, shows how customer drivers may be plotted two-dimensionally, the y axis measuring the importance of the drivers and the x axis measuring the extent to which they are discriminating.

Those factors which are given a low rating on both axes – the poorer returners – will give you, the insurance company, a relatively poor return on your investment if you should decide to spend time and effort on them. So the provision of web-based information, to take an obvious example, will offer you relatively little by way of return since, in this instance, it is of little importance to your customers nor is it a factor which will help to distinguish you from the competition. It may not be a factor which should be totally ignored, especially if the investment required to offer it is low, but, compared with all the other services you may be able to offer, it is one of the least likely to attract customers or prospects.

At the other extreme are the biggest business winners – the customer drivers which are not only inherently important but also highly discriminating. Whichever way you may wish to look at these factors, they are to be given the highest priority.

The remaining two boxes are the most interesting because they represent the areas of greatest neglect, potential confusion and, as a result, poor decision making. The business losers are those customer drivers which, while relatively important, are relatively non-discriminating. They are commonly referred to as the 'givens' or 'table stake' issues; financial probity is a prime example of this since no insurance company would be expected to operate fraudulently! It is crucially important, therefore, that the insurance company should do everything it can to ensure that it meets the highest ethical standards. The business implications of *not* operating ethically can be dramatic – and it is for this reason that the factors in this box are called the business losers: meeting high ethical standards, where such standards are expected as the norm, won't *win* you any business, but failing to do so will most certainly *lose* you the business. We can think of examples of business losers in all businesses – for food manufacturers and distributors, food hygiene would be an example; for airlines, safety; for drug manufacturers, even a relatively rare occurrence of life-threatening side effects.

The final box – the balance tippers – is perhaps the most intriguing, possibly because it is the most neglected. This box contains all the issues which, though not inherently the most important, remain discriminating in that they could tip the balance in your favour, especially when the margin of difference between what you and your competitors otherwise have to offer is very slim. In an increasingly competitive environment, the role of the balance tippers – those 'little extra somethings' – becomes ever more crucial. In the insurance industry example shown, proactive suggestions represent the extreme example of the balance tipper: customers don't regard the provision of proactive suggestions as being nearly as important as the provision of some of the other services shown and they probably don't expect to receive them; however, precisely because they are unexpected, the insurance company offering them to customers is likely to steal a march over the competition, especially since the environment is so competitive that the more obviously important services are probably being offered equally well by all the insurers anyway.

The balance tippers, and their opposite pole, the business losers, represent the extreme examples of why it is true to say that the most important factors won't necessarily win you business. This kind of analysis, delving beneath the surface response about what is important or unimportant to customers, enables you to win against the competition in a way that attention to the obvious customer drivers alone will not. Therefore, beware of the marketing expert who says that, because something is not 'important' to customers, it should always be ignored!

Figure 3.2 showed a purely hypothetical example, from the insurance industry, of how business winners may be identified. In reality, however, a number of companies across the world – including Allianz, one of the world's leading insurance companies – have grown to recognise the distinction which we have made between what is important and what is discriminating. Allianz is a good example of a company that has successfully used the approach described in this section to ensure that it focuses its resources on the truly business winning issues.

As mentioned earlier, many of the concepts mentioned here could equally apply when seeking to understand what drives other stakeholders. To take an obvious example, for a bank lending you money creditworthiness is highly likely to be a 'business loser' (in that if the bank should have any reason to doubt your creditworthiness it will cease to do business with you); having said this, there may well be other factors influencing the bank's willingness to deal with you – like ease of doing business – which, even if less important, may tip the balance in your favour should the bank have other organisations beating a pathway to its door.

'BACK-OF-MIND' AND 'FRONT-OF-MIND' ISSUES

The analysis of customer drivers should also address the need to recognise the role of 'back-of-mind' as well as 'front-of-mind' issues. The simple point here is that customers will not always tell you explicitly what drives their decision making. This is one reason why the feedback gained from sales staff, although always potentially useful, may not provide the full picture about what the real customer drivers are. There are back-of-mind issues which customers fail to verbalise, either unconsciously, because they don't realise themselves how important they can be in influencing their decisions, or deliberately, because expressing opinions about them may be too revealing or embarrassing. There was a time when a luxury car (which will remain nameless) had a poor record for reliability, yet this had no material impact on sales of the car: were customers going to admit to the world at large (as well as possibly to themselves) that an important reason why they continued to buy the car was that it was a status symbol?

As a result, the customer will be tempted to attribute more importance to front-of-mind issues than is justified by their real role in influencing decision making. Price is a prime example of a front-of-mind issue: emphasising the importance of price suits customers because it earns them brownie points to negotiate the supplier downwards and because it may be seen as a safe bet: who can possibly argue that, at some level, price has to be important to customers?

We referred earlier to the caution which may need to be applied to the feedback given to sales staff, because of the tendency to overemphasise the importance of front-of-mind issues. How, you may ask, can back-of-mind issues be identified if they are not verbalised? The answer lies in eliciting the answer from customers without directly asking them questions about what is important to them.

There are a number of ways of doing this, based on statistical techniques which research methodologists have developed to a fine art, and about which many learned tomes have been written. However, a simple (some might say, simplistic) explanation of the principle behind these techniques would be as follows: let us say that most of your customers stated that they were highly satisfied with your overall performance, according you an average score of 8.5 out of 10; let us also postulate that, when asked about specific factors potentially influencing their perception of your overall performance, those same customers rated you highly on, say, delivery lead time performance (a score of 9 on average), and relatively poorly on price (a score of 6 out of 10). The statisticians would say that, in this scenario, delivery performance is highly correlated to overall performance whereas there is a relatively low correlation between price and overall performance. In layman's terms, this means that doing well on delivery lead time is likely to have significantly more impact than offering a low price. It stands to reason that, if customers are giving you a high score on their overall satisfaction with you, price cannot be an important driver because if it were the overall satisfaction score would have been dragged down by the relatively low price score. The point of this simple example is to show that it is possible to deduce the role of the various customer drivers without asking a single question about their importance. It is highly likely that, if questions *had* been directly asked about importance, price would have emerged as being more 'important' to customers.

So what do we do with this information? Clearly, if we know that there are unstated back-of-mind issues, we need to recognise them, but where these issues are potentially sensitive the message we convey to customers must be correspondingly sensitive. The buyers of unreliable luxury cars are hardly likely to appreciate being told: 'We appreciate that status is important to you'! At the same time, front-of-mind issues should be explicitly recognised, even though you may realise that, in the customers' decision making, they may not always be as important to customers as they are stated to be. If price is stated as being important, customers are likely to be put out if you appear arrogantly to be ignoring their stated concerns about price. Some recognition of the role of price may therefore be offered – by, for example, clearly communicating and justifying to customers why your price is on the high side (if that is indeed the case) – without having to take any action to reduce your price (especially when it is known that price is not in practice a key driver of customer choice).

Front-line staff are likely to be more effective in their dealings with customers if they are sensitive to the back-of-mind issues which can drive customer attitudes and behaviour. The story goes that an irate customer of the UK department store John Lewis came to return a teapot he had bought the previous day because the spout had fallen off. When informed about this, the immediate response of the sales assistant was to express concern about whether he had scalded himself. This was quite different from the reaction the customer had expected – an argument, an excuse or, at best, a standard apology. Whether intuitively or whether she had been trained to respond in this way, the sales assistant identified a back-of-mind issue likely to be a key driver of the customer's behaviour – the need to feel cared for – which was quite possibly of greater importance to the customer than the front-of-mind reason for returning to the store (the faulty teapot). The story ends with the customer leaving John Lewis with his loyalty to the store strengthened by his experience. It may be a platitude to say that every customer complaint represents an opportunity, but the John Lewis example illustrates *how* this can happen – namely, through the insightful recognition of the deeper needs, often unrecognised by the customers themselves, which can motivate customer behaviour.

Another organisation that turned a potentially difficult situation to its advantage, by recognising back-of-mind issues, was

Lexus. When it had to recall several thousands of its vehicles for engine modification, it was determined to ensure not only that the technical problem it faced was tackled as quickly as possible but that the car owners affected were really satisfied with the quality of the company's customer care: engineers were sent out to make the necessary engine modification in customers' drive-ways, company car parks and even at the roadside – in short, in any way and at any time which minimised the inconvenience to customers. This was followed up by contacts with customers to double check that all was well with their cars and to ask them if they could suggest ways in which their experience of Lexus's service could have been even better. The next month, Lexus sales – far from suffering a setback – rose by over 5%. Lexus understood that addressing the front-of-mind customer problem – the need to get the engines modified – was clearly the most immediate task, but that this needed to be followed up with actions which recognised the more back-of-mind need of customers to feel cared for.

A number of organisations, particularly those operating in consumer markets, appear to have made a conscious attempt to tap into the back-of-mind drivers which may motivate customers even more powerfully than the obvious front-of-mind benefits which they seek: Starbucks, for example, sought to offer a 'Star-bucks experience' which extended beyond the provision of a good cup of coffee, and Ikea has surrounded the provision of household products at its retail stores with children's play areas and cafeterias offering Swedish food – all apparently designed to transform the shopping experience into an enjoyable family outing. In both instances, the companies have sought to differentiate themselves from the competition by selling not only the front-of-mind product – coffee or household furnishings – but also by aiming to create an environment which satisfies the back-of-mind emotional needs and wants of their customers. One could argue that a moti-vation behind going to Starbucks or Ikea – an enjoyable, social

experience – is not really back-of-mind since visitors may consciously decide to go to those venues because they find them more
pleasant (and not just to drink coffee or buy furnishings); the
fundamental point still holds, however, that the front-of-mind
rationale for the visit is the product (the coffee or the furnishings
– you don't go to Starbucks if you want to buy yourself a beer),
but the front-of-mind motivation is unlikely on its own to explain
why people go to these outlets rather than others. In this context,
it is the emotional and social back-of-mind needs that they satisfy
which help them to differentiate themselves from their competitors
(and win more business).

Business-to-business organisations have also recognised the
importance of back-of-mind issues. Earlier, we had cited Allianz
as an example of a company which had succeeded in identifying
the business winning factors driving its marketplace. It has also
been quick to recognise that it is not enough to work on the
'obvious' issues driving customer decision making – in the insurance industry the level of premiums (the 'price' issue) would be
a case in point – and that, to gain competitive advantage, it is also
important to identify and work on the less obvious back-of-mind
issues.

Figure 3.3 provides a summary illustration of the way in which
back-of-mind and front-of-mind issues can be addressed so as to
make the most positive connection with your customers and
prospects.

As mentioned earlier, the same line of thinking may be applied
to other stakeholders: if, for example, you are a large multinational
wishing to invest in a new plant which could have an impact on
the environment, the opposition you face from environmental
pressure groups may well arise from 'rational' concerns about the
adverse effects of your actions on the local environment; but the
strength of the opposition could also stem from a less overt anti-
big business stance which may be colouring the reaction of the
pressure groups. Your task, given such a situation, would be to

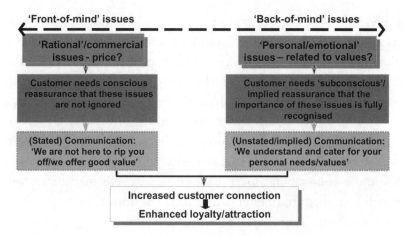

Figure 3.3   Identifying 'back-of-mind' as well as 'front-of-mind' issues

do everything feasible to offer a caring, 'human face' to your organisation by engaging with the pressure groups, demonstrating what you may be able to do for the local community, and so on.

THE ROLE OF INTANGIBLES

Back-of-mind issues are often, though not always, the more intangible factors related to reputation, image, relationships, and so on. Perhaps not surprisingly, front-of-mind issues tend (again, by no means always) to be the more tangible factors such as product quality, price, service performance, logistics, and so on.

It is critically important to recognise that, whether or not they are back-of-mind, the intangibles can play a crucial role in customer decision making. The introduction to this book started by stating 'If it's Tuesday, it must be segmentation and customer satisfaction and branding and…'. The point was being made there in the context of the need to have a holistic view of all the areas influencing how your target market feels about your organisation. However, the point also has a specific resonance when we think about tangible and intangible factors. The world of marketing has tended to separate tangible factors – gathering them under the umbrella of 'customer satisfaction' – from the intangible factors – which tend to be linked to the areas of branding and reputation. Our point is that such a separation is an artificial one, often made for entirely understandable practical reasons: for example, most organisations separate out the corporate marketing function, concerned with branding, positioning, corporate communications, and so on, from product marketing, sales or service functions, which tend to focus more on the tangibles offered; similarly, if you wish to embark on a market survey, it is often too time consuming to cover both satisfaction and brand-related topics in the same survey.

Our view, however, is that, because the intangible and tangible factors go hand in hand in shaping market views, they should be considered side by side. This is for a number of reasons:

- As already mentioned in the introduction, since the impressions of those you are targeting are shaped both by their experience and by their image of your organisation, separating satisfaction from brand issues flies in the face of the reality of the marketplace.
- Often the intangibles – for example, reputation/image-related issues – can be the single most important drivers influencing customer decision making.
- There is a body of evidence, revealed in business literature, showing how strong brand equity increases customer loyalty.
- A strong brand can have a 'halo' effect on satisfaction with the tangibles you offer: if you offer a strong brand and also perform well on the tangibles, while your competitor has a weaker brand but performs equally well on the tangibles, it is quite possible that customer satisfaction with the tangibles you

offer will be greater than customer satisfaction with the tangibles offered by your competitors.

- Similarly, the relationships customers have with you – their feeling of 'customer affection' – can have a material impact on their overall attitude towards you: how many of us, for example, have continued to put up with our banks' inefficient service because of the relationship, based on trust, that we have with our bank managers?

WHAT MAKES FOR VALUE IN YOUR BUSINESS?

An understanding of what the real customer drivers are should be set in the context of the fundamental nature of your business. It is useful, every now and then, to take a step back and ask what really makes for value in your business. This can be done by creating a simple quality/cost matrix, as shown in Figure 3.4.

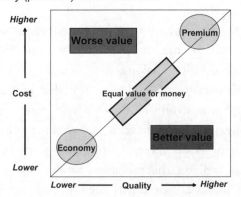

Figure 3.4 What makes for value in your business?

The subject of value has been tackled in depth, most notably by Bradley Gale and Ray Kordupleski (Gale 1994; Kordupleski with Simpson 2003). The purpose of this section is not to repeat this work but rather to raise some basic questions: Where would you plot your organisation in Figure 3.4? Where would you plot your competitors? Are you an economy brand, a premium brand, or something in between? Is this position where you *wish* to be? Are you above the 'equal value' line – in which case why do you think you are offering relatively poor value and what can you do to enhance the value you offer?

Conversely, are you in the fortunate position of being below the line? Or is it fortunate? Do you really wish to offer quality at a relatively low cost? Could there be an opportunity to charge more and thereby enhance your profits, quite possibly reinforcing, through a higher price, your reputation as a premium brand (assuming that the premium position is where you aspire to be)? Our experience shows that there are many organisations which would actively wish to move from the 'better value' area to a position nearer the premium end of the equal value line. For them, the better value box represents not only a lost profit opportunity but also an erosion of the premium image they would wish to project to the marketplace.

The discussion surrounding Figure 3.4 has focused on where you believe you are positioned. However, Figure 3.4 can also be used to show where you are positioned *in the view of your target market*. You can then compare where you see your organisation with your target market's perceptions; if, for example, you see your enterprise as falling in the premium value zone but your customers and other stakeholders position you in the 'worse value' area, that perceptual gap should surely call for some serious thought about how that gap can be narrowed.

This situation is illustrated in Figure 3.5 which shows how, if you see your organisation as being more of a premium brand than your target market does, you are in danger of being seen to offer

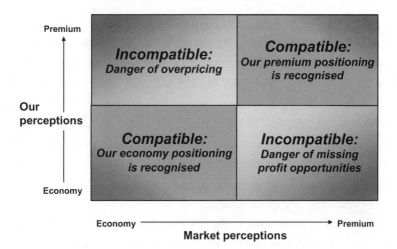

Figure 3.5 Does the market position us the way we position ourselves?

poor value for money because you will charge a higher price than the market believes to be justifiable. At the other end of the spectrum, if the market feels that your organisation is more at the premium end of the market when you feel that your organisation's positioning is of an economy brand, you may be in danger of missing the opportunity to charge a higher price and therefore improve your profits.

In addition to comparing how you see the positioning of your organisation with how your target market sees it, you should also take into the account the needs and *expectations* of the market you are serving. Figure 3.6 shows how you can plot your own current or desired positioning against market expectations; since these expectations may vary by market segment, you may wish to create variants of Figure 3.6 for each of the segments you serve. In Chapter 2 (on market segmentation), we saw how Dow Corning

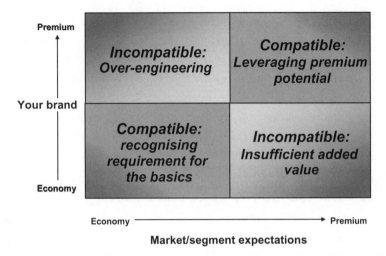

Figure 3.6 Does your value proposition match market/segment expectations?

found that its overall premium value proposition did not match the expectations of a specific no frills segment. For that segment the company found itself in the 'Over-engineering' box shown in Figure 3.6, and we have already seen how it took the radical step of creating a new brand to make the positioning compatible with the nature of that segment.

The simple message in Figure 3.6 is that your positioning on the economy–premium spectrum should be compatible with the expectations of the markets you serve. There is nothing inherently good or bad about aiming to be an economy or premium brand (or something in between) as long as you don't lose sight of your marketplace – in terms of both its *perceptions* of your organisation and its *expectations*.

So, when looking at the whole issue of value in the context of your business, you need to address three questions:

1. What is our positioning, as we see it, on the economy–premium spectrum, and have we come to this positioning because it is the *desired positioning* we have worked towards?
2. What are *market perceptions* – that is, does our marketplace see our positioning in the same way?
3. What are *market expectations* – that is, does our marketplace want us to occupy the position we desire?

Figure 3.6 can be adapted by again plotting market *perceptions* (rather than your own views) of your positioning against market expectations. Now suppose you fall into the 'Insufficient added value' box. If you believe that you do in fact offer the value expected by the market, but that this has not been recognised by your target audience, then the conclusion is that you need to understand why your target market has this perception if you wish to alter it through an appropriate communication campaign. The opposite situation can also occur: the market believes you to be a premium (and therefore high-priced) brand when the market expects to be given an economy offering. In this situation you would be seen to be charging prices which are too high. If, in fact, your prices are not significantly higher than average, your task now would be to inform the market that you in fact offer better value than target customers believe you do.

So how in practice do you ensure that your organisation's position and value proposition match market expectations? It may well be that you are convinced that you are offering the right match, but if you are not or if you feel that your business performance could be improved, you may wish to undertake a market investigation to establish whether or not there is a close match, and, if not, why not and what action needs to be taken to bridge the gap.

One result of such a market investigation could be Figure 3.7, which shows an example of what is described as a value or attributes tree.

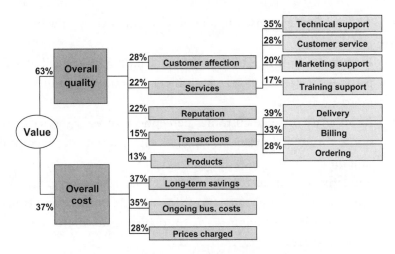

Figure 3.7 Identifying the key customer drivers of value

The value tree-based methodology is described in detail in Ray Kordupleski's book *Mastering Customer Value Management*. The purpose of this is to show the relative importance (in percentage figures) of the various factors which may influence your customers' view of the value they ultimately receive from their suppliers. So, in the example shown, technical support is the single most important driver of perceptions of the services you offer, services in turn are slightly less likely than customer affection to drive perceptions of quality, and finally quality is far more important than cost in driving value perceptions.

Because quality is more likely to drive value than cost, the chart describes a market in which a premium offering should succeed. This point is further reinforced by the fact that, among the cost factors, the actual price charged is the least important to customers, long-term savings and ongoing business costs being more likely to drive cost perceptions. Some of the conclusions you would draw from the illustration would, therefore, be as follows:

- This market lends itself to a premium, rather than an economy, positioning.
- In order to enhance your premium standing, you need to pay particular attention to customer affection, services and reputation.
- In order to enhance customer perceptions of your services, the single most important area of focus should be technical support.
- Similarly, you need to act on the key factors influencing customer affection and reputation (for reasons of space it has not been possible in Figure 3.7 to disaggregate these and the 'Products' area).

As with much of the earlier analysis, the approach represented by Figure 3.7 can be applied not only to the customers who buy your products and services but also to other stakeholders who may or may not be involved in the purchasing process itself: as we will see in Chapter 6, staff views about what makes for value in your business can be usefully compared with those of customers. Similarly, if you are operating in a business characterised by intermediaries, you could apply the process described to understand the factors most likely to drive their recommendation of supplier. If you are in the financial services sector, for example, brokers' views may well influence the decisions of the end users who are your customers; in the construction sector, the opinions of architects may well influence the choices made by contractors; if you are a pharmaceuticals company selling over-the-counter medicines, the views of chemists may well influence the purchase decisions of your end customers.

THE EXECUTIVE SELF-ASSESSMENT CHECKLIST: DELVING INTO THE MIND OF THE MARKET

Question	Yes, confident +3	Yes, tentative 0	No −3	NA
Are we able to make the connection between the actions we take to improve our market position and our ultimate business performance?				
Do we understand that market loyalty/attraction is not necessarily the same thing as market behaviour (as exemplified by customer retention)?				
Do we consistently and regularly keep abreast of all the key factors which drive the decisions made by our target market place?				
Do we know what quality means to our customers and prospects?				
Do we know what cost means in our business (whether it boils down to price, or whether it is something more than price alone)?				
Do we seek to measure the impact of the actions we take on our overall business performance?				
Do we know what the most important market drivers are in our business?				
Do we know what the business winners are in our marketplace?				

Question	Yes, confident +3	Yes, tentative 0	No −3	NA
Do we know what the business losers are?				
Do we know what the balance tippers are?				
Can we cite instances of how working on the business winners/ balance tippers has made a difference to our business?				
Do we know what are the back-of-mind issues of our customers, prospects and other stakeholders?				
Have we worked on these back-of-mind issues, and thereby gained competitive advantage?				
Do we recognise the role of intangibles in driving the decision making of customers and other stakeholders?				
Do we recognise that intangibles and tangibles should be brought together and compared for their impact on the decision making of our customers, prospects and other stakeholders?				
Do we know what the key intangibles are in our business?				
Have we acted on those intangibles to gain competitive advantage?				
Do we know where we are positioned in the economy–premium spectrum?				
Are we happy with that positioning?				

Question	Yes, confident +3	Yes, tentative 0	No −3	NA
If not happy, do we have an action plan to change the positioning?				
Does our positioning match market expectations?				
Do we know if our view of our positioning is compatible with our target market's perception of our positioning?				
If we do know, are the two positions compatible?				
If not, do we have an action plan to align the different positions?				
Do we know if our target market's perception of our positioning is compatible with market expectations?				
If we do know, are market perceptions and expectations compatible?				
If not, do we have an action plan to align market perceptions with expectations?				
Do we know enough about what drives the perceptions that stakeholders (other than customers) have of us?				
GRAND TOTAL SCORE				
NET ABSOLUTE SCORE				
NET AVERAGE SCORE				

Now, taking each of the above questions, what in practice are we doing?

CHAPTER 4

FROM CUSTOMER SATISFACTION AND BRANDING TO LOYALTY AND ATTRACTION

WHY CUSTOMER LOYALTY IS IMPORTANT – AND WHY CUSTOMER SATISFACTION DOESN'T GIVE YOU THE WHOLE PICTURE

Reference has already been made to the pivotal role of market loyalty in leading to favourable market behaviour and, ultimately, to improved business performance. As mentioned in the last chapter, when we speak about 'market' loyalty we are referring not only to the loyalty of our customers but of all the players in the marketplace whose loyalty may have an impact on our business. These could include, for example, our staff and our suppliers as well as our customers – in other words, market players who are not necessarily involved in the actual purchase of our products and services. Later in this book we refer to why the loyalty of these different parties is relevant – for example, in Chapter 6, where we discuss staff motivation and loyalty, and in Chapter 7, where we show how intelligent management of suppliers can result in stronger relationships and potential cost reductions.

In this chapter, however, we will focus on 'customer' loyalty: for the purpose of the discussion which follows, the term 'customer' will exclude players like staff and suppliers but will include *all* the market players who are engaged in the specification and purchase of products and services. This means that whereas the points made in this chapter about customer loyalty are clearly relevant to the customer contacts we normally deal with they may be equally relevant to, say, end customers (our customers' customers), intermediaries, advisers/consultants and different members of the distribution chain (major wholesalers, smaller distributors, retailers, etc.). To take a few obvious examples, if we are food manufacturers we need to win the loyalty of both the major retailers who may stock our products and that of the end consumers (the consumers who buy from the retail outlets); similarly, if we are manufacturers of automotive components or accessories, our 'customers' can include not only the original equipment manufacturers (the car or commercial vehicle manufacturers) but also fleet operators, the retail outlets selling our products and the end users (the car or commercial vehicle drivers) – the relative importance of each customer group depending on whether the sale is for new vehicles or replacement parts.

There is a considerable body of literature on why customer loyalty is important, so let us confine ourselves to a summary of the key reasons:

- It normally costs far more to acquire new customers than to keep existing ones.
- Loyal customers tend to buy more from you than those who are not loyal and are more likely to be receptive to your cross/up-selling initiatives.
- They generally place more frequent, consistent orders, and so are usually less costly to serve.

- They may be less likely to complain, so it can be less time consuming and costly to keep them happy.
- They are likely to be more forgiving of the odd lapse.
- They are your advocates and often your best 'sales people'.
- They may well be less concerned about the price you charge.
- You are less likely to lose them to the competition.

For all the above reasons, much of our discussion focuses on existing customer loyalty rather than on new customer attraction – a point already made in the last chapter. Additionally, many of the actions required to consolidate and increase customer loyalty also apply to new customer acquisition: the importance of identifying business winners and back-of-mind issues, for example, is at least as relevant to new customer attraction as it is to existing customer retention. So – perhaps with some adaptation – we can apply many of the points made in this chapter, as well as the previous one, to new customer attraction as well as existing customer loyalty.

It may be argued that loyal customers may well be *more* difficult to handle than those who are not – for example, companies may find that it is more difficult to command a price premium the longer a customer stays with them. Whereas this may well be true (particularly in business-to-business markets where customers may be relatively hard-headed in their relations with their suppliers), there is a danger here of confusing loyalty with customer retention. It is certainly possible to cite examples of long-term customers who put price pressures on their suppliers as a condition for their continued business – but it is arguable whether such customers can be regarded as truly loyal; the relationship here is more akin to that of commercial blackmail. For a genuinely loyal customer, doing business with you should not depend primarily on price. Equally, this does not of course mean that you have the licence to get away with charging a higher price just because your customer is loyal. Loyalty, as we see it, is a two-way process based on trust.

We may confuse loyalty with customer retention if we have lost sight of the point made in the previous chapter – that customer loyalty, as we define it, is all about feelings, and should not be confused with favourable purchase behaviour. However, favourable purchase behaviour should be an outcome of loyalty – otherwise there wouldn't be much point in having loyal customers. Although it is intuitively obvious that, if customers are loyal to you, they should buy more from you, this common sense view is supported by a great deal of empirical evidence. Figure 4.1, drawn from some work conducted by Dow Chemical, shows how loyalty is directly correlated with share of spend – a useful purchase behaviour measure in business-to-business markets typified by multisourcing customers.

The chart leads us to two conclusions:

- First, and most obviously, that there is a clear connection between increasing loyalty and increasing share of account, as one may expect.
- Second, that the relationship is not a straight line one: in this particular example, there is a trigger point between the first four

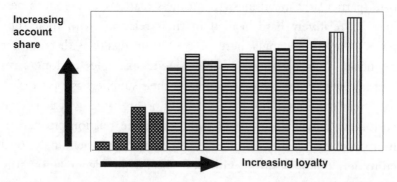

Figure 4.1 Loyalty links with business performance metrics. (Reproduced by permission of Dow Chemical Company)

bars and the next set of bars at which increased loyalty has a particularly dramatic effect on purchase behaviour: clearly, the message in this instance is that if there are disloyal customers residing in the area represented by the first four bars, the most urgent task is to move their loyalty upwards by investigating and acting upon the reasons for their disaffection.

But why do we focus on customer loyalty rather than customer satisfaction? Well, clearly the two are connected: all other things being equal, a satisfied customer is likely to be more loyal than a dissatisfied one. However, given that most of us operate in a competitive environment, customer satisfaction alone is not sufficient to secure your position: customers who are quite satisfied with your performance do not necessarily feel loyal towards you, and without that feeling of loyalty, they cannot be relied upon to remain with you if, say, a competitor comes up with an exciting new offer. In the absence of a genuine feeling of loyalty, customers have not made the emotional investment in the relationship with you which would bind them to your organisation. So satisfaction and loyalty, though linked, should also be seen as separate, and the focus should be on maximising loyalty as the ultimate goal to be achieved. The assumption here is, of course, that the customers whose loyalty you seek are those whom you wish to keep − unprofitable customers are hardly likely to be a target for a customer loyalty programme!

There is another, more tangible, reason why customer satisfaction cannot be equated with loyalty. Figure 4.2 shows how the relationship between satisfaction and loyalty can vary when we look at how satisfied customers are with specific aspects of their suppliers' offerings.

In this example, adapted from some work undertaken for a bank, we can see that, as satisfaction with personalised customer service grows, there is a discernible improvement in feelings of loyalty; in other words, those customers who are not satisfied with the customer service they get because they don't believe it to be

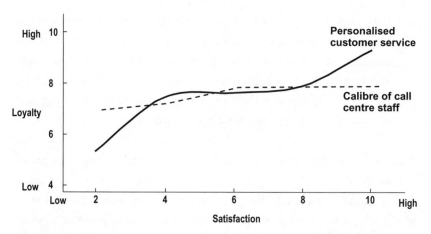

Figure 4.2 The link between satisfaction and loyalty can vary by customer driver

sufficiently personal are clearly less likely to feel loyal to their bank than those who are satisfied. However, the same is not true for the calibre of call centre staff: here improvements in satisfaction levels seem to have little impact on feelings of loyalty. How can this be?

One obvious explanation for this difference could lie in less importance being placed by customers on call centre staff calibre than on personalised customer service; this would mean that improving call centre performance would not have the same impact on loyalty as improving customer service would. In this case, however, the reality was that call centre performance *was* regarded as important, but customers could not see much difference between the performance of the various banks on this aspect: the majority of customers gave the banks they used a relatively poor rating on this aspect and the smaller number who were more satisfied tended to believe that the banks were generally on a par with one another. If the expectation was that there was not much difference between the banks on call centre staff, this factor would not be a major driver of loyalty towards a particular bank. Conversely, personalised customer service was felt by customers to vary more significantly from one bank to the next, with the result that this factor had a greater impact on their loyalty.

There is a connection between the outcome shown in Figure 4.2 and the discussion in the last chapter about the difference between 'discriminating' and 'important' factors. In that chapter, we referred to discriminating customer drivers as those which you can focus on as a way of differentiating your organisation from the competition. The reason why they are discriminating could be that customers don't expect you to offer them and so they are pleasantly surprised when you do offer them; but the reason could also simply be that the performance of the various players in the market varies significantly from one supplier to the next, in which case good performance on those factors is likely to have a greater impact on feelings of loyalty than good performance on factors where suppliers generally perform well.

We have been referring to 'feelings of loyalty' and earlier we had also made reference to a 'loyalty programme'. This brings us to the question of precisely how loyalty should be defined. What we are certainly *not* talking about is the 'incentivised loyalty', based, for example, on loyalty points, favoured by airlines, super-markets or service stations. Nor are we talking about 'price loyalty', which is almost a contradiction in terms: as mentioned earlier, customers who are 'loyal' to you because they can push you down on price are liable to switch their 'loyalty' the moment a competitor comes along with a lower price. When we are referring to loyalty, we are talking about any indicator of the feeling which binds customer to supplier – this could be, for example, the willingness to recommend the supplier to a friend (in consumer markets) or to a business colleague (in business markets), or the desire to allocate a greater proportion of business to the supplier. Or, as was the case in the example shown in Figure 4.1, it could be a 'loyalty index' based on some combination of the factors which represent the feeling of loyalty in your business.

As we mentioned in the last chapter, much of the recent literature on the subject has been concerned about fine differences
between 'loyalty' and related concepts concerned with 'trust',
'commitment', 'advocacy', and so on. Or you may see references
to 'emotional connection' and 'emotional branding', which, quite
rightly, stress the importance of the emotional, sometimes uncon-
scious, drivers of customer decision making. Our view, however,
is that, whatever the terminology used, this in itself matters less than
the underlying principle – the genuine *feeling which binds customer to
supplier*. Having said this, if you wish to find out directly from your
customers how loyal they really are, care should be taken to ensure
that the wording of your questions really comes to the nub of the
matter if you are not to draw the wrong conclusions: asking your
customers whether they intend to purchase more (or less) from you
may not be enough because their overall demand may be increasing
(or decreasing) and they may therefore intend to purchase more (or
less) from all their suppliers. Equally, however, asking them whether
and how the share of business which they give to you is likely to
change may not provide you with the full answer you need since
it is possible that a recent price change made by you or the competition may encourage them temporarily to switch a greater proportion of their business to, or away from, you; in this situation,
they should be asked how your share of their total business would
change assuming that all their suppliers' prices remained unchanged.
The precise definition and wording you use may be adapted to suit
your business as long as the fundamental principle – of a feeling
binding your customer to you – remains intact.

When we refer to a feeling we are not, however, talking about
a soft-headed approach based on an irrational, 'blind' loyalty – it
is debatable as to whether such loyalty ever exists, especially in
business-to-business markets. To assume that your customers are
blindly loyal to you is, in any case, dangerous, since their loyalty
can never be taken for granted and needs to be nurtured if it is
to be sustained. Inherent to a mutually trusting, loyal relationship

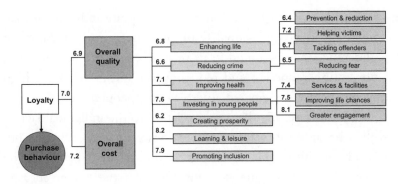

Figure 4.3 Loyalty should lead to favourable purchase behaviour

is the assumption that it should always lead to a 'win–win' situation; if an imbalance creeps into the relationship, in which one party feels taken advantage of by the other, the feeling of loyalty will be eroded.

Figure 4.3 illustrates how loyalty should lead to but is not the same as favourable purchase behaviour, and how loyalty in turn is influenced by satisfaction with your performance on the factors which drive customer choice. The chart is an adapted version of Figure 3.7 (shown in the last chapter), a key difference being that this time the numbers are not percentages reflecting the weight of factors in driving customer choice but rather performance ratings. It can also be adapted to include the concept of value (as we have shown in Figure 3.7) so that quality and cost lead up to value. However the table is adapted, it is a powerful yet simple way of showing, at a glance, where your performance is relatively strong or weak, both at a top line level (quality, cost, loyalty, etc.) as well as at more disaggregated levels. This way you know what actions you need to take to improve your overall performance in the marketplace.

The chart shows the (hypothetical) situation in which a public sector authority may find itself: on reducing crime (6.6 out of 10) its performance is felt by customers to be significantly worse than on investing in young people (7.6), and the primary reasons for this difference may be found in its relatively low satisfaction rating on prevention/reduction and reducing fear and its relatively high rating on greater engagement (with young people).

As with Figure 3.7, the results relating to the individual factors can then be traced forward to perceptions of quality and cost and, ultimately, in this instance, to loyalty and purchase behaviour. The numbers shown in Figure 4.3 only describe the perceived performance of the public sector authority, since it has no direct competitors. In a market characterised by more direct competition, however, it would be more appropriate to look at both the organisation being assessed and the competition so that its performance can be compared with that of competitors on the individual factors as well as the 'top line' issues like quality, cost and loyalty. Later in this chapter we will discuss in more detail the importance of benchmarking against the competition.

The approach described in Figure 4.3 (and Figure 3.7) has been successfully used by a range of companies in sectors as diverse as the oil industry, chemical catalysts and mobile communications. A number of organisations regularly undertake this type of market analysis to enable them to assess quickly not only their overall performance but also the specific areas which require their greatest attention. The information shown in Figures 3.7 and 4.3 is useful, therefore, not only for the CEO, general manager or marketing director who wishes to have a helicopter view of market drivers and where the organisation stands on those drivers; it is also valuable for the functional managers who may wish to focus on their particular areas of responsibility: the managers responsible for product performance, for example, may wish to pay particular attention to the part of the tree relating to product quality, customer relationship managers may focus on those aspects concerned with customer relations, the corporate communications team can examine the factors influencing the company's overall reputation, and so on.

We showed in Figure 4.2 how improving satisfaction on a specific factor may well not yield the same outcome, in terms of enhanced loyalty, as improving satisfaction on another factor. The same can be true when we look at the relationship between loyalty and purchase behaviour. Although, as Figure 4.1 (describing Dow Chemical's experience) showed, it is generally the case that strengthened feelings of loyalty should result in more favourable purchase behaviour, the extent to which this happens can vary depending on the sector in which you are operating. If, for example, you are in an industry characterised by high switching costs, customers are less likely to move their business than if you are conducting business in an area where it is relatively easy to switch – even if they feel very negative towards their existing suppliers. Going back to Figure 4.1, if the switching costs in Dow's business had been higher, the slope of the line linking loyalty with purchase behaviour (in this instance, account share) could well have been less steep. All this reinforces the importance of avoiding confusion between loyalty and purchase behaviour, not least because such confusion can lead suppliers to rest on their laurels, with dangerous consequences: if you believe that long-standing customers are, by definition, loyal to you, you may be in for a rude shock when, one day, they decide to move their business away from you; the reason for remaining with you may lie in extraneous factors which have hitherto made them reluctant to switch, but if they feel that they have been taken for granted for too long they may reach a tipping point which overcomes their inertia and results in loss of business for you.

INPUT–IMPACT ANALYSIS OF ACTIONS TAKEN

Figure 3.1 in the last chapter showed how the actions you take can have an impact on market perceptions and, potentially, on customer loyalty and business growth. Figure 4.3 provides an illustration of how this can happen in practice. Therefore, one of the first tasks any organisation faces in its drive to enhance the loyalty of its customers is to ensure that the actions it takes are most likely to have a favourable impact on market perceptions and, ultimately, on loyalty. Much of Chapter 3 in fact focused on how you can identify and act on the factors most likely to have a favourable impact on your standing in the marketplace: if, as was shown in Figure 3.7, technical support is a significantly greater driver of service performance than training support, then, all other things being equal, you should place greater focus on technical support if you are to achieve maximum market impact. This point would be reinforced if it were also the case that your performance on technical support was regarded by customers to be weaker than the competition's. So:

$$\begin{array}{c}\text{Importance}\\\text{of a factor}\end{array} \times \begin{array}{c}\text{Your relatively}\\\text{poor performance}\\\text{on that factor}\end{array} = \begin{array}{c}\text{Impact of the action}\\\text{you take on that factor}\end{array}$$

This simple formula doesn't mean, of course, that if you are performing *well* on an important factor, you should neglect that factor: clearly, you should capitalise on your strength because that continues to give you competitive advantage. If you perform poorly on an important factor, however, you need to pay more urgent attention to it if you are not to lose business to the competition.

Having said all this, it would be simplistic to suggest that the way you allocate your resources should be dependent solely on the impact of the actions taken. Your decision must also take into account the input required to take the necessary action. This input may be measured in terms of cost, effort or speed – or some combination of the three. 'Quick wins' are certainly worth going for, especially if they are relatively inexpensive to implement. A chemicals company found out that customers rated its HSE (health, safety and environment) service as being run of the mill and worse than the competition's. The company knew that this was not in fact the case and that its HSE performance was superior to that of the competition. It required relatively little time, cost or effort to embark on a customer education campaign, through items of information provided in its regular newsletters, which very quickly resulted in far more favourable customer attitudes towards the company's HSE performance. Even though HSE was not the most important factor driving customer decision making, it was still important enough for the investment required to make the necessary correction to be well worthwhile.

Figure 4.4 provides a simple illustration of how the input–impact analysis can be done.

Box A (May as well do it?) reflects a relatively low input–low impact scenario. An example here would be the provision of information about your organisation, in newsletters, websites, etc., which may not have an immediate or measurable impact but which requires

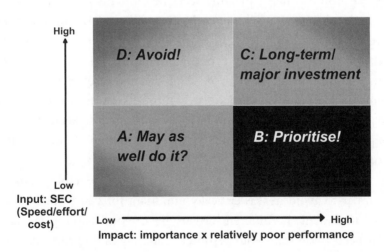

Figure 4.4 Input–impact analysis

low incremental cost, time and effort. Regular items on new products developed or the development of a letters page in a company newsletter are possible examples of 'may as well do it' actions.

Box B (Prioritise!) reflects the most desirable scenario, where a relatively low input action results in high impact. The example of the chemicals company providing HSE information in its newsletter is a possible case in point: the impact was relatively high, and the input was so low that this was an obvious course of action for the company to have taken. Box B is often characterised by situations where there is a need to correct a market misperception, which, if allowed to go uncorrected, could result in significant harm to the company or which could result in lost opportunities: obvious examples would be of the company being wrongly associated with poor product or service performance, or inadequate knowledge of the company's products or services (which can result in significant loss of business).

Box C represents the situation where there is a need to make a major and/or long-term investment because the impact of that investment is significant. Whereas Box B is often concerned with the need for communication, Box C typically involves product/ service improvements or large-scale investments (for example, to upgrade plant and machinery). In Boxes A and B, the company could be faced with a negative market view based on a misconception which is relatively economically corrected through appropriate communication; in Box C, if the company faces criticism about its products or services, it is more likely that this criticism is justified and that substantive improvements are needed which require a far greater investment than a programme of communication in newsletters!

Box D quite obviously represents the least desirable scenario. In order to avoid it, it is critically important for you to understand how important the different drivers are in your marketplace since you need to allocate your resources carefully and ensure that you don't spend them on actions which offer you a low return.

BRINGING CUSTOMER OPINIONS TO LIFE

One of the criticisms levelled at customer satisfaction surveys, often justifiably, is that they say the 'same old thing' year in and year out and that it is often difficult to link customer opinions with the precise actions which suppliers need to take. Both criticisms can be addressed by developing the insights into customer decision making described in Chapter 3 in particular and many of the insights offered in the rest of this book.

The second criticism often arises because very little connection is made between what customers are saying and what the supplier is offering in practice: if, for example, customers give you a mediocre rating on delivery lead time (let's say an average rating of 6 out of 10), what does that mean in terms of actual delivery days or hours and what practical improvements need to be made to bring delivery up to the desired standard?

Figure 4.5 shows the benefits of making a linkage between the views of customers and the internal measures you have at your disposal.

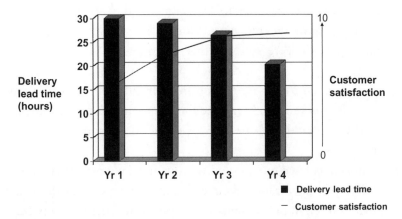

Figure 4.5 Linking customer views with internal measures

Here we see that, from year to year, customer opinions about your delivery performance have tended to improve as you have improved your actual delivery performance from 30 hours to 20 hours. We see that in year 1, the average customer rating is around 5 out of 10, which means that on average a rating of 5 equates with a lead time performance of 30 hours. Now, if you can map the lead time being enjoyed by those customers who are highly satisfied with you – let us say that you receive a rating of 9 when you offer a lead time of 25 hours – then you may conclude that, in order to increase customer satisfaction significantly, you need to reduce your delivery lead time from 30 hours down to 25 hours. By linking the customer ratings with actual delivery performance measures, you are able to take the practical action necessary to make your customers significantly happier. Making this linkage is also useful when you are undertaking the input–impact analysis mentioned in the last section: by knowing that you need to reduce delivery lead time by five hours you are likely to have a clearer picture of the magnitude of the input involved in achieving that objective.

Figure 4.5 does, however, reveal something else: whereas the general direction of the satisfaction curve is upwards as performance improvements are made, between years 3 and 4 the dramatic reduction from around 25 to 20 hours yields very little by way of further improvements in customer satisfaction. There are a number of possible reasons for this outcome:

- For your customers, a reduction from 30 to 25 hours is *good enough* – there is really no need to make further improvements, and you would be better off investing your resources in something else.
- Customers have got so used to your improvements that, ironically, you have raised their expectation levels, with the result that further improvements fail to make the desired impact.
- In year 4, competitors started offering even further reductions in hours and this again raised customers' expectation levels.

- Customers have got so used to your improvements that they no longer notice them – in which case the message is that you should *communicate* more effectively to remind them about the benefits they are now enjoying.

Figure 4.5 shows a hypothetical scenario, and you may well find that, in your case, the linkage between the internal and external measures is consistently positive – that is, every improvement in your actual performance results in a corresponding improvement in customer perceptions. However, making the linkage is always valuable because, first, it shows you what precisely needs to be done in practice to increase customer satisfaction; and, second, it may reveal instances where improvements made are not having the desired effect on customer perceptions – in which case you could be saving your organisation a lot of time and money by using your resources more effectively.

The linkage between internal and external measures is a desirable, although not always easily achievable, objective; not easily achievable for two reasons: first, whereas delivery lead time can be quantified in terms of days or hours, this cannot be done so easily with softer issues (like friendliness of service); and, second, organisations often simply do not have the internal records necessary to make the kind of connection suggested. However, if you don't have the records which you should have, perhaps this is an area of activity which you may wish to work on.

THE WORLD IS A COMPETITIVE PLACE!

Notwithstanding what would seem to be a truism for most of us, there remain far too many instances of companies who lose sight of the need to benchmark their performance against their competitors'. How often have we experienced disappointment when we have felt confident of winning a new prospect because our bid was well received, only to find that the contract went to a competitor? The obvious point is that, whereas we may have been very good, the competition was even better.

So, when assessing how we are seen in the eyes of our customers and other stakeholders, we must look at our perceived performance relative to that of the competition – are we regarded as being better or worse than the competition, or are we seen as the same? The fact is that even today there are companies which undertake customer satisfaction or brand equity surveys in which attitudes towards the competition don't feature. This is hardly surprising when one considers that some of the KPIs (key performance indicators) promoted by marketing gurus and professional bodies as measures of how we are seen by our marketplace still fail to include the competitive dimension. To really understand how strongly we are positioned in the marketplace, we should seek to know the following:

(a) *How our customers compare us with the competition*: This provides a measure of *how loyal our customers are and how likely they are to move more of their business to competitors*: this is particularly relevant if our customers multisource (that is, they buy from us as well as our competitors), because we can measure their satisfaction with both us and the competition to arrive at an assessment of how likely they are to switch loyalties; if, conversely, our customers single-source (that is, only buy from us), they cannot compare us with the competition in this way – although they can make a comparison of our brand/reputation with that of the competition, since they do not need to have experience of a brand to form general perceptions about it.

(b) *How our competitors' customers – our prospects – compare us with their suppliers*: This indicates *how likely we are to attract new customers from the competition*; since these prospects are not currently using our products/services, this comparison can only be made if they have a general impression of our organisation.

(c) *What our prospects know and feel about us, compared with what our competitors' prospects know and feel about them*: This provides us with the means of comparing our overall market profile and the impact we are making in the marketplace with the corresponding profile and impact of our competitors – showing *whether we or the competition are more likely to make inroads into the wider market.*

(d) *How our standing among our customers compares with the standing of our competitors among their customers*: By providing a like-for-like comparison, this provides the most objective way of assessing *whether we are, in the eyes of the marketplace, better or worse than our competitors*; if we wish to measure satisfaction levels, this comparison is particularly valuable when at least some of the customers are single-sourcing, because our customers can talk about their satisfaction with us while our prospects can talk about their satisfaction with their suppliers.

(e) *How other stakeholders and influencers – end consumers, distributors, consultants, the media, and so on – regard us vis-à-vis the competition*: This provides us with a measure of *our overall market standing.*

The comparisons above are summarised in Figure 4.6.

Later we refer to the various ways in which we can glean information about how we are seen in our marketplace. One obvious

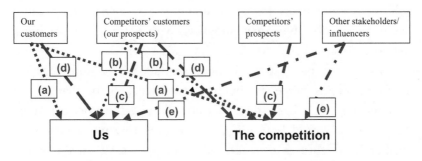

Figure 4.6 How does our market compare us with the competition?

source of valuable information is our customer-facing staff – sales executives, customer relations managers, and so on. However, an important reason why we cannot place too much reliance on their feedback is precisely the fact that they may not be the best placed to obtain objective information about how their own organisation is doing vis-à-vis the competition: first, customers may not always reveal the full details of what they know or feel about the competition; second, sales people and other customer-facing staff may be heavily dependent on feedback from their customer contacts, whose views, particularly in business-to-business organisations, may not be wholly representative of the opinions of all the relevant parties within the customer enterprise (see a more detailed discussion of this in Chapter 5 on customer decision making dynamics); and, finally, the customer-facing staff are liable themselves to have some bias in the way they interpret and communicate the information they receive from their customer contacts. For all these reasons, it is important to supplement the feedback we receive regularly from our staff with other sources of information, most notably periodic market surveys which are designed to be as objective as possible by eliciting information directly from customers, prospects and other stakeholders and influencers.

When conducting such market surveys, we should be careful to ensure that the sample of people we talk to is as unbiased as possible. For example, going back to the multisourcing scenario ((a) above), we should make sure that the customers we have selected are not likely to be favourably biased towards us because we happen to be their main suppliers, with competitors playing a subsidiary role.

So far we have stressed the importance of comparing our performance, as perceived by the marketplace, with that of the competition. This gives us a measure of our *relative* performance. However, it would be a mistake to assume that we need go no further if we find that we are performing better than our competitors. It is also important to examine our *absolute* levels of per-

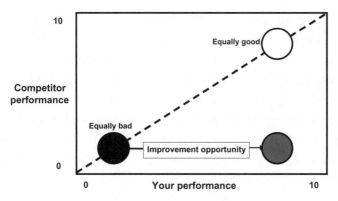

Figure 4.7 Look at relative *and* absolute performance

formance. Figure 4.7 shows a simple example of why this is necessary: if our performance is on a par with our competitors', the absolute level will tell us whether we are equally poor, equally excellent or somewhere in between. Clearly, if we are all performing excellently, our primary aim should normally be to maintain our position; conversely, if we are performing equally poorly, we have the opportunity to gain competitive advantage by raising our game.

The focus of the discussion in this section has been on how we compare with the competition in the eyes of the various players in our marketplace. Although understanding market perceptions is critically important, we also need to obtain information about the competition at other, more fundamental levels:

• Keeping up to date with news and developments relating to the competition – knowing what is happening with the competition, what our key competitors are actually doing and planning to do, whether there are new competitors emerging, etc. – all in the context of what is happening in our own organisation: all the information which is commonly understood to be part of *competitor intelligence.*

- Making an inventory of offerings to our marketplace – our offerings as well as those of the competition; what products and services we offer and how they compare with those of each of our main competitors: a *product/service audit.*
- Developing a parallel assessment of how aware and knowledgeable the market is about the products and services offered by us and by the competition (see more on awareness and knowledge in Chapter 8 on communication): an *awareness/knowledge comparison.*

We mentioned earlier that too much reliance should not be placed on customer-facing staff if we need to obtain objective information about how we are seen by customers and other stakeholders. However, sales and other customer-facing staff can be a very valuable source of competitor intelligence because they are well placed to find out, in the course of their direct contacts with customers, about the latest developments with their competitors. They can be the most up-to-date providers of competitor information precisely because they are in day-to-day contact with their marketplace. For the same reason, the incremental cost of gaining this information is relatively low. If, however, we seek to use our customer-facing staff as a source of information about the competition, are we confident that we are making the most of this valuable information source? If, for example, we regard the primary role of our sales executives to be to sell our products or services, are we offering them the incentive they need to engage in information gathering activities which they may regard as a distraction from their main job? Unless they see some reward for their competitor intelligence activities, such activities are liable to be haphazard and sporadic, and as such we are potentially squandering a valuable intelligence gathering resource.

Competitor intelligence is important, as is the product/service audit briefly referred to above. However, the reason why this book focuses on market perceptions is that many companies already undertake competitor intelligence and product audit tasks, albeit not always as thoroughly and systematically as they ideally should. This is because we can, at least in part, use our internal resources – our staff – to undertake these activities. To gain an objective understanding of market perceptions, on the other hand, often requires, almost by definition, the use of a third party (like a market research company), since using internal staff is liable to result in biased information.

The objective, therefore, should be to come as close as possible to obtaining a 360 degree view of the competitive scenario, both in terms of 'what's happening' with the competition (through competitive intelligence and product audits) and in the context of market perceptions. This information can be gathered and organised in many different ways. For example, at a 'corporate' level, we may wish to know what the competition is doing overall, how knowledgeable the market is about our competitors vis-à-vis us and what the market feels about our competitors compared with our organisation. At a more specific 'product' level, we may wish to know what the competition is doing within each of the product/service areas in which we operate, how knowledgeable the market is about the competition and about us as providers of each of the products/services, and what the market feels about us versus the competition within each of the product/service areas. Equally, the information may be analysed by each of the key market segments in which we operate, as we have already mentioned in Chapter 2 on segmentation.

Figure 4.8 shows a hypothetical example, drawn from the industrial lubricants business, of how we can achieve a holistic view of our position versus our competitors' in each of a number of key product areas.

In the example shown, in addition to all the latest news and developments concerning our competitors, we can also draw some interesting conclusions about our competitive strength within each

	Gear oils	Metal forming fluids	Metal cutting fluids	Hydraulic oils	Process oils	Greases	Etc.
Are these the main products offered?							
Our company	☆	☆	☆	☆	☆		
Company A		☆	☆	☆	☆		
Company B	☆			☆	☆	☆	
Company C		☆	☆				
News/devpts							
Our company	(To be completed)	(To be completed)	(To be completed)	(To be completed)	(To be completed)	(To be completed)	
Company A							
Company B							
Company C							
Market awareness/ knowledge (strong = ☆ weak = 0)							
Our company	0	☆	☆	0	0		
Company A		☆	☆	☆	0		
Company B	☆			0	0	☆	
Company C		☆	☆				
Market reputation (strong = ☆ weak = 0)							
Our company	0	☆	☆	0	0		
Company A		☆	☆	0	0		
Company B	0			0	0	☆	
Company C		☆	☆				
Customer satisfaction (10 = highest, 0 = lowest)							
Our company	4	7	7.5	6	5.5		
Company A		8	7.5	7.5	6.5		
Company B	9			7	7	8.5	
Company C		9	8.5				

Figure 4.8 How we compare with the competition: a 360 degree view

of the product areas: although our company offers the first five products shown, we are only really well known for metal forming and metal cutting fluids, where we have a strong reputation, but our customer satisfaction in these areas falls behind that of the competition, particularly behind Company C, which is a specialist in these product areas. In short, it looks as though we are relatively strong on the range of products we offer but we are not leveraging that strength because our customer satisfaction levels are not as strong as those of some of our competitors.

The information shown in Figure 4.8 can be adapted and expanded according to our needs and circumstances: we can add an assessment of the products offered by our competitors, compared with our own, as part of an overall product audit to show whether our products are in fact on a par with or superior to those of the competition. If we haven't already done so, we can also add an up-to-date SWOT analysis for ourselves as well as for each of our competitors, so that we can keep abreast of our competitive advantages and disadvantages in terms of a range of topics – from product offerings and innovation to distribution networks and internal cost structures.

BUT BENCHMARKING AGAINST THE COMPETITION ALONE CAN LEAD TO WASTED RESOURCES

In our anxiety to beat the competition, there may be instances when we are *too* fixated about our competitors' performance and, as a result, waste our precious resources.

How can this happen? Most obviously, when we are focused on factors which are not important to customers. A bank, for example, laid great store by the online transaction facility it offered its customers, only to find that the customers placed this facility lowest in the list of all the services they expected from their banks. It was of no interest to them, therefore, whether or not the bank surpassed, or even matched, its competitors in this area.

But there is another, less obvious, situation where our performance against the competition may not be so relevant – namely, when we have lost sight of our customers' expectations: whether or not we match or beat the competition, are we matching or exceeding customer expectations? Is it possible that, by failing to take customer expectations into account, we may not be doing enough (even if we are performing better than the competition)? Or that we may be doing *too much* (even if we are lagging behind the competition)?

There are indeed many instances in which we do misallocate resources because we do not take customer expectations sufficiently into account. To go back to the example of Dow Corning Corporation, which had discovered a no frills segment, in so far as competitors continued to offer a bells and whistles service to this segment, they were ignoring the expectations of this segment, and consequently wasting resources which could be better allocated elsewhere. The lesson here was that the no frills service was *good enough* for this segment because it met the needs of the customers – if the chemicals company had remained in thrall to what the competition was doing it may never have developed the additional business stream it succeeded in creating through the introduction of its new Xiameter brand.

One of the reasons why we fall into the trap of going along with the competitor bandwagon is that we fail to question received wisdom: we must, we are told, never lag behind the competition; and we must always 'exceed customer expectations'.

The truth is that we *don't* need to match, let alone beat, the competition in all instances and we *don't* need always to exceed customer expectations. Let us for a moment consider what we understand by the term 'expectations'; a distinction needs to be made between what we may call 'realistic expectations' and what we may refer to as 'target expectations':

- Realistic expectations reflect customers' *experience*; here the customer may say: 'My suppliers are all pretty bad and I don't expect any of them to do any better.'
- Target expectations reflect customers' *aspirations*; here the customer says: 'None of my suppliers achieves this level, but if one of them did I would give them more of my business.'

If customers are talking about realistic expectations, those expectations clearly should be *exceeded*. If, however, they are referring to target expectations, those expectations should be *met*; and if the

© Farrokh Suntook

Figure 4.9   How you match up against realistic and target customer expectations

competition exceeds those target expectations, they are wasting their resources and you should resist the temptation to follow them. A word of caution, however: expectation levels can change over time and must therefore be monitored, especially when there is a continual trend towards the upgrading of performance.

Figure 4.5 showed how improvements in delivery lead time from the third to the fourth year had little impact on customer perceptions, and one of the reasons given was that customers' expectations – in this case, target expectations – had already been met in year 3. Figure 4.9 shows a hypothetical example of how we can map the different expectation levels and how we perform against them.

- The area represented by 'Realistic expectations' shows where the majority of customers find themselves; these expectations must clearly be *exceeded*.
- The star represents the target expectation level – every im-provement in satisfaction up to that point has a clearly positive impact on customer loyalty (as represented by the relatively

steep slope of the line up to that level); this is the level of expectation to be *met*.

- The area represented by 'Reallocate resources' reflects the fact that exceeding the target expectation level results in virtually no improvement in loyalty.
- The total area leading up to the star represents the competitive playing field in that it is in our interest to beat the competition in this terrain because performance improvements significantly increase customer loyalty. If we lag behind the competition, customers are liable to switch their loyalty to our competitors; even if we beat the competition, there may be mileage in improving performance further, widening the gap between our organisation and our competitors, because we will succeed in entrenching customer loyalty.
- The area beyond the star represents the 'plateau of no return' where there is not much advantage in our seeking to beat (or even match) the competition, given that we have limited resources which may be put to better use elsewhere.

To summarise, therefore, when assessing the strength of your position in the marketplace, your competitor benchmarking should be done, wherever possible, in the context of customer expectations.

One final point here: in addition to competitor benchmarking and the 'benchmark' represented by customer expectations, there is another form of benchmarking highly attractive to many organisations: 'best in class' benchmarking. Here you are comparing the performance of your organisation against that of non-competitive organisations, often operating in different sectors, generally recognised for their excellence in the area of activity you wish to benchmark. A public sector authority may, for example, look at the experience and achievements of private sector organisations to learn how they have achieved excellence in customer service.

Indeed, the expectations of your marketplace may well be shaped by customers' experience of suppliers *outside* your market who, they may feel, set the standards which you should meet. For example, a customer of First Direct, a UK bank highly regarded for its customer service, may well – consciously or unconsciously – expect the same level of service to be provided not only by other banks but also by, say, the utilities companies who supply to him; this is especially likely to happen if he does not regard any of the utilities companies as setting a high standard themselves. If you operate in a business which is generally not highly regarded for its service performance, there is a danger of complacency setting in because you feel that customers are unlikely to move away from you to the competition. However, if you benchmark yourself against outside best in class suppliers you have the opportunity to gain competitive advantage by offering a standard of service which your marketplace isn't used to – and, if you don't, you face the risk of losing business to a competitor which has improved its service (quite possibly because it decided to undertake its own best in class benchmarking activity!). A word of caution, though: benchmarking against organisations that share little in common with your own field of activity may not always be of practical value. A high street bank may, for example, usefully look at the activities of successful FMCG companies because, although the industry sectors are quite different, their target market – the consumer – is the same; if, however, the bank is an investment bank dealing with corporate customers, FMCG companies may not offer the most appropriate role model.

THE PERFORMANCE/EQUITY GAP

In Chapter 3, the point was made that intangible as well as tangible factors should be taken into account when seeking to assess the role of the drivers that influence customer choice. So, for example, the strength of your brand as well as the quality of your service should be considered side by side because they both play a role in shaping the view that customers and other stakeholders have of your organisation.

At the same time, it can be valuable to separate out and compare how you are seen to stand on the intangibles and the tangibles. In this context, we are associating your brand equity with all the factors – often the intangibles – that make your brand what it is in the mind of the marketplace; and we are linking the tangibles with your performance in satisfying customers. The term 'brand equity' has been defined in a number of ways, but its essence is that it is an indicator of the strength of your brand, a strength which has been developed historically through your past actions and the image/position you have occupied over time in the minds of customers, prospects, other stakeholders and even the public at large. In current literature, brand equity is often defined in terms of the financial value of the brand and there is much debate as to how one may arrive at this value. We are applying the term, however, in the context of market perceptions – what customers, prospects, other stakeholders and quite possibly the public at large feel generally about your brand. These perceptions are not necessarily based on any experience or deep knowledge of the brand; they reflect a view held about your brand, whether or not that view is borne out by the 'reality' of the brand.

Conversely, 'performance' relates to all the actions that you are currently taking which affect your customers, distributors or any other parties with whom you engage commercially – be they the quality of the service you offer, the products you sell, or the way in which you transact with these stakeholders. So, whereas brand equity is relevant in the context of the wider marketplace – as we have seen, not only customers but also prospects, other stakeholders, and so on – performance tends to be associated with those who have had experience with you – most obviously, your customers.

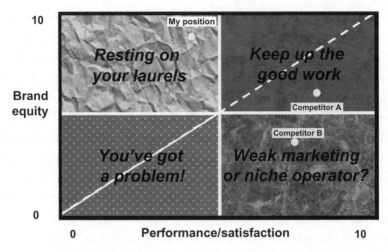

Figure 4.10 The performance/equity gap: compare your performance with your brand equity/image – and compare yourself with your competitors

Figure 4.10 shows the 'Performance/equity gap'. This is a simple strategic tool which helps you to define where you are positioned when brand equity and performance are separated out.

The diagonal line represents any position where your brand equity and performance are on par – which could, of course, mean equally strong or equally weak. The two boxes, 'Keep up the good work' and 'You've got a problem!', broadly describe these two areas. Clearly, if you are in the 'You've got a problem!' zone, you need to think seriously about how you have got there and how you can migrate north-eastwards.

Perhaps the greatest strategic value of the performance/equity gap is when you find that there is a disconnect between your brand equity and your performance. If your brand is clearly stronger than your performance, it means that the equity you have developed over time is no longer matched by the quality of your current or recent performance – in other words, you are, possibly quite unwittingly, resting on your laurels. This is a dangerous position to be in, since it is untenable in the long run: at some point in time, your relatively poor performance will catch up with you, dragging your brand down and quite probably losing you business and even your stock market standing. When discussing this scenario, many business executives have cited Marks & Spencer as the classic example of a company that found itself in this box, with the negative consequences of which we are all too aware. The good news is that, with effort, it is possible to recover from this position, as we know Marks & Spencer successfully did with its improved clothing range and well-judged advertising. Indeed, in *Management Today* magazine the retailer won the accolade in December 2007 of being the UK's 'most admired company' out of a total of 220 companies – achieving an aggregate score which was the highest winning total ever achieved by a company in this ranking; no one survey can tell the whole 'truth', but in a subsequent study, 'BRANDZ™ Top 100 Most Powerful Brands', reported by Millward Brown in April 2008, Marks & Spencer ranked 68th globally out of a total of some 40 000 brands (4th in the UK alone) and, significantly, of the top 100 brands achieved the highest (192%) improvement in brand value over the previous year.

The polar opposite of resting on your laurels is represented by the 'Weak marketing or niche operator?' box. Here, your brand lags behind your actual performance, a situation which may result from two possibilities:

• You are not capitalising sufficiently on your real, tangible assets because you are failing to market and communicate what you have to offer sufficiently or effectively.

- You are a niche operator – highly regarded by the relatively small customers who know you but otherwise a comparatively unknown quantity in the marketplace at large.

In the first scenario, you clearly need to invest in increased marketing, communications and PR activity. In the second scenario, you may need to do nothing if it is your objective to remain a niche operator.

If given the choice between the 'Resting on your laurels' and 'Weak marketing or niche operator?' boxes, we would normally say that it is better to find oneself in the latter than in the former: if you wish to move from the latter, you need to focus on communications activity – far less costly and risky than an overhaul of the tangible products and services (as well as the communications activity) which the former would call for.

As Figure 4.10 shows, you can plot your organisation against the competition. This provides you with a more complete basis for evaluating where you are positioned and what you need to do. Clearly, if a competitor is in the 'Keep up the good work' zone, and you are not, the need to take action is likely to become all the more acute.

Figure 4.10 represents a powerful but very simple exercise which the senior management in any organisation should undertake. This is because it forces you to take a step back and a hard look at exactly where you are positioned; if you can also position the competition, all the better. By utilising this tool, you are armed with a trigger to take measures *before* things get worse. And if you come back to it every now and then, you will be using the tool as a dynamic lodestar for the way in which you should be monitoring your operations. At the very least, it will reveal that you are not quite sure where you stand – in which case that alone should be a wake-up call.

COMPARING NORWEGIAN APPLES WITH ITALIAN ORANGES

One final word of warning when you look at your market standing across different parts of your marketplace. If you were to undertake a survey of how well you were regarded in different market sectors, demographic groups or countries, could you confidently take the results you received at face value? If, for example, your customers in Norway gave you an average brand rating of 7 out of 10 and your Italian customers gave you a rating of 8, would it be right to conclude that your position in Norway was weaker than your position in Italy and that, therefore, you needed to take corrective action in Norway which you would not need to take in Italy? Not necessarily, according to the market research company Harris Interactive, which found, from a survey conducted among over 70000 consumers, that Norwegians were inherently 'harder graders' than Italians. In other words, if Norwegians were asked to give a rating on a 10 point scale, they were, compared with the Italians, more inclined to use the lower end of the scale, *irrespective* of the product or brand under consideration. A lower score given by the Norwegians didn't therefore mean that they were necessarily less happy with the brand than the Italians. It meant quite simply that Norwegians tended to give lower scores for the same degree of satisfaction or admiration than the Italians might have for a brand. As Figure 4.11 shows, it was found that, when asked to rate on a 10 point scale, on average Italians tended to give a score as much as 1.16 points higher than Norwegians. If the Norwegians and Italians were your customers, this would mean that if the Norwegians gave you an average rating of 7 and the Italians gave you a rating of 8, you could conclude that, if anything, you were doing *better* in Norway than in Italy!

The possibility of grading bias of the type described also means that we have to be very careful about absolute scores which some

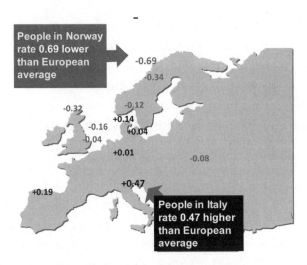

Figure 4.11 Nationality effect within Europe – rating scale differences from European average. (Reproduced by permission of Harris Interactive)

marketing gurus may declare to be 'gold standard' magic numbers which we should all aspire towards achieving: it is understandable for us to ask what a target performance score should be, and it is equally tempting for the 'experts' to provide a pat answer – for example, we are sometimes told that, on a 10 point scale, a score of 8 is 'good' but that the aspirational score should be 9 or more because it is 'excellent'. The reality may be that, to take the example of Italians and Norwegians, a score of 8 may be 'reasonably good' for Italians but 'very good' for Norwegians. To depend on a single score to represent a standard of performance in all circumstances may therefore be simplistic and misleading.

Clearly, the information in Figure 4.11 related to a group of consumers interviewed at a particular time, and it could well be that if we took different markets or time periods the precise results would not be the same. The fundamental point, however, is that you cannot always compare at face value the responses of different groups of people. This is one more reason why competitive benchmarking is so important: if Norwegians are likely to give lower scores they are likely to do so when rating your competitors just as they are when rating your own company, and the same would be true for Italians or any other group. This means that the *relative* score – how you compare with the competition – remains unaffected and you can then compare the relative score you have achieved in Norway with that achieved in Italy.

Some would say that even this is not enough, since the grading bias occurs at the level of the individual person and the bias is not caused solely by country differences but can also be related to other factors (like age or gender). This means that one Norwegian may be a harder grader than another and it is quite possible that any one Italian may also be a harder grader than any one Norwegian (although on the whole Italians are not). If, therefore, you were comparing how your customers felt about your organisation with how competitors' customers felt about the competition, competitor benchmarking may not always give the most accurate results: were it to be the case, for example, that older people tended to be easier graders than younger people and, for whatever reason, the age profile of your customers in Norway was higher than that of a competitor's Norwegian customers, you may wrongly conclude that your customer satisfaction is better than your competitor's when in reality your apparently higher score may again be down to grading bias (this time age related). It is possible, through a statistical procedure, to adjust the biased scores to arrive at a more accurate reflection of the true feelings of the different groups which comprise your market, but you would need to enlist the assistance of a research methodologist or statistician to make that adjustment. Short of being able to undertake this statistical exercise, the use of competitor benchmarking can provide a reasonable safeguard against drawing the wrong conclusions, especially if there is no reason to believe that the profile of the group assessing your organisation is materially different from the profile of the groups assessing the competition.

THE EXECUTIVE SELF-ASSESSMENT CHECKLIST: FROM CUSTOMER SATISFACTION AND BRANDING TO LOYALTY AND ATTRACTION

Question	Yes, confident +3	Yes, tentative 0	No −3	NA
Do we have an ongoing plan of action to ensure that we retain and strengthen the loyalty of our customers?				
Do we know the trigger points at which improvements in customer satisfaction have the strongest impact on the loyalty of our customers?				
Do we know when our performance is good enough and no further improvements are required?				
Are we able to link the views of our customers to internal measures of performance?				
Do we use these internal records on performance measures to help us make confident judgements about what precise improvements we need to carry out?				
Are we confident that we are allocating our resources to those areas most likely to result in greater customer loyalty?				
As well as the impact of the actions we might take, do we also take into account the input – in terms of cost, effort or time – required to take those actions?				

Question	Yes, confident +3	Yes, tentative 0	No -3	NA
Do we benchmark our organisation against the competition by finding out how customers and prospects compare us with competitors?				
Do we benchmark our organisation against the competition by finding out how other stakeholders and influencers compare us with competitors?				
Are we careful not to be overdependent on our own staff's feedback when we benchmark ourselves against the competition?				
Do we benchmark our performance against that of best in class organisations outside our business?				
Do we undertake a 360 degree assessment of how we fare against the competition, taking into account both the 'hard facts' on what we/ the competition are doing and market perceptions of us versus the competition?				
Do we know what customers' and prospects' expectations are?				
Do we know how well our organisation meets or exceeds those expectations?				
Do we know when we need to exceed (or even meet) expectations?				
Do we recognise that we don't always need to beat, or even match, the competition?				

Question	Yes, confident +3	Yes, tentative 0	No −3	NA
Do we know when we need to beat the competition, when we need to match it and when lagging behind the competition is acceptable?				
Do we plot our organisation's position on a performance/equity map?				
Are we confident we know what our position is?				
If we are not in the 'Keep up the good work' segment, do we have a plan of action to improve our position?				
Have we succeeded in moving to a stronger position?				
Are we aware of the pitfalls of making face value comparisons when we wish to assess how well we are doing in different countries, among different age groups, etc.?				
GRAND TOTAL SCORE				
NET ABSOLUTE SCORE				
NET AVERAGE SCORE				

Now, taking each of the above questions, what in practice are we doing?

CHAPTER 5

DECISION-MAKING DYNAMICS

INTRODUCTION

We may all recognise in principle that the market contacts with whom we directly deal are liable to be influenced by other stakeholders and influencers. In practice, however, how vigilant are we in seeking to identify these parties and find out precisely how they influence the decision making of our contacts? How often do we question whether the people we deal with are always the key decision makers? How often do we ensure that we are dealing with all the parties who may have a role in influencing the decisions made? How sensitive are we to the needs – emotional as well as rational – of these people?

Why are these questions relevant? Because the market-sensitive organisation will recognise that it will be more effective in its transactions with its direct contacts if it can understand and take into account the environment in which they are operating. In personal dealings, an individual with a high emotional intelligence quotient will instinctively seek to understand the feelings and behaviour of others in the context of their upbringing and environment; disturbed people, for example, may be better understood if we know that they have had a traumatic past. It may not be carrying the analogy too far to say that organisations can similarly better understand and manage those with whom they deal directly if they take into account and understand all the influences to which their targets may be subjected.

Broadly, the influencers/stakeholders having an impact on the decision making of our direct contacts reside:

- within our own organisation – the internal stakeholders, who are our staff (the subject of Chapter 6)
- within the customer or prospect organisation or household with which we are dealing; the way in which they influence and interact with one another and our most direct contacts is the subject of this chapter
- outside the customer/prospect; these are the other external stakeholders and influencers, who are the subject of Chapter 7.

The rest of this chapter focuses on those decision makers and influencers – commonly referred to as the 'decision-making unit' – operating within our customer/prospect organisation or household. As in the previous chapter, when we refer to customers or prospects, we are including not only the customers who are using our products and services but also all the other players who may be involved in the specification or purchase of our products and services. To take an example from the construction industry, if we are suppliers of building products some of the organisations we deal with have more of a specification/advisory role, others more of a purchasing role, but it may be important for us to understand the decision-making unit operating within all the key parties involved – from architects and quantity surveyors to contractors, housebuilders and developers.

The term 'decision-making unit' (DMU) has been used for many years to describe the collection of individuals, particularly within business-to-business organisations, who are involved in the decision to buy a product/service and choose a supplier. Most of us are, in all probability, quite familiar with this term. However, we will touch on this topic in this chapter because the role of other members of the DMU can go a long way in helping to explain the decisions which influence our business – especially, decisions which may appear to be anomalous: how often have we come away from a meeting, convinced that we have won the contract discussed, only to discover that we have lost to a competitor? As we mentioned in the last chapter, this outcome could be explained by the fact that, however well we performed, the competition performed even better; but it could also be explained by our focus on those whom we know – our direct contacts – and our failure to connect with others whose importance in the decision-making process we simply failed to recognise.

In order to avoid this situation, we need to:

- identify the different functions and, among business customers, the levels of seniority of the potential decision makers and influencers
- assess their roles
- understand their distinct needs, interests and desires
- understand the 'psycho-cultural' environment in which they are operating
- ensure that all these individuals have been covered through appropriate approaches which take their needs and concerns into account
- update the customer database and include within it a profile of all the potential decision makers and influencers so that the information on their different roles, needs and so on is formalised and accessible to all those who may need to interface with them.

FUNCTIONS/LEVELS OF SENIORITY

Among business customers, typical functions/titles of those involved in purchase decisions can include administrative staff, purchasing managers, technical executives, production staff, marketing managers or general management/board members. The precise function is liable to depend on the products or services you are selling and the decision the customer has to make. If, for example, you are offering a courier service, you are likely to be dealing with administrative staff on a day-to-day basis, although the decision as to whether your company is to be chosen to be the supplier may well be influenced by others further up the hierarchy.

In consumer markets, the decision-making unit is likely to be based around the household. Clearly, the household may only comprise one individual, but where more than one individual is involved, the possible influence of all these individuals – not just the person being targeted – should be taken into account; to take obvious examples, if you are a toy manufacturer you need to recognise the influence of parents as well as the children you are targeting, and if you are a supplier of paint to dual occupancy households you may need to target both occupants, not just the man who may be (possibly wrongly) assumed to take on the main decorating role.

ROLES

The roles of the individuals involved in decision making may be viewed in a number of different ways. For example, they may be defined in terms of the *nature of the influence* of the individual: in *The New Strategic Selling* by Robert B. Miller and Stephen E. Heiman (Miller and Heiman 2005), buying influences are split into four categories – economic buyers, user buyers, technical buyers and coaches. The book goes into considerable detail in explaining these buying influences, but in simple terms we would understand them to be as follows:

- *Economic buyers* are those individuals who are concerned about the return on investment of the choices made; they typically occupy a senior position and hold the purse strings.
- *User buyers* are those who will actually use the products or services chosen; they are concerned about the direct impact of the choices made on themselves and the departments which they represent.
- *Technical buyers* are those responsible for technical specifications and the screening out of products or services which don't meet those specifications.
- *Coaches* are those within the organisation whom you should nurture since they can provide you with the guidance and inside track on how best to succeed in winning business from the organisation.

Another way of defining roles, however, is to consider how individuals fit at the various *stages of the decision-making process*. The precise definition and sequence of the various stages may well depend on your particular business, but some or all of the steps shown in Figure 5.1 are likely to be broadly relevant, especially in a business-to-business environment.

The stages may be summarised as follows:

- *Specification of initial need*: Who specifies the initial need, requirement or desire for the product or service being considered. This is the first stage, before any individual supplier is considered.
- *Authorisation in principle*: Who agrees that the stated need, requirement or desire is justified – that is, who provides the authorisation, in principle at least, that the product or service should be considered.

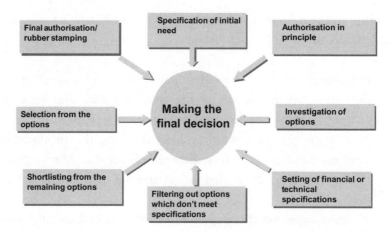

Figure 5.1   Possible stages of the internal decision-making process

- *Investigation of options*: Who investigates the various product/ service and supplier options likely to meet the stated need, requirement or desire.
- *Setting specifications*: Who influences and/or sets the specifications – financial or technical – for the products/services and suppliers being considered.
- *Filtering out options*: Who further examines the options to filter out those which don't meet these specifications.
- *Shortlisting*: Who produces a shortlist from the remaining options.
- *Selection*: Who selects the option chosen.
- *Final authorisation*: Where the *de facto* final decision has been made, but formal authorisation to go ahead is required, who provides that rubber stamp.

It may well be that the same individual is involved in more than one stage, or that, conversely, more than one individual is involved in any one stage. For example, there may be no separation between the selection and final authorisation stages because there is no need for a rubber stamp.

The complexity of the decision-making process can be illustrated by the example of a business-to-business software services provider who needs to deal with at least four layers of people in the customer organisation:

- *Procurement*: These are the people who negotiate the initial contract and are concerned with contract renewals.
- *The users*: These include people in functional departments within the customer organisation – for instance, the finance department – as well as the IT department who support the software solutions; all these people are the actual users of the software service provider's offerings.
- *The managers*: These comprise the project managers concerned with the implementation of the software solution (which can take more than a year to be completed).
- *The 'C'-suite/director level*: These are the most senior people in the organisation, whose sign-off is required before the solution is adopted.

It is also possible to link buying influence classifications of the type produced by Miller and Heiman to some or all of the stages mentioned earlier. Figure 5.2 provides an illustration of how this linkage may occur within a business-to-business customer organisation, although it should be recognised that, from one company to the next, there may be differences in the relative importance of the various buying influences at each stage of the decision-making process.

In practice, of course, the buying influences will be defined in terms of their functions or job titles. In business-to-business markets, some buying influences can be virtually self-defining – for example, technical managers or engineers will often fulfil a technical buying role involved in product specifications. However, this

Stage	Possible buying influence
Specification of initial need	User buyer
Investigation of options	User buyer or technical buyer
Influence on technical specifications	Technical buyer or coach
Setting of technical specifications	Technical buyer
Setting of financial specifications	User buyer or economic buyer
Filtering out	User buyer or technical buyer
Shortlisting	User buyer, technical buyer or (indirectly) coach
Final selection	Economic buyer and/or user buyer

Figure 5.2 Linking buying influences to stages of the decision-making process

is not necessarily the case for all buying influences: for example, the purchasing manager, because of his concern about price/commercial considerations, could in certain situations be the economic buyer, but so could the general manager or chief executive.

Although much of the discussion relating to the DMU is particularly pertinent to business-to-business markets, we must recognise that in consumer markets as well the decision-making process may involve more parties than may initially be assumed. For example, when a family embarks on a holiday, the choice of the holiday is influenced by a combination of preferred destination, type of holiday sought, price, and so on; and the way in which the decision is made will also be influenced by family circumstances, the ways in which information can be accessed, etc. A hypothetical scenario involving a working father and a mother looking after young children could therefore be as follows:

- Who specifies initial need/requirement or desire? – children desiring an activity holiday.
- Who agrees in principle to go along with the children's desire for an activity holiday? – both parents.

- Who investigates holiday options? – mother, by searching on the internet.
- Who filters the options (bearing in mind financial or other considerations)? – father, with mother's involvement.
- Who agrees the shortlist? – both parents.
- Who makes the final decision? – both parents, ensuring that the children are happy with it.

Clearly, the value of the item of expenditure being considered by the customer can have a major bearing on the complexity of the decision-making process – the greater the value the greater the number of people who are likely to be involved in the decision making because more is at stake. To take an obvious example, the child's desire to buy a lollipop is unlikely to involve the same degree of family involvement as his wish to go on an activity holiday!

Not recognising the role of the different parties involved at various stages of the decision-making process can mean lost opportunities and lost business; if, for example, you focus your sole attention on the individual you normally interface with, but your competitor recognises that there is also another individual fulfilling an 'economic buyer' role at the crucial final selection stage, you should not be surprised if you find that you are losing business to the competition.

NEEDS, INTERESTS AND DESIRES

Implicit in much of the discussion so far is the importance of understanding the specific needs, interests or desires each individual within the DMU has in the outcome of the decision-making process. In the example above, the interest of the children is to have a holiday which will keep boredom at bay by offering a range of activities; at the other extreme, the father is the obvious economic buyer – a key interest for him is to ensure that the holiday comes within his budget. Similarly, when a couple is engaged in decorating their home, it may be that the male partner will choose paint for its performance and ease of use – because he will be doing the bulk of the paintwork – whereas the female partner may be more involved in the softer aspects concerned with paint colour, the scope for colour matching, the ambience intended for the home, and so on.

Of course, this stereotypical role playing may not always apply, and we should be careful to ensure that we are reasonably confident about the different roles of all the parties concerned. In the real world, the roles and needs/wants of the various individuals involved in decision making are seldom totally distinct. However, although there can be some blurring between them, it is worth establishing who is *primarily* engaged at the various stages of the decision-making process and what their primary concerns are.

PSYCHO-CULTURAL ENVIRONMENT

In business-to-business markets, closely allied to the needs and wants of the individuals with whom we are dealing is the 'psycho-cultural' environment in which these individuals are operating. By this we mean, first, the overall corporate culture of the organisation in which the individuals are working; and, second, the morale of these individuals, which can be affected by organisational culture and/or the attitudes of their closest colleagues and managers.

Overall corporate culture will determine whether, for example, the customer organisation has an aggressive, 'macho' approach to business, is highly focused on cost reduction, is concerned with short-term, bottom-line results, won't take 'no' for an answer, demands exacting time schedules, and so on; or, at the other extreme, whether the organisation has a more collegiate, partnership-based approach, more concerned with quality issues and its long-term position. Vast differences in corporate culture can prevail even within the same industry; by way of example, two of the leading companies within a certain sector of manufacturing are regarded very differently by some of their suppliers – one is consistently seen to be the 'nice' company which everybody wishes to deal with and the other is seen as the 'client from hell'.

Understanding the culture in which your customer contacts operate can help you to interpret and filter their responses to your advantage: let us say, for example, that it is virtually habitual for your contact to be in panic mode because the culture of his organisation seems to encourage neurosis; being aware of this will enable you to respond in a way which is sensitive to the pressures under which he is operating. In some instances, this could even give you the opportunity to be the comforting shoulder to cry on, thereby enabling you to develop a relationship in which your contact becomes ever more reliant on your guidance and help.

Corporate culture may influence the morale of the individuals you are dealing with, but morale can be influenced by more immediate circumstances as well; your contact, for example, is reporting to a difficult or insecure manager, or he is operating in a 'dog eat dog' team within which all the people feel the need to look over their shoulders when they make decisions. By understanding the personal, as well as corporate, pressures, to which your contacts are being subjected, you can handle them more sensitively and even turn the situation to your advantage. You can gain even greater advantage if you can apply this understanding to all those involved in the decision-making process – whether they perform the role of user buyer, technical buyer or economic buyer, or whether they be your day-to-day contacts or their immediate managers.

One final point: an earlier section referred to the needs, interests and desires of the individuals within the DMU. These were discussed in the context of 'rational' motivations – the child wishes to go on an activity holiday because it is fun, the technical manager is concerned with technical issues not least because it is part of his job. What drives the individual to behave the way he does can also, however, be understood in the context of 'emotional' motivations; just as we discuss staff motivation in the next chapter, so we can seek to understand the emotional motivations of our contacts within the customer organisation.

These motivations will be closely connected with corporate culture and with the morale of the individual. The technical manager's rational requirement may be to ensure that products meet specifications, but if he is operating within a highly demanding corporate culture he may well be correspondingly more demanding of the service you offer him: if he feels that his every decision is being scrutinised, he will have the emotional need to over-scrutinise everything you offer him as well. If you can make a shrewd assessment of this situation, you will know that you need to respond to his emotional as well as his rational need by making every effort to allay his anxieties. Returning to the discussion in Chapter 3 about back of mind issues, you will be recognising the need to fulfil an unstated requirement – in this case, reassurance. By so doing, you will be better placed to win his trust and consolidate his loyalty to your organisation. You will, in effect, have demonstrated how an organisation can be emotionally intelligent in its dealings with its customers and how the application of such 'corporate emotional intelligence' can benefit your own organisation.

APPROPRIATE APPROACHES

Recognising that there are different parties involved in the decision-making process can also materially influence the way in which you go about approaching them. Take the example of companies engaged in the personal selling of high value items to households; the more professional organisations – whether they were selling encyclopaedia sets or white goods – learned over 30 years ago that, when the household included two partners, it was critically important to ensure that *both* partners were present at the time of the sales pitch. The suppliers may not have known what the precise role or interest of each partner was but they did know that, if only one partner was present, the other partner was liable to pour cold water on the potential purchase; a sales opportunity would be lost, even if the partner present had been convinced about the value of the product at the time the sales pitch was being made. In short, by engaging with all the potential decision influencers, you are increasing the likelihood of their buy-in and therefore the probability of making the sale.

Some organisations have developed their sales approaches to a fine art by applying their understanding of the emotional responses of customers: at least one supplier of educational books had found that a salesperson visiting the home of any couple should be careful about how the individuals in the room sat; if the salesperson was male, it was important when demonstrating the books he was selling to ensure that both he and the couple sat on the same sofa, but, crucially, that the male partner sat in the middle so that there was a separation between the salesperson and the female partner. The company had evidently found that close proximity between the salesperson and the female member of the household would generate feelings of insecurity within the male partner – which would kill off the possibility of making a successful sale!

If you know the precise roles and needs of the different parties involved in the decision making, you are in a position not only to engage with them all but also to approach them with messages which are likely to be most effective in winning their attention. It stands to reason that if you are operating in business-to-business markets and you need to speak to a technical manager or engineer, you are likely to focus your message on quality-related issues; with the purchasing manager or finance director you may stress value for money or return on investment; with the CEO/board you may dwell on the long-term value of the product/service being considered and the ways in which it can help the customer organisation perform better in its own business. In all instances, if you also understand the emotional needs of the parties involved, you are well placed to make an even more powerful impact.

When approaching business-to-business organisations in particular, one of the challenges we face relates to how we can define and understand the 'customer' view when there may be a number of different parties with different priorities and attitudes. How, for example, can we measure how satisfied a particular customer organisation, as a single entity, is with our service, if the individuals within the organisation have different views about us? One option is to decide who the single most important individual is within the customer organisation and use that person's views as a surrogate for the 'company view'. This option is clearly problematic since the assumption that any one individual represents the company view may well not be a supportable one. Also, it assumes that you are accurate in identifying the individual who is most likely to 'represent' the company.

Another possibility is to take into account the relative importance of the different parties within the DMU and come to a 'weighted average' view. If you know that the finance director as economic buyer accounts for 50% of the decision, the technical buyer 30% and the purchasing manager 20%, you may decide to weight their respective opinions by these percentages to come up with an overall company view. This is precisely the approach taken by the business-to-business software services provider referred to earlier: this company places the greatest weight on the C-suite individuals, after whom managers are given the most importance, with the user and procurement people being accorded the lowest importance. This approach is, however, fraught with problems:

- Taking a weighted average view can be misleading precisely because it may hide significant variations.

- The approach assumes you have succeeded in identifying all the parties accurately.

- It assumes that you know how to weight their importance. However, when this sort of weighting has been attempted, it has usually been done subjectively, based typically on the experience of the individuals within your organisation who have had most contact with the customer. This approach is highly likely to result in bias: for example, salespeople may, quite understandably, overemphasise the importance of those with whom they are most frequently in contact. Seeking the opinion of the customer contacts themselves is liable to result in even more bias – in favour of the individual customer contact whose opinion you seek. A further complication arises from the difficulty in applying a generalised rule across your market. The weights may vary by geography – for example, women in some non-western societies are unlikely to have the same role as those in western societies; or by company size – in SMEs, for instance, managing directors are likely to play a more active role in purchase decisions than their counterparts in larger organisations.

Rather than weighting the role of individuals involved in the decision making, it may be more realistic to treat each of these decision makers as a 'mini-target' within the customer organisation. Returning to the household decorating example, you may communicate the softer issues of colour, home decorating, etc. to the woman, advertising in women's magazines; conversely, the 'harder' messages relating to ease of application, performance, etc. could be directed at the male audience (assuming that these somewhat stereotypical roles do apply), possibly using DIY journals as one method of communication. In business-to-business markets, you may wish to target, on the one hand, purchasing decision makers (focusing on commercial aspects like value for money) and, on the other, technical or production managers (emphasising performance aspects in technical journals, for example). It is true that, by focusing the sales and marketing activity on each of the individuals involved in the decision-making process, you may not be making optimum use of your resources, since in reality it is quite likely that one individual will have a greater impact on the final decision than another. Some qualitative judgement may, therefore, be required about the amount of attention each individual warrants; that may be appropriate as long as this judgement is applied in a self-critical manner which recognises the potential danger of biases creeping into the judgements being made.

Potentially a significant amount of time and effort can be invested in ensuring that your approaches are adapted to cater for the different needs, interests and wants of the various parties involved in the decision-making process. For practical reasons, you may wish to focus most of your efforts on those customers who account for a relatively large proportion of your business. This is another reason why the discussion surrounding the identification of the different parts of the DMU is normally held in the context of business-to-business markets, where the 80/20 rule is far more likely to apply than in consumer markets.

UPDATING THE DATABASE AND PROFILING THE DMU

A final point: it goes without saying that you should update your database as you refine the information you have about the various individuals involved in purchase decisions. The sad truth is that even the most sophisticated multinationals have been found to struggle with keeping their databases clean and up to date, their customer lists often containing inaccurate telephone numbers, addresses and even, in some instances, names of individuals who are deceased! Your database and your CRM tools are critical to the way in which you approach your customers and prospects.

The individuals in your database must therefore be frequently reviewed so that your staff can approach them in the confident knowledge that they are covering off all the people on whom they should focus their attention, not just those with whom they have historically had the greatest contact.

Particularly in the case of business-to-business customers, the database should as far as possible include a profile of each relevant individual within the customer organisation. This profile should include all the most pertinent information about each individual (role, key concerns, involvement in decision-making process, etc.). This information would considerably enhance the data typically provided about individuals, often confined to job titles. Figure 5.3 is an adapted version of Figure 2.4, giving the example of a single hypothetical company, Abacus Ltd. Figure 2.4 showed how a database can be enhanced by showing the likely market segment to which an individual customer organisation may belong; Figure 5.3 now shows how the database can be rendered more powerful by providing further information about each relevant individual within the customer organisation.

Comp-any name	Address	Post code	Likely segment	DMU Details					
				Initial	Surname	Function	Role	Primary interest – rational (R) and/or emotional (E)	Stage of Decision
Abacus Ltd	3 Sorbonne Close	M26 4CA	3	A	Birt	Chief buyer	User buyer	R – value for money E - job security	- Needs specification - Shortlisting - Final selection
				B	Cape	Technical engineer	Technical specifier	R – performance to specs E – risk aversion	- Technical specification - Filtering out - Shortlisting
				D	Earl	Finance director	Economic buyer	R – contribution to bottom line E – ambition to be CEO	- Initial need specification - Final selection

Figure 5.3   Enhancing the contact database through detailed profiling

THE EXECUTIVE SELF-ASSESSMENT CHECKLIST: DECISION-MAKING DYNAMICS

Question	Yes, confident +3	Yes, tentative 0	No −3	NA
Do we recognise that the decision-making unit can include more than one individual involved in purchase decisions?				
Are we confident that we have identified who these individuals are?				
Do we know what the key stages of the decision-making process are?				
Do we know what the roles are of all the individuals involved at all the key stages of the decision-making process?				
Do we know what their functional/rational requirements and motivations are?				
Do we know what their emotional motivations are?				
Do we approach all the individuals involved in the decision-making process?				
Do we adapt our approaches to them to cater for their rational needs?				
Are our approaches also sensitive to their emotional needs?				

Question	Yes, confident +3	Yes, tentative 0	No −3	NA

Do we have an understanding of the corporate culture of the customer organisations we are dealing with?

Do we have an understanding of the immediate pressures being exerted on the contacts we normally deal with?

Are we sensitive to those pressures in the way in which we deal with our contacts?

Can we think of examples of situations where we have won (or lost) against the competition because we succeeded (or failed) to recognise the role of all the key parties to the decision-making process?

Have we been able to turn a difficult client situation to our commercial advantage by recognising the emotional needs of the relevant parties involved in the decision-making process?

Do we feel that we are successful in adapting our messages to answer the different needs of the different individuals within the DMU?

Is our database continually reviewed so that we have an accurate and up-to-date record of all the key individuals operating within the customer DMU?

Question	Yes, confident +3	Yes, tentative 0	No −3	NA
Does our database include information about these individuals' roles and interests, and the stages where they become involved in decisions?				
GRAND TOTAL SCORE				
NET ABSOLUTE SCORE				
NET AVERAGE SCORE				

Now, taking each of the above questions, what in practice are we doing?

CHAPTER 6

STAFF MOTIVATION AND PERCEPTIONS

SOME INTRODUCTORY THOUGHTS ON STAFF MOTIVATION

Today, more than ever, staff motivation and retention are critical issues for the success of any organisation. Talented and experienced staff are essential to any enterprise seeking to gain and retain an edge over the competition. Organisations must (although they do not always) recognise that staff are a precious resource: just as they are faced with increasing competition in the external marketplace, they also face increasing pressure to retain high quality staff. Similarly, just as it costs far more to win new external customers than to keep current customers, so it is far more expensive to recruit new staff than to retain existing employees. Research undertaken at Manchester Business School in 2005 by Dr Ram Raghavan (currently Director of Talengene) has shown that on average a company loses six months' worth of man-days for every vacancy that needs to be filled. An organisation's success in retaining the right staff can, therefore, have a significant impact on its bottom line. In a sense, a high staff turnover is even more problematic than a high customer churn rate because there is a specific risk attached to new staff – the risk that the new employee may simply not match the quality or the experience of the person who left the company or may fail to fit into the culture of the company. This is quite possible because it is precisely the best employees who are in most demand and therefore most likely to leave. By contrast, there is no reason why a lost customer should be *inherently* more valuable than a new one.

At the same time, survey after survey has demonstrated how staff motivation, by influencing staff retention and customer satisfaction, ultimately has an impact on business performance: to take one example, a study of 90 000 workers worldwide, conducted in 2007 by Towers Perrin, showed that, whereas only 23% of workers currently felt engaged at work, firms with the highest percentage of engaged employees collectively increased operating income by 19% whereas those with the lowest percentage showed a 33% decline in operating income.

It is intuitively obvious that there is a link between happy customers and happy staff: no customer wishes to deal with a grumpy member of staff and equally no staff member wishes to face an irate customer. More positively, motivated and happy staff communicate their positive attitude to customers, and, in turn, staff find it rewarding to deal with happy customers. But there is also a considerable body of evidence which supports the view that staff motivation and customer satisfaction are interlinked: as far back as 1998 we learnt how Sears Roebuck found empirically, through information gathered from their stores, that a given increase in employee satisfaction had a positive impact on customer perceptions and, ultimately, financial performance (see Rucci *et al.* 1998).

It may be a hoary cliché, but no less true for that, to say that staff represent the 'internal customers' of the organisation. Senior management should therefore treat their staff as though they form an 'internal marketplace'. Since they represent the organisation's internal stakeholders, their critical role in its future success should be obvious. Some organisations seem to have gone further by ensuring that their staff have a very direct stake in them: in the UK, the staff of the department store John Lewis feel that, as co-owners (or 'partners', as they are called) of the store, they are in effect working for themselves, not for a 'separate' employer; the lack of a 'we/they' mentality means that staff at all levels feel that they are working together as a team and benefit to the same degree from the success of the organisation – a point vividly illustrated by the announcement in March 2008 of a bonus for all John Lewis staff equivalent to 20% of their salaries, beating the 18% awarded in the previous year. And it is difficult not to see the connection here between the high morale this engenders and the performance of the company in terms of customer satisfaction and financial results: in the 2008 Consumer Satisfaction Index survey, conducted among 6 000 shoppers by Verdict, the retail consultancy, John Lewis and its supermarket subsidiary Waitrose occupied first and second place, respectively (and they had similarly occupied the top two positions in 2007). It is perhaps no coincidence that John Lewis also happens to be one of the few retailers announcing good sales results – announcing profits of £380 million, a 19% rise over the previous year.

The reality, however, is that some companies continue to treat their staff in a way which they would never dream of treating their external customers. For all the companies like John Lewis and Waitrose, there are far too many that need seriously to examine how they motivate their staff. They don't appear to be able to make the connection between happy customers and happy staff, and as a result fail to focus on staff satisfaction in the way they focus on the satisfaction of their external customers.

A number of the questions so far raised in the context of external customers may therefore be applied, with some adaptation, to staff:

- What really motivates your staff?
- Do staff attitudes vary by type, function, seniority, or location, and, if so, how?
- What do staff feel about your organisation as a place to work?
- What do staff feel about your organisation's brand?
- What do staff feel about their colleagues and superiors?
- How loyal are your staff?
- Are your staff your best ambassadors?
- What, and how well, do you communicate to your staff?
- Is the corporate culture of your organisation collegiate and participatory or hierarchical and threatening?
- What needs to be done to entrench staff loyalty?

The list of topics could be extended, to parallel many of the topics already covered in the context of external customers. To illustrate the point, we will confine ourselves to one example: just as there may be 'balance tippers' which move customers to give you their business over the competition, equally there may be similar 'little extra somethings' which may help to bind staff to your organisation. Figure 6.1 shows a few examples of the different ways in which companies listed in the *Fortune Magazine* and the *Sunday Times* 100 Best Companies to Work For rankings have sought to motivate their staff.

What is noticeable about the offers shown here is that, in many cases, they represent benefits which may not be expected but, perhaps precisely because they are unexpected, are quite likely to delight the recipients of those benefits – another way of describing the balance tippers mentioned in Chapter 3. They sometimes represent a relatively small financial investment on the part of the company concerned, an investment which is likely to be far outweighed by the return in terms of motivation and loyalty. Some – like Google's contribution to the purchase of hybrid or electric cars, Genentech's subsidy for minimising the use of cars, and Arup's sabbaticals for help in disaster zones – are apparently designed to

- Prayer/meditation rooms with pillows and tatami floor mats (eBay)
- A $4 per day subsidy for coming to work by bicycle, on foot or in a car pool (Genentech)
- $1000 towards purchase of a hybrid or electric car (Google)
- Dollar for dollar match of employee charitable contributions up to $12 000 (Microsoft)
- Flexible work patterns, such as job sharing and compressed/staggered hours, and the absence of the long hours culture typical of banks (Handelsbanken)
- Fully-paid 3-12 month sabbaticals to help with natural and man-made disasters (Arup)
- Daily fresh fruit and free homemade soup and crusty bread every Friday (Jones Lang LaSalle)
- Purchase of bicycles, wine club membership and use of accountants to fill out tax returns (The Wrigley Company)

Figure 6.1 Staff benefits which could be 'balance tippers'

show that these companies are sensitive to environmental and community issues, thereby cleverly combining the provision of employee benefits with a reinforcement of their desired values and reputation. Others, through apparently trivial gestures, such as Jones Lang LaSalle's provision of homemade soup, are indicating to their staff that the company cares for them.

Many of these companies, it seems, demonstrate a 'corporate emotional intelligence' which seems to elude many other organisations, by recognising a simple truth: that staff motivation does not boil down solely to material rewards and is also about the deeper feelings of being genuinely appreciated and of 'doing good' – working with employers whom staff can feel proud of because they offer moral leadership.

It doesn't, however, necessarily require companies to make glamorous or quirky gestures for staff to feel appreciated. A survey of 1003 full-time employed adults in the US, conducted by Maritz Poll in October 2006, found that people are motivated in different ways, and that some of us are particularly strongly motivated by praise. A genuine 'thank you' is gratifying for most of us (and doesn't cost the company any money), and it can work wonders for the 'praise cravers', the term coined by Maritz for the group most strongly motivated by a pat on the back. The operative word here is 'genuine': thanking staff today only to make them redundant next week is hardly going to engender feelings of trust and loyalty. A survey reported in late 2007 stated, however, that a third of workers complained that they were never thanked for their efforts, a sad reflection on the emotional intelligence of their bosses.

However, just as it is important for companies to engage in staff motivation programmes, it is equally important to ensure that the right programme is chosen. This is particularly important when individual staff are being singled out for particular recognition: for example, a survey conducted among insurance company salespeople in the UK found that the jamborees (high profile trips abroad, for example) awarded to 'high flying' sales executives were, on balance, having a *negative* effect on staff. This was because the majority of the salesforce – those middle level, competent staff who provided the bread and butter of the business, but who weren't regarded as star performers – felt positively demotivated by the feeling of being left out of the accolades awarded to the minority who had been given 'public' recognition. Companies should, therefore, be sensitive to the possibility that, in ostentatiously rewarding the few who are seen to have performed outstandingly, they do not turn off the many who may be doing reasonably well. In these cases, a quieter, less high profile way of rewarding those selected may be the more appropriate route to adopt.

The example of insurance industry salespeople indicates that inappropriate ways of rewarding staff may actually have a harmful impact on the performance of the organisation, demotivated staff being more likely to defect to the competition. There is considerable evidence which shows that the right type of incentive can, by contrast, lead to concrete benefits: a study by Hewlett-Packard and the Mind Lab Group, for example, showed that flexible working hours and the provision of up-to-date technology reduced stress levels and enhanced IQ performance, enabling staff to better retain and process information when they were spending long periods of time at their desks.

A few final points on the subject of staff motivation:

- Those organisations that already undertake staff surveys are quite possibly ahead of those that don't – at least in so far as they have taken a practical first step in recognising that staff opinions do matter. However, staff surveys – like external customer surveys – can be worse than useless if the results of the surveys are not seen to be honestly acted upon; surveys done from one year to the next without any tangible outcome benefiting staff will only be seen by staff as a cynical ploy to keep them quiet and may even encourage disaffection.

- It is noticeable how many organisations fail to apply 'joined-up' thinking on the twin questions of staff retention and recruitment. New staff are recruited because of a perceived gap to be filled, but organisations often fail to pay adequate attention to the impact of such recruitment on existing staff: a typical scenario may be one where someone is recruited to occupy a position which an existing staff member may have felt quite capable of filling, the result being resentment and disaffection. The organisation may well be aware of the views of the existing staff member and may feel that this person is overestimating his/her abilities – but how much effort is made to explain the rationale of the recruitment so that any potential feelings of resentment are addressed?

  More to the point, how often do organisations link the issues of staff recruitment and internal staff progression? Rather than thinking piecemeal – 'We need to recruit someone to fill this vacancy' – it may be far more productive to take a step back and think about all the pieces which may need to be moved around to enhance staff motivation and performance: this could involve, perhaps, redefining and expanding the roles of existing staff members and, only in that context, thinking about how a new recruit would fit into the organisation – indeed, quite possibly even *whether* a new recruit is required after all. In other words, new staff recruitment and existing staff progression should be seen as two sides of the same coin. Instead of starting with the premise that new staff need to be recruited, the starting point should be an examination of how best the talents of existing staff can be harnessed, with the new staff member being just one of a number of pieces to be considered. This is not to advocate a cynical policy of recruitment freezes designed to 'economise' by squeezing more work out of existing staff – a policy which many organisations seem to be adopting without any thought about its effects on staff morale. Our suggestion stems from quite the opposite premise: that staff are a precious resource whose feelings and motivations should be given time and attention if they – and therefore the organisation they work for – are to prosper.

The US retailer Nordstrom, which has a strong reputation for customer service as well as happy staff, appears to understand the need to make the connection between staff recruitment and the motivation of existing staff so that all staff, new and existing, can work happily together from the start as members of the same team: this is achieved, for example, by hiring people who seem to share the values of the company, and by adopting a 'democratic' recruitment procedure, involving existing staff in the interviewing process when new recruits are likely to be their peers.

- The issue of staff motivation is relevant across all levels of staff. There is a tendency for organisations to think of staff motivation and retention from a top-down perspective, the focus of attention often excluding the most senior levels of staff. Arguably, however, if a board director were to feel disaffected, the ripple effect across the organisation is liable to be far greater than if someone lower down the hierarchy were to resign.

STAFF PERCEPTIONS: INTRODUCTION

Whereas much has been written and spoken about staff motivation, less attention appears to have been paid to staff perceptions about the business in which they are operating. This seems to be reflected not only in the number of papers and books written on the subject of employee motivation but also in the way in which organisations in practice address staff issues: this seems to be very much the domain of the human resources function, with HR personnel often taking the initiative in this area.

Although it is quite right that HR managers should concern themselves with matters concerning the well-being of staff, there is a role for general, and in particular marketing, management when staff *perceptions* are being considered.

The term 'perceptions' is used here to mean something distinct from 'motivation': motivation is concerned with the emotional side of employees' working lives, whereas staff perceptions relate to the employees' beliefs about the market in which they are operating and their understanding of the organisations for which they are working. Motivation is about heart; perception is about mind.

There are two broad areas of staff perception which we will address:

- Are staff in touch with the marketplace in which they are operating?
- Are processes and opinions within your organisation aligned?

ARE STAFF IN TOUCH WITH THE MARKETPLACE?

If your organisation is to truly understand the market, you need to ensure that, in most cases at least, this understanding filters through all the relevant parts of the organisation. By 'relevant parts' we mean in particular staff who operate in functions which are in any way market facing (from receptionists and call centre operators to marketing, sales and general management personnel). If we are genuinely to become market-sensitive, this understanding should not be the preserve of a few but should inform the behaviour and actions of all staff who are, directly or indirectly, in contact with the marketplace.

However, are you confident that staff in your organisation are really in touch with your marketplace? We have experience of many companies – a few examples of which are cited later – where staff have seriously misunderstood their customers, making assumptions and decisions which do not reflect the reality of their markets. It is important, therefore, that companies regularly undertake a 'health check' on staff understanding, much as they do when they carry out staff motivation surveys.

The key is to identify any significant gaps between staff thinking and marketplace reality, and then to act on bridging those gaps. It is only by finding out opinions directly from staff that the existence and extent of a gap can be revealed and so corrective action – by way of internal communication/education or staff training – can be taken.

We have referred to marketplace 'reality'; in practice, sometimes that 'reality' may be based on the customers' own misunderstanding or ignorance – for example, when customers are not aware of a particular service you may be offering. In that case, the gap is narrowed by educating customers about the service in question. In so far as the customer is never 'wrong', it is up to you to make the move to bridge the gap – after all, it is ineffective communication on your part which has resulted in the customers' misperception. The customer view, whether 'right' or 'wrong', must, therefore, always represent the reality you face – and it is your job, not the customer's, to take the appropriate action.

It should be noted that, when referring to staff opinions, we could be talking about two interlinked but separate sets of views:

- What staff themselves believe about a particular topic.
- What staff believe to be the view of the marketplace (which may not be the same as their own view).

It is possible, for example, that staff may believe that a particular aspect of the service they offer is mediocre but at the same time believe that customers view the service as being satisfactory. This could arise from the inside knowledge staff have that the actual quality of the service offered could be significantly improved, although they also believe that customers are not aware of this. In this scenario, there are in fact two possible gaps:

> What staff themselves believe ↔ What staff believe to be the view of the marketplace ↔ What the marketplace actually believes

If it were found, however, that the marketplace realises that the quality of the service is in fact mediocre, then the staff view that they don't realise this represents a potentially dangerous gap, whatever the staff's own beliefs happen to be. Arguably, if staff themselves believe the service to be mediocre, customers may in time detect the employees' real attitude, which may only serve to antagonise customers by emerging as being cynical. In addition, if staff believe that they are offering a mediocre service but that they are being expected by management to 'pull the wool over the eyes' of the customer, the organisation could well be faced with staff morale problems.

Having said this, if staff genuinely believe that the quality of the products and services they offer is good when customers in fact believe it to be mediocre, that would indicate that:

- staff are genuinely out of touch with customer views, and
- if staff views are based on fact – namely, that the quality of the products and services offered *is* indeed good – the organisation has failed to communicate this important fact to customers.

For the rest of this chapter, any reference to staff opinions may encompass the staff's own views, the staff's views about market opinion, or both. The fundamental gap we are concerned with is the one existing between staff opinion (however defined) and market opinion, and this will be the focus of the discussion that follows.

So where can the gaps between staff and the marketplace be found? We will consider four key scenarios:

- *What drives choice of supplier?* What do staff think compared with what actually drives customers and prospects?
- *How satisfied are customers?* What do staff think compared with actual levels of customer satisfaction?
- *What is the image/standing of the organization?* What do staff think compared with the views of all stakeholders and opinion formers whose views are important to the company? These stakeholders and opinion formers could include, in addition to customers and prospects, financial analysts, the media, shareholders, the community at large, and so on.
- *The market?* What is staff opinion and knowledge about the market compared with the actual profile of the market? This would include the size of the market, its structure, competitor activity, market growth, future prospects, SWOT (the strengths, weaknesses, opportunities and threats in the market), and PEST (political, economic, social and technological issues); this is one area where the staff whose opinions matter are likely to be mainly those in a general and marketing management function.

Scenario 1: What drives choice of supplier?

If staff are consistently out of touch with what drives customers' choice of supplier, the consequences can be serious:

- Misallocation of resources/faulty decision making in terms of:
  - products
  - services
  - pricing
  - marketing and communications.
- Potential customer defection or failure to attract new customers.
- Potential revenue/profit decline.

A few examples of Scenario 1:

- Key customer-facing staff in the UK, working with a global insurance provider, believed the company's international coverage and expertise to be a major attraction to their customers. The insurer found out from its customers that being international was in fact of little relevance to UK customers, for whom the insurer's domestic offering was the prime consideration. The fact that this gap was clearly highlighted brought home to management (who had themselves believed that global standing was a major competitive advantage) the need to educate themselves and the rest of the relevant staff that they should shift their marketing and communications away from the 'international' theme. This meant both improved resource allocation and a more hard-hitting and effective message to their target market.
- Many companies, especially those operating in consumer markets where they are reliant on call centres, seem to have lost sight of customers' need for a personal service. Some, like the UK bank First Direct, with its strapline 'real people to talk to', or the UK insurer Direct Line, strive to be highly customer focused, recognising, for example, that callers would far rather deal with human beings than with machines – a point strongly emphasised in their advertising. To most consumers, this preference would seem to be blindingly obvious, yet management in far too many organisations (some utilities being a prime case

in point) appear to be oblivious to how out of touch they are with customer opinion, seemingly unaware of the intense annoyance of consumers asked to press innumerable buttons before they can finally speak to a person who can deal with their issue. Or, quite possibly, these companies have deliberately chosen to prioritise internal 'efficiencies' over the long-term care of their customers. As a result, customer-facing staff are often astonishingly insensitive to the needs of customers, a point borne out by the very mediocre satisfaction ratings which many organisations, from retail banks to utilities, continue to receive, notwithstanding the lip service given by these organisations to the maximisation of customer satisfaction. To take a small anecdotal example, a consumer recently complained to his household insurance company about the vast number of different parties (from loss adjusters to builders to 'trace and access' specialists) with whom he had been obliged to deal in the course of a home insurance claim; the response of the person handling the complaint was that it was 'only natural' that he would need to deal with these different parties! Setting aside whether or not it is 'natural' to deal with seven different parties, the response reflected a total ignorance of the way a customer might think and a complete lack of training in knowing how to handle a customer in this type of situation.

- Staff at a petrochemicals company believed that their customers were driven by price and product considerations significantly more than was actually the case. Conversely, they underestimated the importance to customers of issues concerned with service and relationships. Figure 6.2 illustrates this gap.

What Figure 6.2 reveals is a classic error many companies are prone to make: a tendency to focus on the tangibles they can offer at the expense of the more apparently 'marginal' – often softer – issues which customers may be concerned with. So, almost predictably, staff regarded price and performance to

Gap analysis: Internal staff versus external customer opinions

Drivers of long-term satisfaction

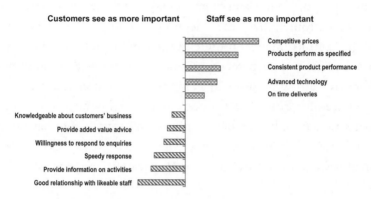

Figure 6.2   Assessing your staff perceptions

specification as being more important than did customers, and, at the other end of the spectrum, underestimated the importance to customers of interpersonal relationships and information provision. As Chapter 3 revealed, it is often these softer issues which tip the balance in favour of one supplier over another, a point not fully understood by the petrochemicals company. It should be noted that price and product performance *were* important to customers, but not *as* important as staff believed them to be; what is relevant here is the gap, not the absolute opinion.

Some organisations have made huge efforts to ensure that they are in touch with their customers' expectations. Going back to First Direct, here is a bank which has invested significant amounts in training its employees. Whereas many organisations record telephone conversations with their customers 'for quality and training purposes', First Direct management, unlike that of many other companies, does appear to act on what it has learnt: staff undergo a continuous training process to ensure that they are really in touch with customer needs, and regular and immediate feedback is given on the appropriateness and effectiveness of the response they have given to customers over the telephone. Doing so has helped the bank to keep its fingers on the customer pulse and ensure that the gap between its own perceptions and the real needs of customers is kept as narrow as possible. This type of action has produced tangible results: First Direct is consistently highly rated for its customer satisfaction, having been reported in early 2008 to have been Britain's top bank for customer service in a survey of over 13 000 individuals conducted by the market research company Mintel.

Scenario 2: How satisfied are customers?

If staff are consistently misreading how customers view the organisation's performance, there are a number of potential consequences:

- Perceived weaknesses are not addressed.
- Perceived strengths are not sufficiently capitalised upon.
- Resources may be misallocated and wrong decisions may be made regarding:
  ○ products
  ○ services
  ○ pricing
  ○ marketing and communications.
- Consequently customers become disaffected.
- Revenue and profits decline as a result.

A few examples of Scenario 2:

- Nowhere is the gap in perceptions more vividly illustrated than in the case of the oil company which succeeded in reducing its delivery lead time by more than half a day as a result of a TQM programme on which it had embarked. Staff prided themselves on their remarkable achievement, one of the results of a programme which had required an investment of millions of dollars. The sad news was that, in the course of a market investigation, company management found out – quite by chance, as it happens – that customers did not regard their delivery lead time to be better than that of any of their competitors. What was even worse, over 80% of their own customers had not even registered that there had been an improvement in delivery performance! In effect, most of the efforts made to make delivery improvements were wasted: there was hardly any point in making improvements if the customers did not recognise them. This case study recalls the year 3 – year 4 scenario described in Figure 4.5.

Again, the company had fallen into the proverbial trap of being internally focused: because it had made a significant improvement in delivery performance, it assumed that this was obvious and would be attractive to customers. Well, the reality was that it was not obvious to customers, and, even if it had been, it is debatable as to whether the advantage staff saw in this achievement would have been seen to the same extent by customers. The lesson for the company was that there was no point in spending huge resources on a service until it was clear that the service was appreciated (and noticed!) by its customers.

- In the 'input–impact analysis' section of Chapter 4, we referred to a chemicals company which had found out, through a market investigation, that customers rated its HSE (health, safety and environment) service as being worse than the competition's even though the company believed that it was in fact superior. Initially, there were howls of protest from senior managers but they quickly, albeit reluctantly, recognised that the 'fault' didn't lie with customers, and that a 'customer education' campaign was necessary to bridge the gap between the customers'

misconceptions and the reality of the company's actual performance. The interesting lesson that management drew from this
experience was not only that customers had a negative impression of the company's HSE performance but also that the company's staff had been clearly out of touch with customers'
opinions until they undertook the market investigation.

The examples cited reflect instances in which the company needed
to reallocate resources or educate/communicate to its staff. There
are, however, many instances when there is a need to implement
real service improvements. This would be the case where it is
found that staff have underestimated the extent of dissatisfaction
felt by customers and that this dissatisfaction is justified because
the performance of the company is not up to scratch or materially
worse than competitors'.

By contrast, some organisations have pre-emptively sought to
ensure that a gap is not allowed to develop between the perceptions of their customers and their own assessment of how they
stand with customers. The international financial services company
Prudential plc, for example, seeks to keep its fingers constantly on
the pulse of the market it serves by surveying new customers when
they receive their welcome pack, inviting existing customers to
give their feedback at the end of a telephone call, holding Meet-
Pru sessions where customers can meet board members, running
a Pru-Bus which tours to hold focus groups, and ensuring that
customer complaints are properly dealt with by a specialist customer relations unit.

Scenario 3: What is the image/standing of the company?

Chapter 7 will be addressing the need to take into account the
views of external stakeholders and influencers – pressure groups,
analysts, media, and so on – as well as those of the more obvious

customer and prospect targets. Suffice it to say at this stage that on matters relating to the corporate image and overall standing of your organisation, it is particularly important to identify and measure the extent of any gap between the views of all these stakeholders and the staff who communicate with them directly or indirectly. Relevant staff here would include those involved in such areas as corporate marketing, communications, investor relations and PR, as well as general management and marketing/sales staff directly interfacing with customers and prospects.

One instance of the critical importance of being aware of market image was the case of the international bank whose management believed that the bank was highly regarded for its ethics and probity. This was not, however, a view shared by certain sections of the media who, it was discovered, associated the bank with secret bank accounts connected with an unsavoury regime during the Second World War. Even if the reputation of the bank was being unfairly tarnished, management recognised that speedy action needed to be taken to address this perception if real damage was not to be done to the bank's image.

Scenario 4: The market

Your organisation needs to be in touch not only with the requirements, opinions and attitudes of those you wish to influence – customers, prospects and other stakeholders – but also with the 'harder' aspects of the market itself: the size of the market, competitor activity, future prospects, customer activity, and so on. It is self-evident that such basic knowledge is essential for your market strategy and growth plans, but it is also true that this information can also enhance your customer understanding. To take an obvious example, if you can anticipate that your business-to-business customers will increasingly find themselves operating in a tougher competitive environment, let's say because of the growth of low cost Indian and Chinese competitors, you will be better able to cater for their future requirements and attitudes; in this example, this could take the form of greater price sensitivity in the purchase of your products or a greater need for your support in helping them to offer *their* customers an added value service which cannot be matched by the new low cost competitors. It is valuable, therefore, to contextualise the requirements and attitudes of your customers and prospects by ensuring that your organisation keeps up to date with general market trends. Do you believe that your staff are on top of these trends, and what measures – in the form of training, for example – have you taken to maximise the likelihood that they will be in touch with market conditions?

ARE PROCESSES AND OPINIONS WITHIN YOUR ORGANISATION ALIGNED?

We discussed earlier the connection between happy, motivated staff and satisfied customers and we have also stressed that staff should be in touch with market needs and attitudes. Extensive research conducted by Manchester Business School has shown, however, that happy and informed employees do not automatically mean happy customers. There is an intervening variable – processes – which can either help or hinder the consistency and repeatability of the deliverables to the target market. Often gaps between staff and customers can arise from, or be exacerbated by, internal misalignments. Two ways in which such misalignments can occur are as follows:

- *Internal process misalignments:* Management believes that customers will acknowledge and recognise what is being delivered to them, but fails to realise that process misalignments within the organisation make the final deliverables to the customer

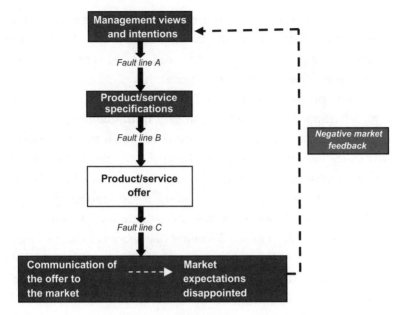

Figure 6.3   Internal Process Misalignments

different from what it had in mind. This point is well illustrated in the schematic shown in Figure 6.3.

Here we see a number of fault lines, the first of which (Fault Line A) describes how management views and intentions are not fully reflected in the way products and/or services have been specified. This situation can be aggravated, in turn, by the failure of the product and service offer fully to reflect the stated specifications (Fault Line B).

Fault Line C then describes the extent to which the products and services offered fail to fulfil the promise of the messages communicated to the market, resulting in market expectations being disappointed. This could well result from the fact that the communication reflects the original views and intentions of management which, as we have seen, have become distorted by internal slippages.

The net result of this misalignment is negative market feedback resulting from the disappointment felt by customers when their perceptions of the products or services actually delivered fall short of their expectations.

The precise ways in which this sort of misalignment takes place within an organisation can vary from one instance to the next. The worst case scenario is one in which there is slippage at every one of the stages shown in the diagram – the corporate equivalent of Chinese whispers – but it can take only one fault line for management intentions to be scuppered.

- *Misalignment of opinions within the organisation:* Although not explicitly stated, Figure 6.3 implies that there is some misalignment of opinions between management and the staff responsible for implementing the policy of management. This misalignment of views can happen between many different types/levels of staff, for example:

  - by seniority – where the vision or guidance of the leadership may not be clearly transmitted through the rest of the organisation
  - by function – where, for example, customer feedback transmitted by front line staff like salespeople is not adequately acted upon by support or technical staff or by senior management
  - by structure/location – where staff operating within subsidiaries may not feel that their knowledge of local operations is respected or acted upon by headquarters management.

Such misalignment can have serious consequences for the way the external customer is likely to view your organisation. A number of surveys in business-to-business markets have shown that customers feel frustrated when their immediate point of contact (let's say the relationship manager) within the supplier organisation does not have the authority to make on-the-spot decisions and has instead to refer back to head office to get a green light. This also causes the relationship manager to feel frustrated and demoralised. Not only does this give the signal that the local point of contact cannot be trusted to make the right decision but also that his viewpoint may not reflect that of senior management at head office. Whether or not a misalignment of views exists, the impression given to the customer is that it does. At a more strategic level, if all members of staff do not understand or share the vision of the organisation's leadership, there is a serious possibility that not only will there be confusion and morale problems within the organisation but also mixed, if not conflicting, messages being conveyed to the external marketplace. If, therefore, you have a mission statement, you may wish to check whether staff even know what it is (let alone understand or believe in it)!

Quite possibly the first action you need to take is to ensure that members of the management team are themselves in agreement about your organisation's visions and goals. A survey of senior executives within Fortune 500 companies conducted by William Schiemann & Associates found, for example, that as many as 30% of the respondents mentioned that there was 'lack of management agreement on business strategy'. If one considers the number of people who may not have mentioned this, either deliberately or because they did not know, the actual proportion could have been even higher. If there is confusion at the top it is hardly surprising that this confusion should filter down through the rest of the organisation.

At a more operational level, you may wish to consider the practical implications of gaps within different areas of your organisation, for example:

○ There is a gap between customer-facing staff and management; this could be because:
- the staff have failed to communicate adequately to management the views of the customers they deal with – for example, because they have no particular incentive to

do so (a point referred to in Chapter 4 in the section 'The world is a competitive place'), and/or

- management fails to listen adequately to what staff are telling them.

As a result of this situation, management is out of touch with the views of the customer, and since it is management that ultimately decides about the deliverables offered to customers, the net impact is liable to be lower customer satisfaction.

Poor communication within an organisation can result from a 'shoot the messenger' culture which makes staff concerned about the repercussions of any bad news they may feel they need to convey to management. Conversely, some companies have positively encouraged a free flow of information: John Lewis staff, for example, have a hotline to top management which enables them to offer them honest feedback whenever they feel that there are matters of importance, which could include customer service issues, to be dealt with. This type of open communication seems to be the hallmark of similarly well-managed companies, like Southwest Airlines, where a caring management ensures that staff can feel free to express their opinions about the customer feedback they receive.

○ The customer-facing staff are themselves out of touch with or turn a blind eye to customer views; this can happen when:

- they cling on to views with which they feel comfortable ('all the customer wants is a lower price', for example)
- they do not understand the customer – perhaps a new customer segment is emerging which staff are slow to recognise
- inadequate information is provided by management to customer-facing staff – information which may, for example, come from market research, industry sector information, or the provision of enhanced database/

CRM systems; we have already seen in Chapter 2 how the provision of information about the needs segments to which target prospects belong can empower sales executives in their approaches to individual customers. Similarly, a study by the Aberdeen Group (*Sales Effectiveness: Getting Sales Back to Selling*) showed that companies that were best in class in terms of sales effectiveness were those that adequately armed their sales teams with information on the company's (and competitors') products and how the products matched the needs of customers and prospects. Yet another survey, from Beagle Research Group, showed that 50% of the salespeople interviewed did not believe that they were adequately supported by their companies.

- Even though management is doing its best to provide valuable support and information, the customer-facing staff do not wish to know. For example, management offers staff suggestions on the ways in which customer service may be enhanced, but implementing these suggestions may mean that the chances of a quick sale are reduced; in this situation, staff may be tempted to take the easy, short-term option because they feel their sales commission is jeopardised. For them, the bird in the hand is worth two in the bush. Management must make them realise, through appropriate incentivisation, that the two birds are not hidden in the bush but rather firmly within their grasp.

What this last example illustrates is the point that, whatever the reason for the staff's failure to keep in touch with or follow up on customer views, it is management's responsibility to tackle such misperceptions – since your organisation's business will clearly suffer if your customers feel misunderstood or ignored by the very people with whom they are most likely to deal on a day-to-day basis.

THE EXECUTIVE SELF-ASSESSMENT CHECKLIST: STAFF MOTIVATION

Note: Since staff motivation and staff perceptions are distinct concepts (although they have both been addressed in this chapter), we have created a separate checklist for staff perceptions, which follows the one on staff motivation.

Question	Yes, confident +3	Yes, tentative 0	No −3	NA
Do we truly recognise that our staff are a precious resource and do what is necessary to keep them happy and motivated?				
Do we clearly demonstrate to our staff – with a genuine 'thank you' – that we appreciate them?				
Do we apply 'joined-up' thinking, looking at new staff recruitment and existing staff progression as two sides of the same coin?				
Do we seriously consider the impact of the actions we take on staff morale?				
Do we really know what motivates staff?				
Do we have a formal, tested and ongoing programme designed to motivate, grow and retain staff?				
Do we know what the business winners and balance tippers are in helping us to retain our staff?				

Question	Yes, confident +3	Yes, tentative 0	No −3	NA
Do we know what the key business losers are which drive staff away from our organisation?				
Can we cite instances of how working on the business winners/ balance tippers has made a difference to our staff retention?				
Are we confident that the incentives we offer our staff do have a positive impact on morale?				
Are our staff really happy to be working in our organisation?				
If they are not as happy as they should be, do we know why not?				
Do staff attitudes vary by type, function, seniority or location, and, if so, do we know how?				
Do we know whether our staff have bought into the vision/ mission of our organisation?				
Do we know whether there is agreement within the management team itself about the vision/ mission of our organisation?				
Do we communicate well with our staff?				
Do we conduct regular staff surveys?				
Do we act upon the results of those surveys?				

Question	Yes, confident +3	Yes, tentative 0	No −3	NA
Do we know whether staff regard those surveys as a genuine way of listening to their wants and concerns?				
Is our corporate culture participative and collegiate, rather than hierarchical?				
Do we know what our staff feel about our organisation as a place to work?				
Do our staff trust their colleagues and managers, and feel free to express their opinions?				
Do we benchmark what we offer our staff with what our competitors offer theirs?				
Do we benchmark our performance against that of 'the best companies to work for' outside our business area?				
Do we know whether we are more or less successful in retaining our best staff than are our competitors, and why?				
Do we keep track of changing staff expectations?				
Do we meet and manage those expectations well?				
Are our staff loyal to and proud of our organisation?				

Question	Yes, confident +3	Yes, tentative 0	No −3	NA
Are we confident that our staff will represent our organisation to the outside world as we would wish them to?				
Have we succeeded in creating an increasingly happy and productive workforce over time?				
GRAND TOTAL SCORE				
NET ABSOLUTE SCORE				
NET AVERAGE SCORE				

Now, taking each of the above questions, what in practice are we doing?

THE EXECUTIVE SELF-ASSESSMENT CHECKLIST: STAFF PERCEPTIONS

Question	Yes, confident +3	Yes, tentative 0	No −3	NA
Do we regularly check whether our staff are in touch with our marketplace?				
Do staff recognise that the customer is never 'wrong'?				
When there is a gap between staff and customer thinking, do we know where the gap lies?				

Question	Yes, confident +3	Yes, tentative 0	No −3	NA
Do we know how to bridge that gap?				
Do we take the action necessary to bridge the gap?				
Are we successful in bridging the gap?				
Are staff in touch with what drives the marketplace?				
Do we know where, if at all, there is a 'disconnect'?				
Are staff in touch with how satisfied customers are with us?				
If not, do we know where and why not?				
Are staff in touch with how the marketplace as a whole sees our organisation, what it stands for, and its image?				
Do we know where, if at all, there is a disconnect?				
Do our staff tend to overestimate, or underestimate, what the market thinks about our organisation?				
If they overestimate or underestimate, do we know where and how?				
Are staff in touch with our own customers' opinions?				

Question	Yes, confident +3	Yes, tentative 0	No −3	NA

If they are not always, do we know where they are out of touch?

Are staff in touch with our prospects' opinions?

If they are not always, do we know where they are out of touch?

Are staff in touch with other stakeholders'/influencers' opinions?

If they are not always, do we know where they are out of touch?

Where there are gaps, do we know where the widest gaps are (e.g. in product, service, image, relationship issues, cost)?

Are staff in touch with the market (its size, growth, industry trends, new opportunities, competitor activities, etc.)?

If not, do we know where they are out of touch?

Is there alignment in thinking across all areas of our organisation (between different functions, between geographies, between different levels of seniority, etc.)?

Where there is misalignment, do we know where and in what way such misalignment occurs?

Question	Yes, confident +3	Yes, tentative 0	No −3	NA

Where there are process misalignments, do we know where and how these are taking place? Do we have plans of action/ training programmes to bridge the gap wherever we find that staff are out of touch with the market or where there is misalignment within our organisation?

Are we confident that these action plans are effective and properly implemented?

Do we know where and how the barriers to implementation arise?

Do staff feel free to provide feedback about their customers and prospects, without fear of repercussion if there is bad news to give?

When necessary, are staff encouraged (through appropriate incentivisation) to offer customers and prospects services and solutions which do not result in a quick return?

Are we confident that staff feel adequately supported in terms of information they need from management in order to keep in touch with the market?

Question	Yes, confident +3	Yes, tentative 0	No −3	NA
Do we empower our front line staff in their dealings with the market, in the confident knowledge that they will speak for what our organisation stands for and offers?				
Do staff communicate effectively with the marketplace?				
If not, do we know why not?				
Do staff manage customer expectations effectively?				
Do we have training programmes in place to help staff communicate/ manage expectations better?				
When there is a gap to be filled, do we know whether the gap needs to be bridged through more effective communication, a reallocation of resources, or an increase in resources (e.g. because services need to be improved)?				
GRAND TOTAL SCORE				
NET ABSOLUTE SCORE				
NET AVERAGE SCORE				

Now, taking each of the above questions, what in practice are we doing?

WHO ELSE SHOULD BE ON YOUR RADAR SCREEN – THE ROLE AND MOTIVATION OF OTHER EXTERNAL STAKEHOLDERS AND INFLUENCERS

INTRODUCTION: WHO ARE OTHER EXTERNAL STAKEHOLDERS AND INFLUENCERS?

We have already discussed the role of your internal stakeholders (staff) in the last chapter and in Chapter 5 that of individuals within your customer decision-making unit who may have an influence on the choices made by your direct customer contacts. The focus of this chapter will be on other external stakeholders and influencers whose views and actions can have a powerful impact on your customers' decision-making process.

Before moving further into this topic, it is relevant at this stage to elaborate on the terms 'other external stakeholder' and 'influencer' in the context of the discussion which follows.

The term 'other external stakeholder' refers here to any party, other than customers/prospects and staff, with an interest in the outcome of a situation concerning your organisation or a decision you may wish to make; if, for example, you are making a major investment decision, your shareholders, your suppliers or the local community directly affected by the investment would be obvious stakeholders.

The term 'influencer' is used for any party that influences the choices made by your customers. These would include 'pure influencers' – that is, opinion formers whose role is solely to comment as external observers and whose views may shape your customers' views; the media and financial analysts would be obvious examples of pure influencers. But there are also 'hybrid influencers': these may be 'customer influencers' – those whose views influence customer decision making but who may also be customers themselves (an insurance broker, for example, influences the end customer but is also a direct source of business for the insurer); and they may also be 'stakeholder influencers' – trade unions or local pressure groups may be examples of parties who have an interest in the outcome of, say, an investment decision you make, but, by being vocal about their opinions, they are also likely to influence the views of other interested parties.

Why are the views of external stakeholders and influencers potentially important to you? The following are some typical scenarios where their opinions can be highly relevant:

- *Scenario 1 – You wish to assess the impact of influencers on your customers' attitudes/behaviour.* This is the most obvious scenario, where the targets are your *customers or prospects*, and you wish to assess how *influencers such as the media* can have an impact on the targets' decision making.
- *Scenario 2 – Some influencers are also your customers or at least may play a direct role in the purchase or specification of products/services*: Here, you need to target your sales and marketing activity directly at the *customer influencers* (like financial intermediaries or architects in the construction industry) who play a direct role in the purchase or specification of products/services.

- *Scenario 3 – You wish to enhance your overall standing*: Here, you need to address not only *primary customers/stakeholders*, like your direct customers or intermediaries, but also *influencers*; these can be both *pure influencers*, like the media and financial analysts, and *stakeholder influencers*, like environmental pressure groups – and the influencers can also be the *customers* themselves, who can influence one another through word-of-mouth communication.
- *Scenario 4 – You are making a major decision or taking an initiative, e.g. investing in new plant affecting local infrastructure*: When you wish to test opinion on any major initiative or decision, you need to know the views of both your target *stakeholders* and *influencers* whose views are important.
- *Scenario 5 – You are engaged in a damage limitation exercise, e.g. faced with an environmental scandal*: Here you wish to mitigate the negative impact of circumstances that you would have certainly wished to avoid; you need again to target those key *stakeholders* most affected and those *influencers* whose reactions are most likely to have an impact on the amount of damage done.

Figure 7.1 summarises these scenarios with examples of the most likely customers/stakeholders and influencers in each instance. In some instances, the same parties are mentioned twice (both as customers/stakeholders and as influencers) – this would apply when the same party has more than one function; in Scenario 2, for example, some of the influencers are also customers.

The scenarios shown in Figure 7.1 offer examples of typical situations in which various types of stakeholders and influencers may have a role to play. You need to decide for yourself which scenarios are most relevant and which types of stakeholders/influencers are most likely to play a role in your business. Figure 7.1 and the discussion that follows are intended, therefore, to provide little more than guidelines on the ways in which you may need

Scenario	Primary customers/other stakeholders – some examples	Primary influencers – some examples
Scenario 1: You wish to assess the impact of influencers on your customers' attitudes/behaviour	• Customers • Prospects	• Media • Peer groups (customers/prospects influencing one another through word of mouth) • End customers (customers' customers)
Scenario 2: Some influencers are also your customers or at least may play a direct role in the purchase or specification of products/services	• Financial intermediaries • Architects • Consultants	• Financial intermediaries • Architects • Consultants • Trade press • Peer groups • End customers
Scenario 3: You wish to enhance your overall standing and, ultimately, your business performance	• Customers • Prospects • Intermediaries • Banks/creditors • Suppliers • End customers • Shareholders	• Peer groups • Financial analysts • Media • Intermediaries • Pressure groups • End customers
Scenario 4: You are making a major decision or taking an initiative – e.g. investing in new plant affecting local infrastructure	• Suppliers • Local community • Employees/trade unions • Government • Regulatory/quasi-regulatory authorities • NGOs • Environmental groups • Shareholders • Public at large	• Media • Financial analysts • Local community • Employees/trade unions • Government • Regulatory/quasi-regulatory authorities • NGOs • Environmental groups
Scenario 5: You are engaged in a damage limitation exercise (e.g. faced with an environmental scandal)	• Shareholders • Public at large • Local community	• Media • Government • NGOs • Environmental groups

Figure 7.1 Stakeholders and influencers who may play a role in different scenarios

to think about and handle all the stakeholders and influencers relevant to your business. You need to adapt the schematic shown in the figure to make the scenarios directly relevant to your business.

Let us look a little more closely at these scenarios and how, within each scenario, you may need to address the various stakeholders and influencers.

SCENARIO 1 – YOU WISH TO ASSESS THE IMPACT OF INFLUENCERS ON YOUR CUSTOMERS' ATTITUDES/BEHAVIOUR

Here, the stakeholders are your customers (or prospects), and this scenario describes the obvious situation in which the customers' decision making is potentially influenced by other parties. Your task here is not only to understand the requirements and attitudes of your customers but also to ensure that you have identified who their influencers are, the ways in which they influence your target customers and the extent of the influence they have. You also need to understand the attitudes of these influencers towards your organisation, how they have arrived at these attitudes and the factors which are important in shaping those attitudes. You may, for example, be a manufacturer of industrial products which are commented on in the trade press, or a food supplier serving super-markets whose stocking policies are inevitably strongly driven by consumer demand. In the first instance, you clearly need to under-stand press attitudes (as well as the attitudes of the customers of your industrial products); in the second, you need to understand what drives consumer demand even if your immediate purchasers are the supermarkets. On the basis of this information you can target the influencers directly, addressing any negative views which they may hold and capitalising on the positive influence they may have on your direct customers. Many of the lines of enquiry and analytical approaches mentioned in Chapters 3 and 4 of this book would, therefore, apply if influencer attitudes are to be properly understood and addressed.

You may feel that, on the strength of your experience in this market, you already have this information, or you may need to undertake a market investigation to confirm your views.

Typical influencers in this instance would include the media; peer groups, who may influence customers through word of mouth; or end customers (the customer's customers) whose opinions and demands may exert an indirect pressure on the choices made by your customers.

SCENARIO 2 – SOME INFLUENCERS ARE ALSO YOUR CUSTOMERS

Here you wish to understand how the influencer as 'customer' rates your organisation; this scenario is relevant when any influencer is also directly engaged in the decisions relating to the purchase of your products or services.

In this scenario, the influencer may be operating as an intermediary or a specifier. In addition to the insurance broker example mentioned earlier, other typical customer influencers could be architects, subcontractors or engineering consultants in infrastructure or construction projects; their role can extend beyond the provision of an opinion, in that their specifications can have a direct bearing on the particular product or supplier chosen. Construction or engineering projects often involve channels of distribution and decision-making processes which can be quite complex, involving a number of parties operating, to a greater or lesser degree, at various stages of the process; here, the lines of division between the 'customer' and the 'influencer' can be so blurred that to seek to make a distinction between the two can sometimes feel like an academic exercise.

The role played by intermediaries depends in large part on their relationship with the end customers they serve. To take an example from the financial services sector, the financial adviser serving a high net worth individual may, at the one extreme, offer a discretionary service through which the adviser manages the client's portfolio and therefore strongly influences the products bought on behalf of the client, who is content to depend on the adviser's recommendation; or, at the other extreme, the adviser may have relatively little influence (because the client is more confident and proactive in specifying the products to be chosen), in which case the adviser's role is confined to monitoring and operating like a time-saving buying channel rather than like a genuine influencer. In the first instance, the intermediary, rather than the high net worth individual, is, for all practical purposes, the main customer to whom the provider of financial products should pay particular attention.

The insurance sector is another example of a business where the extent of the influence an intermediary exerts on the customer can often depend on the type of customer (whether the customer is a consumer, an SME, a large corporate, etc.). Whereas consumers requiring personal or household insurance may rely on little or no input from the intermediary, it is equally true, perhaps not surprisingly, that many will have little confidence or interest in insurance-related matters and will therefore be inclined to depend on the opinions and advice of the broker. Conversely, whereas there may be corporate customers who place great reliance on the broker's advice, many in the corporate sector believe that it is their job to have a professional awareness of insurance-related matters and that, for this reason, they have no need to lean heavily on the broker, instead being more inclined to use the intermediary as no more than a channel or sounding board.

In Scenario 2, the relevant lines of enquiry are similar to those that would apply to the customers in Scenario 1: you need to know what drives the decisions and choices made by these customer influencers, how satisfied they are with your service compared with the competitions', how loyal they are to you, and so on. Many of the analytical approaches mentioned in Chapters 2, 3 and 4 of this book would, therefore, apply to customer influencers (as they do to 'pure' customers) – how to unearth the factors truly driving the loyalty of the customer influencers, what level of performance is required to delight them, how best to allocate resources, and so on. To take a major player in the insurance industry, Allianz is a prime example of a company doing precisely this, by looking at both brokers (the customer influencers) and customers (the users of the insurance service) as separate customer groups, while at the same time recognising that the former can shape the opinions of the latter.

SCENARIO 3 – YOU WISH TO ENHANCE YOUR OVERALL STANDING AND BUSINESS PERFORMANCE

Scenario 3 applies when you wish to understand how you are seen as a corporate entity, what your brand equity is, what drives your image in the marketplace, and, ultimately, how you may enhance your business performance.

Customers/other stakeholders

Here, in addition to direct customers/prospects, the targets whose opinions need to be shaped may include, for example, the investment community. Any favourable or unfavourable publicity is clearly liable to affect the purchase behaviour of customers and prospects; but it can also influence the investors' decisions to buy or sell your shares and therefore affect your share price.

Other stakeholders who will be influenced by your overall standing in the marketplace include banks acting as creditors and end customers whose opinion about your organisation can easily be shaped by positive or negative publicity.

In this context, end customers may be operating as stakeholders because they seek the reassurance that their immediate suppliers (your direct customers) are being served by a reputable supplier (namely, your organisation); but they are also operating as influencers in that their positive or negative views can affect the decisions made by your direct customers. With respect to end customers, therefore, you may wish to engage in back selling activity designed to maximise the chances of their recommending the use of your organisation to their suppliers (your immediate customers).

Your suppliers may also have a role to play: first, because it is in their interest to be associated with a reputable organisation; and, second, because the quality of the products and services you acquire from them will in turn affect the quality of your offering and, ultimately, your standing in the marketplace. How you manage your suppliers can have a significant impact not only on your relationship with them but also on your profitability: one reason cited for Wal-Mart's success as a retail giant is its partnership approach towards its suppliers; this has enabled it to achieve cost efficiencies through just-in-time delivery, helping to reduce overheads, and through better terms obtained from the suppliers.

In order to enhance your standing among all your target customers/stakeholders, you may need to engage in corporate marketing and communications as well as investor relations activity. This should be designed to address in particular any weaknesses in your corporate positioning which may need to be corrected. However, attempts to enhance your image could emerge as a cosmetic exercise if there are no corresponding efforts to address the substantive issues which may be giving rise to negative perceptions: we have seen in Chapter 4 (Figure 4.10) how you can go down a slippery slope if you rest on your laurels by not making performance improvements when they are called for.

Influencers

Clearly, your customers and prospects themselves can have a major influence on your overall market standing, through word-of-mouth communication with other customers and prospects. But outside influencers can also have a direct bearing on the standing of your organisation, potentially influencing customer decision making and, ultimately, sales and stock market performance: the media can influence general opinion, vocal opposition from pressure groups can result in negative reporting, your image among end customers can influence your immediate customers' decision making, and financial analysts can directly influence your stock market rating.

The evidence shows that, if we ignore the role of these influencers, we are liable to become confused and make the wrong decisions: reference has already been made in the last chapter to a major international bank which found that its image among corporate prospects bore little relationship with the efforts it was making, through advertising activity, to raise its profile; further examination showed that this was because its profile was more strongly influenced by press reporting – much of which negatively focused on the bank's previous association with a dictatorial government – than by any of the bank's own marketing efforts. The message was that its advertising activity would ring hollow until the root source of the negative reporting was addressed directly, and this required far more engagement with the media than it had hitherto embarked upon.

Sometimes the negative reporting can occur because of a perceived inability or unwillingness to tackle a real problem: to take an obvious example, the media criticism suffered by British Airways for its baggage handling was hardly going to go away as long as the airline's rate of baggage loss continued to be reported as being significantly above that of the industry average. The airline's problems continued in late March 2008 with the baggage handling delays at the newly opened Terminal 5, which resulted in numerous flight cancellations. No amount of advertising about being the world's favourite airline could undo the damage being caused by this negative reporting. Prior to the problems at Terminal 5, an unplanned – and near disaster – situation may have done something to salvage the airline's reputation as one of the best in the world: the skilful and courageous conduct of the pilots of the aircraft which crash landed at Heathrow airport in January 2008, favourably reported all over the world, may well have caused many to wonder how many other airlines would have, through such professionalism and experience, saved the lives of all its passengers. However, whatever goodwill that incident generated appeared to have been undone by the unfortunate opening of Terminal 5.

SCENARIO 4 – YOU ARE MAKING A MAJOR DECISION OR TAKING AN INITIATIVE

Stakeholders and influencers can have an important role to play when you are planning to make key decisions, especially when you are taking an initiative about which influencers and stakeholders may have strong views. These decisions may have a long-term impact, because they are strategic, or a shorter-term impact, because they are more tactical. The following are some examples:

*   *New positioning/branding*: We have already referred to the Dow Corning Corporation, which successfully developed a new no frills brand – Xiameter – to meet the needs of a specific segment of its market. The success of the brand was down not only to the company's shrewdness in spotting a business opportunity, but also to its promotion activity, undertaken primarily in the US, Europe and the Far East, which ensured that all relevant stakeholders and influencers understood the reasons for the new brand and the value it would bring to the market.

    Another example is that of the major multinational which, when divesting itself of part of its business, sought to develop a new brand name which needed to be tested among analysts, government departments, the media, etc., as well as key customers. This activity, undertaken in Europe, North America and the Middle East, contributed to the brand name development as well as to a better understanding of how the new brand should be introduced to the target marketplace.

• *Investment in new plant or products/services*: Suppliers are clearly important stakeholders when you are considering a new investment: they have an obvious interest because the investment offers them the potential opportunity to increase their business with you. But you are also dependent on them – to provide you with the right product at the right time.

But other parties are also likely to have a role to play when you embark on a new investment. For one thing, there are government/regulatory authorities to contend with: if you are a food or pharmaceuticals manufacturer in the US, there is the FDA (the Food and Drug Administration); if you are a financial services provider in the UK, you need to think of the FSA (the Financial Services Authority); if you are a manufacturer of a whole range of products in Germany, you may need to be prepared to have your new product tested by Stiftung Warentest, a quasi-regulatory testing authority supported by the German federal government.

A range of stakeholders and influencers can become involved when major infrastructure projects are being undertaken. These can often have a negative impact on an organisation's image; the building of a dam, a new highway, a new housing complex or an airport could well meet with opposition because these initiatives may be seen to destroy the environment and blight people's livelihoods. From the furore caused by the proposed extension of London's Heathrow airport to the Narbada Dam project in central India, infrastructure projects can generate strong feelings on the part of interested parties such as 'green' lobbyists, the local community and transport authorities. These are obvious high profile cases which often make the news, but even if you are making investments on a more modest scale, you would be wise to engage with the stakeholders and influencers likely to be affected by, and influence the outcome of, the proposed initiative: the very act of reaching out and talking to the various interested parties can help you to manage the situation in your favour.

•   *Entering new markets*: As with the investment in new plant or products/services, so any initiative to enter a new market requires identification of and engagement with all the stakeholders and influencers who may have an interest in your arrival – from trade unions, the local community and the local press to environmental pressure groups and government authorities. Some companies have been better than others at engaging with local interested parties: the Swedish company Securitas, for example, set up a European Group Council to provide a forum for discussions between group management and employees in their European operations. This has resulted in a growing emphasis on employee training which the company believes has enabled it to offer higher quality and higher priced services, in turn resulting in better wages and improved morale. Securitas has sought to carry out this policy in all the countries in which it operates; every time it entered a new country it invited employee representatives to join the group council.

•   *Image-enhancing 'do good' initiatives*: A number of private sector organisations seek to enhance their standing – or sometimes counter the effects of negative publicity – by engaging in image-enhancing initiatives which may range from the adoption of a fair trade policy on coffee to investment in local schools, hospitals or community facilities. Here, the key targets are clearly those most likely to be directly affected by the decision – most obviously, the local community itself – but also those who can influence opinion at large – environmental groups or the local and national media, for example.

In the fair trade coffee example, the stakeholders may be the local community or the coffee producers in Africa or South America, and the influencers may be pressure groups, the media, government and non-governmental organisations (like the FDA in the US), and so on. But here the ultimate target which the organisation wishes to impress would be the public at large – who, it is hoped, will be more favourably disposed towards the organisation and more inclined, now or in the future, to purchase its products or services.

An advantage of 'do good' initiatives lies in the fact that they don't necessarily require a large investment and can therefore be worth considering even if you are a small or medium size organisation: getting involved in organising a raffle for a local children's hospice, for example, may require very little financial investment (although possibly a larger investment in time) but is liable to pay huge dividends in terms of goodwill generated within the local community. If the local community includes people who are potential purchasers of the product or service you offer, this goodwill may well result in increased business and therefore a good return on the investment made.

- *Image-enhancing sponsorship activities*: Companies engaged in the sponsorship of sporting events, musical activities, and so on, are doing so in the hope that this will build a positive profile over time. Here, the 'direct customers' may be the individuals who have a specific interest in the activity – the sports or music fans attending the events, for example – and the 'indirect customers' would be the public at large; the influencers may be the events organisers or the media.

Companies engaged in 'do good' projects may feel that there is a moral or a political imperative to get involved in such initiatives, especially if they feel that they need to counter negative associations with their normal business activity; a supermarket flaunting its fair trade credentials, for example, may be doing so precisely because it has been accused in the past of being unfair to its suppliers.

Sponsorship activities, however, are not normally undertaken in response to this kind of pressure; here, the decision to sponsor an event is based on the view that somehow in the long run it will benefit the sponsor in a positive way. Having said this, how often have companies engaged in sponsorship seriously sought to quantify the return on what can be sizeable investments? How often is the decision to sponsor based on the personal preference of the chairman or the CEO? Even if quantification is difficult, what attempts are made to develop measures of the impact of sponsorship on those at whom the sponsorship is targeted? Is there a match between the sponsorship chosen and the business or desired positioning of the sponsor? Arguably, some sponsorships would appear to be natural fits – for example, sponsorship of motor sports by a car manufacturer or a tyre company – but when a company decides to sponsor, say, a classical music festival, for which the market may be relatively small, has it thought through who its customer/stakeholder and influencer targets are and why classical music should be the best way of reaching and eliciting a positive response from those targets? This is by no means an argument for saying that classical music should not be sponsored: there is, for example, a body of evidence which strongly supports the view that children's exposure to this type of music benefits their development. However, the sponsorship activities undertaken by some organisations fail to make the connection with the tangible value offered by this sort of activity and can even have the negative effect of being seen to be elitist and irrelevant to all but a small minority.

SCENARIO 5 – YOU ARE ENGAGED IN A DAMAGE LIMITATION EXERCISE

The damage limitation scenario is distinct from the others in that you are reacting – rather than taking a proactive initiative – to a specific event which you would certainly not wish to have had to face. Obvious examples of such situations, which we have seen in recent years, have been oil spillages, plant explosions and train crashes, all of which lead to highly critical media reporting and awkward questions from government, the communities directly affected and other pressure groups.

There is clear evidence that this sort of disaster can have a long-term impact on the standing of the organisation, people remembering the event many years later. It can also accentuate public cynicism and dent the credibility of the company when it seeks to position itself as a caring or 'green' organisation. Nearly 20 years after the *Exxon Valdez* oil spill polluted Alaska's Prince William Sound, the United States Supreme Court found itself debating in 2008 how much money Exxon should pay in punitive damages. Almost 25 years after the Bhopal disaster, the public at large continues to be reminded of it through full page advertisements in national newspapers. As far as companies like Exxon and Union Carbide are concerned, it is likely that the damage that these disasters caused to their reputations was at least as serious as the financial costs incurred in reparation and compensation.

The obvious solution is to avoid such disasters in the first place but since that can never be guaranteed, the damage limitation needs to focus not only on communication to the customer/stakeholder targets – that is, the public at large, the local community most directly affected by the disaster, or the investment community – but also, equally importantly, on engagement with the influencer parties, such as government, green lobbyists and the media.

In order to be effective in undertaking the damage limitation, it is important for organisations involved in businesses which are vulnerable to disasters to develop *advance plans* in 'preparation' for future occurrences. It would appear that companies are often unprepared for a disaster scenario – given the frequent ineptitude with which they have responded to the damage done; to give the impression of being evasive, defensive or lacking in transparency can only exacerbate a fraught situation. Ironically, the very same organisations may engage in regular safety exercises to ensure that they are prepared to make the appropriate *physical* response in the event of a disaster. But their *communication* in the aftermath – which requires the professional handling of all relevant customers/stakeholders and influencers – is often found wanting. It is a hoary marketing precept that a customer complaint well handled represents an opportunity to enhance our relationship with the customer concerned; although an oil spillage or a chemicals explosion are particularly difficult problems to handle, we would do well to bear this principle in mind: we need to ensure not only that we are taking all the necessary practical steps to mitigate the impact of the disaster but also that we come across as transparent, responsible and sensitive in the way we are handling the situation.

Effective disaster limitation is also helped by ongoing communication about the positive actions and achievements of your organisation. Instead of a flurry of activity to 'justify' your position once the disaster has taken place, you should aim over a period of time to build an image whereby, as far as possible, the disaster is seen as a one-off setback, not something symptomatic of the way in which your organisation conducts itself. In practice, the balance is often not right – the clamour of the disaster tends to drown out any positive perceptions which the public may have of the company in 'normal' times.

MANAGING THE (CONFLICTING) DEMANDS OF DIFFERENT STAKEHOLDERS

The discussion so far has tended to look at the different influences of different types of stakeholders individually. In reality, your organisation may need to address simultaneously the requirements and concerns of a number of different stakeholder groups, often operating in combination but sometimes presenting you with demands which may be conflicting.

When there are conflicting demands, how do you resolve these conflicts? *Is* it possible to resolve them? There are many obvious examples of conflicting requirements:

- The consumer may welcome the possibility of late night shopping at supermarkets but staff unions may be opposed to moves to extend the working hours of their members.
- It would not be surprising if consumers wish to have heavy restrictions placed on energy prices but, if the energy supplier is a privatised company, shareholders may well want to resist such initiatives.
- As the Northern Rock crisis in the UK unfolded in early 2008, there was clearly a conflict of interest between the taxpayer, whose interests the UK government was seeking to safeguard, and Northern Rock's shareholders, who resented the fall in the value of their shares in the bank.
- The adverse publicity about battery-fed chickens in the UK resulted in battle lines being drawn between the lobby calling for free range chickens, supported by some parts of the press and the general public, and supermarkets and other members of the public who focused on the needs of those who couldn't afford the free range alternative.
- We have already referred to the heat generated by high profile projects like the Heathrow extension and the Narbada Dam project, with local communities and environmental campaigners in conflict with government authorities and the investment community.

There is clearly no easy answer to how the conflicting demands of your different stakeholders should be managed. However, there are some guiding principles worth considering, which are summarised in Figure 7.2:

- Prioritise your stakeholders

- Consider the criteria for deciding who matters most

- Think long term

- Make your case

- Recognise that your stakeholders don't operate in silos

- Be sensitive to changes in climate of opinion

- Take initiatives to demonstrate you are concerned

Figure 7.2 Managing the conflicting demands of different stakeholders – some guiding principles

- *Prioritise your stakeholders*: However difficult this may seem, you need to provide leadership by taking a stand on the basis of your judgement as to who matters most.
- *Consider the criteria for deciding who matters most*: You may decide, for example, that because the future of your business ultimately depends on a profitable and growing customer base, it is the customer's opinion that should, in the end, take precedence over other views.
- *Think long term*: The operative phrase in the previous point was 'in the end', and you should not be afraid to ride a storm if you feel that the long-term benefit of doing so will prevail over shorter-term problems.
- *Make your case*: Having the courage to take a stand doesn't mean that you should come across as arrogant and unwilling to listen to the concerns of all the interested parties; you should instead seek to win over the doubters and opponents by arguing as persuasively as possible why it may be in their interest, in the long run at least, to go along with your view.

- *Recognise that your stakeholders don't operate in silos* and that the same individual or organisation may have different stakeholder roles; to take an obvious example, your customer may also be a shareholder and is by definition a member of the general public.

- *Be sensitive to changes in the climate of opinion* in your business and within the broader community; the pressures you face today may become less relevant tomorrow, and this may result in changes in the attitudes and practices of your target groups: for example, today's rabid consumer could become tomorrow's 'green' champion, as environmental consciousness becomes increasingly embedded in the way people think about the world.

- *Where appropriate, take initiatives which demonstrate that you are concerned* about the local community, the environment, fair trade, or any other programme designed to show that you are not solely driven by the short-term need to make money. There is nothing new about this suggestion, and companies have engaged in such activities for many years. However, the point is particularly relevant in the socially and environmentally conscious world of today, where pressure groups, local communities, the media and other stakeholders/influencers are more vocal than ever before. Organisations operating in sectors liable to generate anxiety and even hostility need to be especially sensitive; obvious examples of these are banks, sometimes associated with unscrupulous treatment of customers, energy companies linked with unjustifiable price rises, petrochemical companies associated with environmental pollution, and retailers accused of exploiting their small suppliers. Enterprises operating in such 'politically sensitive' businesses are unlikely to be able to avoid controversy, however hard they might try, so it is in their interest to embark on parallel activities which reveal another, more acceptable persona. The examples mentioned here are of sectors typically characterised

by large enterprises, but even if you are a smaller local operator you may wish to consider more modest initiatives which
demonstrate that you care for the environment or your local
community – thereby ensuring that you too recognise the
needs of the various stakeholders and influencers who have an
interest in your activities.

So what do these principles mean in practice? Here are a few
possible examples:

- If all that your shareholders are concerned about is the short-
  term value of their shareholdings, you may wish to persuade
  them to think long term because a fixation on short-term
  results may well be counterproductive in the long run. Investing in R&D, for example, may not yield immediate returns
  and may well affect your company's short-term bottom line;
  but by managing shareholders' expectations and explaining to
  them how the provision of a higher quality offering will in
  the end result in improved customer satisfaction and loyalty,
  you may be able to convince them that you will be in a
  stronger position to enhance shareholder value in the long
  term.

- The scenario just described requires the leadership mentioned
  earlier: far too often boards of directors seem to be overanx-
  ious about shareholder concerns and the pressures coming
  from financial analysts and the media. Instead of taking the
  lead in explaining and justifying the position they have chosen
  to take, they succumb to a spiral of over-optimistic short-term
  forecasts which are not met, leading to declines in share prices
  and further pressure to take short-term measures to 'appease'
  the market.

- You need to embark on a regular and consistent campaign of
  communication to ensure that those who need to be converted to your view really get the message: to go back to the

example of shareholders, you could seek to show them how their interests and the interests of customers may in fact converge in the long term.

- If you are a retailer feeling caught between the need to offer low price but less 'ethical' food and more 'ethical' but higher price food, it is genuinely difficult to strike a path which is going to satisfy all the parties concerned. What should be avoided, however, is the appearance of seeking to duck the issue: in the course of the 'free range' versus 'battery farm' chicken debate in the UK, a number of the supermarkets came out of the debate badly because, by failing to set out clearly what the pros and cons of the various options were, they appeared not to take leadership on the issue. Perhaps if they had taken the initiative in engaging in and inviting other parties to the debate, they would have avoided giving the impression of shiftiness and embarrassment which only served to undermine their position.

- Some retailers have succeeded in projecting a more caring and socially responsible image, thereby counterbalancing some of the activities with which they may be negatively associated; so we see many UK supermarkets offering Fairtrade coffee (with Marks and Spencer, for example, having ceased to offer any coffee which is not Fairtrade), Dunkin' Donuts in the US similarly joining Fairtrade, and Switzerland's leading retailer, Migros, marketing what it claims to be the first Fairtrade fuel through its petrol pump operator Migrol.

- If you are running an airline, your customer – the airline passenger – may well want you to offer low price tickets, but that same customer may be increasingly concerned about the carbon footprint resulting from low budget air travel. As the climate of opinion becomes increasingly environmentally concerned, there may be an opportunity here to convince your customer that some price premium should be paid to ensure that he/she, together with your airline, makes a contribution to an improved environment. The UK airline easyJet, for example, has introduced a not-for-profit carbon offset scheme which offers passengers booking flights an easy way to offset their CO_2 footprint by making a modest contribution to a UN-certified carbon offset project. Similarly, the online travel company lastminute.com has launched a carbonwise initiative, whereby, when customers book a flight, they are informed of the CO_2 they will produce, and an optional offset charge is added by default. With these initiatives, the airline and the travel agency are seeking to achieve two important objectives: first, enhancing their own image as being environmentally responsible; second, addressing a number of stakeholder audiences – the environmental lobby, their customers, who may need to feel that they are doing their bit towards helping the environment, and the public at large who, it is hoped, will regard these initiatives as evidence of organisations that care for the future of the planet.

CONCLUDING QUESTIONS

This chapter has been designed to provide a framework and guidelines to help you to think about the role of the various stakeholders and influencers who may be relevant to your organisation. How precisely you handle your stakeholders/influencers will depend on the specific nature of your business and the market in which you are operating. You need therefore to adapt the various scenarios and examples discussed here so that they become more relevant to your particular situation. However, the discussion in this chapter does give rise to some basic questions which need to be asked:

- Have you methodically identified *all* the stakeholders and influencers who are relevant to your business?
- Have you assessed their relative importance to your business?

- Have you taken into account how stakeholders and influencers have a role to play in different scenarios, from initiatives to enhance your overall standing to damage limitation exercises?
- Have you considered how their demands, when they conflict with one another, should be managed?
- Are you confident that all the staff who should be responsible for dealing with them are aware of them?
- Are you confident that they are constantly on your organisation's radar screen?
- Do you have a continual process in place to manage all your stakeholders and influencers (not only your direct customers and prospects) appropriately?

If you can answer 'yes' to these questions you will know that you have taken proper account of them when you wish to assess your position in the marketplace and the likely impact of any decisions you may make in future.

THE EXECUTIVE SELF-ASSESSMENT CHECKLIST: OTHER EXTERNAL STAKEHOLDERS AND INFLUENCERS

Question	Yes, confident +3	Yes, tentative 0	No -3	NA
Stakeholders Do we know who all the different types of external stakeholders are in our market?				
Do we know which of these are really important to our business?				
Do we know how they play a role in decisions involving our business?				

Question	Yes, confident +3	Yes, tentative 0	No −3	NA
Do we know and engage with the key stakeholders within each stakeholder category?				
Do we know what really drives their thinking and the way in which they play a role?				
Do we know what their overall opinion is of us?				
Do we know what they believe to be our strengths and weaknesses?				
Do we know whether these views vary by type of stakeholder?				
Is all this knowledge based on solid information, gleaned from the marketplace, rather than on gut feeling or common sense?				

Influencers

Do we know who all the external influencers are?				
Do we know how they play a role in decisions involving our business?				
Do we know what really drives their thinking and the way in which they play a role?				
Do we know what their overall opinion is of us?				
Do we know what they believe to be our strengths and weaknesses?				
Do we know whether these views vary by type of influencer?				

Question	Yes, confident +3	Yes, tentative 0	No −3	NA

Is all this knowledge based on solid information, gleaned from the marketplace, rather than on gut feeling or common sense?

Communication
Is all this knowledge filtered right through our organisation so that all the staff who should be responsible for dealing with stakeholders and influencers know who they are and how to deal with them?

Do we communicate with our stakeholders and influencers on a consistent, ongoing basis?

Scenario 1 – Customer attitudes/behaviour and decision making
Are we confident that we have understood the role of influencers in customers' decision making?

Do we approach the influencers when they have a role to play in customers' decision making?

Do our approaches take into account differences in the extent to which, and manner in which, the different influencers play a role?

Are we confident that our approaches are effective?

Do we know why they are/they are not effective?

Question	Yes, confident +3	Yes, tentative 0	No −3	NA

Scenario 2 – Customer influencers

Are we confident that we have understood the role of customer influencers?

Do our approaches take into account differences in the extent to which, and manner in which, the different customer influencers play a role?

Are we confident that our approaches to customer influencers are effective?

Do we know why they are/they are not effective?

Scenario 3 – Overall market standing

Are we confident that we have understood the role of both stakeholders and influencers in matters concerning our general market standing?

Do we approach the influencers as well as stakeholders when we wish to ensure that what we stand for is properly understood and appreciated?

Do our approaches take into account differences in the extent to which, and manner in which, the different influencers and stakeholders play a role?

Are we confident that our approaches are effective?

Question	Yes, confident +3	Yes, tentative 0	No −3	NA

Do we know why they are/they are not effective?

Scenario 4 – Major decisions/initiatives
Are we confident that we have understood the role of stakeholders and influencers when we make major decisions which can have an impact on our market or on the community at large?

Do we approach the stakeholders and influencers when we make such major decisions?

Do our approaches take into account differences in the extent to which, and manner in which, the different stakeholders and influencers play a role?

Are we confident that our approaches are effective?

Do we know why they are/they are not effective?

Scenario 5 – Damage limitation
Are we confident that we have understood the role of stakeholders and influencers when we have been faced with the need for a damage limitation exercise?

Do we approach the stakeholders and influencers when faced with a damage limitation situation?

Question	Yes, confident +3	Yes, tentative 0	No −3	NA

Do we cater for 'disaster scenarios' in advance?

Do our approaches take into account differences in the extent to which, and manner in which, the different stakeholders and influencers play a role?

Are we confident that our approaches in damage limitation situations are effective?

Do we know why they are/they are not effective?

Managing the (conflicting) demands of different stakeholders

Do we show leadership and clarity of vision in prioritising our stakeholders?

Have we developed criteria for deciding which stakeholders matter most?

Do we take a long-term view which influences the way we manage our stakeholders?

Do we communicate clearly and make our case in order to overcome potential opposition from stakeholders?

Is the way we manage our stakeholders informed by the recognition that the same individual or organisation may have different stakeholder roles?

Question	Yes, confident +3	Yes, tentative 0	No −3	NA
Are we sensitive to changes in the climate of opinion which could affect stakeholders' priorities?				
Do we take initiatives demonstrating our concern about social and environmental issues?				
GRAND TOTAL SCORE				
NET ABSOLUTE SCORE				
NET AVERAGE SCORE				

Now, taking each of the above questions, what in practice are we doing?

CHAPTER 8

COMMUNICATE (AND COMMUNICATE AND COMMUNICATE...)

YOUR COMMUNICATION TARGETS

Implicit in much of the discussion so far is the theme that effective communication is an imperative for any market-sensitive organisation. However well your organisation's products and services perform, if your target market does not know about you or the products/services you offer, much of your effort will be wasted. So you need to communicate to:

- *your customers*, to ensure that
  - you remain on their radar screen
  - they fully understand what you have to offer
  - you fully understand their requirements and attitudes
  - you reinforce your standing with them
  - you engage with all the relevant parties involved in the decision-making process

- *your prospects*, to ensure that
  - they are aware of you
  - they understand what you stand for
  - they know what you can offer to them
  - you pre-empt or correct any negative misconceptions they may have about you
  - you understand what they in turn would expect of you
  - you engage with all the relevant parties involved in the decision-making process
- *your staff*, to ensure that
  - they are motivated
  - they understand where your organisation is heading
  - they are all focused on the same key objectives
  - they communicate with one another
  - they convey the right messages to customers and prospects
  - they listen to what customers and prospects have to say
- *other stakeholders and influencers*, to ensure that
  - they are aware of you
  - they understand what you stand for
  - their attitudes are favourably disposed towards your organisation
  - their positive views will in turn encourage your immediate customers and prospects to give you a greater share of their business.

The term 'communication' is quite often used to mean different things, and it is valuable to make a broad distinction between:

- corporate communication, and
- product/service communication.

Although these two areas of communication are interrelated, we will discuss them separately because their applications are distinct: both are concerned with how to convey information and mould the perceptions of your target markets; however, in the case of corporate communication, this task relates to your organisation as a single entity, whereas, for product/service communication, the application relates to the individual products or services you are offering. It is true that the larger an organisation is the less likely that it will be a 'single entity', in that it is liable to comprise different divisions operating in different geographic markets or industry sectors. In that sense there may be a number of different businesses within the same organisation, each representing a single entity; in addition, in so far as those different businesses are defined on product/service lines, the division between corporate and product/service communication can become blurred. For the purpose of this chapter, however, we will treat corporate and product/service communication separately, with the caveat that in reality there can be a degree of overlap between the two.

CORPORATE COMMUNICATION: INTRODUCTION

When the name of your organisation is mentioned to one of your prospects, is the immediate response:

- a blank look?
- an immediate signal of recognition, but no real knowledge about what you do?
- views about your organisation which indicate confusion about what you stand for?
- favourable views about your organization?
- unfavourable views about your organization?

The list of questions can no doubt be extended and refined, but it is the answers to these questions which will reveal how effective your corporate communication has been.

The two basic criteria for effective corporate communication are that you need to be successful in:

- conveying information about your organisation
- strengthening your corporate brand.

INFORMATION ABOUT YOUR ORGANISATION

It may be obvious, but it is nonetheless worth reminding oneself, that if people don't know about you they won't buy from you. The dissemination of information about your organisation – who you are, what you do, what your recent activities have been, what your future plans are, and so on – is an essential element in any successful corporate communication activity. We have all experienced seeing clever advertisements with witty punchlines which failed nonetheless to communicate clearly the nature of the company's business. The first focus should, therefore, be on the basics:

- *Is our target market aware of us?* Here, awareness can be defined in two ways. First, there is what the market researchers refer to as 'spontaneous awareness' – which describes whether or not you spring to mind when customers or prospects are asked about suppliers in your business. Clearly, if you don't spring to mind, then your prospective customer will not be looking out of his way to purchase your products or services.

  The other form of awareness is 'prompted awareness'. This describes whether or not customers or prospects recognise you as a supplier in your business when your name is mentioned to them. If you fail the prompted awareness test, then there is certainly no way in which customers will go out of their way to buy from you until and unless you succeed in increasing their levels of awareness.

How does all this work in practice? Let us take a simple example: you are a manufacturer of breakfast cereal sold through supermarkets. A customer visits the supermarket to buy breakfast cereal. She has never bought your brand but she is spontaneously aware of it – in other words, it is, probably together with some other brands, at the forefront of her mind; so when she sets foot into the supermarket, she is most likely to know that yours is one of the brands she can buy and she may even actively look out for it. You have therefore passed the first hurdle, since at least there is a chance that she will buy your brand.

Let us now alter the scenario somewhat: the customer has no spontaneous awareness of your brand but, if she were prompted, she would recognise it as a breakfast cereal brand. She now enters the supermarket without any expectation of seeing your brand, simply because she hasn't even thought about it. When she arrives at the breakfast cereal aisle, she *may* become aware of your brand if she happens to set eyes on it, but equally she may not. So this time, there is a reduced likelihood of her purchasing your brand because she needs to be prompted to become aware of the brand.

Now, the worst case scenario would be one in which the customer is not aware of your brand even when prompted. In other words, if asked about the brand, she would not even recognise it as a breakfast cereal brand. Now when she enters the aisle, the likelihood of her noticing the brand is further reduced because, even if her eyes fell upon the cereal packet, it would have little meaning for her beyond what she notices on the packet. It is possible, of course, that the packaging is so striking that this may grab her attention, but eye-catching packaging would be an advantage in any scenario and the lack of any form of awareness prior to going into the supermarket would remain a serious disadvantage for your brand. In this scenario, therefore, the customer is least likely to buy your brand.

The communication task here is, therefore, to ensure that the maximum number of people should be aware of your brand, at least when they are reminded about it but far preferably on a spontaneous basis.

- *Is our target market knowledgeable about us?* Of course, simply being aware of the brand doesn't guarantee that it is going to be purchased. Clearly, the brand must be seen to be attractive enough for the prospective purchaser to consider buying it – to use the marketer's jargon, it should be in the consideration set. But there is another condition which needs to be met, even before the brand can be seen as being attractive: the customer needs to have *knowledge* of the brand – or at least *feel* that she has enough knowledge to make the decision as to whether or not the brand is attractive and therefore worth considering.

In the breakfast cereal example, to make a distinction between 'awareness' and 'knowledge' may seem somewhat fatuous; if a customer is aware of your brand it is highly likely that she will know that it is a breakfast cereal! But she may still not know what the ingredients of the cereal are, how the contents compare with that of other cereals, and so on. So, whereas awareness is a basic first step, knowledge may be necessary for the customer to consider making the purchase, because it is only on the basis of that knowledge that the customer will be able to make a judgement and therefore considered decisions about the brand. Of course, this sort of knowledge becomes relevant if the customer is making a rational decision – for instance, choosing a cereal brand because it is made of natural ingredients with no added salt or sugar. It is quite possible, however, that a decision relating to a consumer product may not be based on 'rational' considerations; the decision may be based on the emotional connection which the advertising of the brand has made with the consumer, quite possibly at a subconscious level. The relevance of knowledge is, for this reason, likely to be greater when the products/services under consideration are business-to-business or industrial – a point made further in this section.

Having said this, the distinction being made between awareness and knowledge is more relevant today than ever before. This is because today's consumers are more conscious than they have ever been about the big issues surrounding them – be they about health and nutrition, energy saving, the environment or world poverty. This has made them feel more knowledgeable about what they should or should not buy; they are, therefore, far more likely than before to know which cereals are healthy (sugar-less, fat free, etc.), which products are being sold on a fair trade basis, which energy supplier is using green energy, which foods are organic, and so on. The increasing take-up of organic and fair trade products provides clear evidence of this trend. This means that suppliers today need to be more careful than before in assuming that consumers will simply buy a product on the strength of attractive advertising or packaging. This is not to say that advertising and packaging don't have an important role to play, or that price doesn't remain a key consideration in consumers' purchase choices. But it does mean that the consumer walking down the supermarket aisle is also more likely than before to be influenced by other issues, such as the nutritional aspects of cereals. Suppliers are therefore more likely to succeed if they recognise that consumers are (or at least feel they are) generally more knowledgeable and if they ensure that information about their products is successfully conveyed to the marketplace.

There is nothing new, one might say, about the need to convey information about the nutritional aspects of breakfast cereals, and indeed there are a number of cereal brands focusing precisely on this. But there are many other consumer products and services which remain overdependent on catchy headlines, big brand names and a long history in the market-place. Surveys about financial institutions, utilities, petrochemical companies, and so on, continue to show negative consumer perceptions which associate them with poor customer service, a cynical attitude towards the environment, and a focus on shareholders and profits at the expense of the community at large. We have a situation here where the consumers' general knowledge of the big issues – the environment and world poverty, for example – is not matched by an equal knowledge about what individual organisations are doing to address these issues. Even if some of these organisations are doing a lot in these areas, they are often failing to communicate this sufficiently; as mentioned in the previous chapter, damage limitation in response to a particular disaster is less likely to be successful if consumers and the public at large are not knowledgeable about all the positive actions taken over a period of time by the organisation causing the damage.

The distinction between awareness and knowledge becomes more relevant and easier to grasp in the case of more complex business-to-business products or services. If you are a manufacturer of a hydraulic pump, for example, your prospective purchasers will wish to know about its performance specifications even if they are fully aware of your brand and what the overall function of the pump is. To take a very different example, if you are a law firm, your prospective clients may well be aware of the fact that you are reputable but they may still need more information about how much you specialise in intellectual property or media law – the areas in which they may have a particular interest.

To summarise, therefore, the basic condition for successful corporate communication should be the effective dissemination of information which will maximise knowledge, as well as awareness, of the brand.

STRENGTHENING YOUR CORPORATE BRAND

Awareness and knowledge, however, are not enough. A brand must be attractive for any prospect to consider buying it. A prospective customer may know a lot about your brand (or at least think he knows) but that is not much good if the image or reputation of your brand is so negative that he would never consider buying it. The customer's knowledge about a bank, say, may be considerable – knowledge about the bank's activities, its geographic reach, its size, and so on; but if all this is associated with an uncaring, impersonal image, this knowledge won't benefit the bank – indeed, it may reinforce the negative image if size, for example, is also linked with being impersonal.

This is not to say that knowledge and brand strength are quite separate. In the previous section, we showed how the right type of knowledge – for example, about the nutritional aspects of a cereal – will attract customers. The immediate impact of this information is a practical one directly related to the product – to induce the customer to buy the product because it is seen to offer health benefits; however, the longer-term impact could be more strategic, being concerned with corporate image – that is, encouraging consumers to link the brand with positive, health-related associations. This offers a cereal manufacturer the opportunity to capitalise on this association if it wishes to extend its product range; now *any* product introduced by the manufacturer may benefit from the health associations of the corporate brand. Smaller cereal producers like Health Valley in the US and Dorset Cereals in the UK have successfully made a name for themselves as suppliers of healthy cereals, so any new product offered by these brands may well become automatically associated with good health.

So knowledge and brand strength can be interlinked, as in the healthy cereal example, but they may be quite separate or even negatively associated with each other, as in the big bank example. The bottom line for successful communication is to ensure not only that your target market knows about your organisation but also that you project the most positive image for your organisation.

Well, what makes for a positive image? Clearly, the precise components of a strong brand will be influenced by your circumstances and your business activity; for example, size or global reach may be a positive attribute for a multinational company that seeks to convince its marketplace about its international presence, but may be quite irrelevant for an SME with no aspirations to operate outside its domestic market – and, as we have seen, may even have negative connotations for the consumer. However, whatever the specific issues relevant to your business, there are 10 generic areas relating to the image of the brand which are broadly applicable irrespective of the type of organisation you are or the marketplace in which you are operating. These are summarised in Figure 8.1.

Figure 8.1 What do we need to work on to ensure favourable brand perceptions?

Not all the generic themes shown in Figure 8.1 are equally relevant to all organisations and all markets, and for this reason you may wish to emphasise some more than others in your communication with your stakeholders. If you are a cereal manufacturer, quality and care are quite likely to be important attributes to be conveyed if you wish to ensure that the product you offer is seen by consumers as being good for them. If you are a manufacturer of luxury goods, the themes of quality and reputation may be the dominant ones on which you may wish to focus, rather than, say, value. Conversely, if you are a financial adviser, you will need to communicate trustworthiness, possibly more than any other attribute. However, it is difficult to envisage any business in which any of the attributes shown in the diagram would be incompatible with the aims and objectives of that business: no organisation would wish to be seen as being untrustworthy, lacking in empathy with customers, offering poor value, or having no enthusiasm for what it is doing!

You will notice that a number of the attributes in Figure 8.1 occur quite frequently in corporate mission statements: for example, we often read how the company aims to be 'innovative' or how much it 'cares' for its customers. 'Customer focus', a favourite with many mission statements, is not mentioned in the diagram because we believe that it is the end result of many of the attributes shown – care, empathy, humility, enthusiasm, and so on. Similarly, mission statements will quite frequently refer to the uniqueness or distinctiveness of the company's offering, but we would regard this again as the outcome of the qualities referred to in the diagram. Sometimes attributes are mentioned in mission statements and other forms of communication (most notably advertising) when they are not relevant or important to the target market. Greg Stuart, co-author of *What Sticks: Why Most Advertising Fails and How to Guarantee Yours Succeeds* (Briggs and Stuart 2006), cites the example of a financial services brand, operating in the consumer marketplace, which had positioned itself as innovative: when market research was conducted, however, it was found that innovation was ranked as the 10th most important reason for consumers' selection of a provider of financial services (see *Missing the Mark* by Greg Stuart (Stuart 2007)). The point being made here was quite simply how wrong organisations can be in the messages they choose to convey and how this results in advertising failing to hit the target.

Conversely, some of the generic themes shown in the diagram don't come up often in mission statements, marketing literature or general business-speak. 'Humility' is the most obvious case in point; in the competitive environment which characterises so many of our businesses, the concept of humility would appear to be at distinct odds with the general focus on being thrusting and go-getting. However, it is precisely because the need for humility is forgotten that its importance as a corporate value should be re-examined. Some years ago, a Ugandan Asian businessman who had achieved huge business success in the UK was asked about the secret behind his 'rags to riches' story; his immediate answer was 'humility'. We would do well to ponder on how much humility we practise in our business dealings. Indeed, does the very idea of humility jar and cause us to cringe with embarrassment?

The generic themes shown are useful as a checklist to ensure that you are communicating the qualities which they embody, but they only come into their own as powerful marketing tools when they are transformed into more specific, tangible attributes which are meaningful in your particular business. We have listed in Figure 8.2 some examples of the specific characteristics that the generic themes may represent; it may be argued that some of these characteristics should be categorised differently, and you should feel free to modify the definitions shown to suit what you believe to be appropriate to your market.

It is noticeable that many of the generic themes, and the attributes associated with them, are concerned with the *emotional*, rather than the purely rational, side of the motivations of your

Generic theme	Specific attributes – examples
Trust	*Reliability, ethics, commitment to deliver what is promised, won't rip you off, transparency*
Care	*Concern for customers' welfare, responsibility to community, concern for environment*
Reputation	*History to be proud of, longstanding presence, experience, track record, name associated with quality*
Innovation	*Leading edge, pioneering, focused on the future, strong R&D, new products and services, ingenious solutions, clever ways of doing things*
Strength	*Size, financial stability, global reach, number one position in market*
Quality	*Professionalism, best in its field, best products/services, premium brand, sound quality management procedures, Six Sigma, knowledge, expertise, competence, safe pair of hands*
Value	*Offering justifies the cost, quality matches/exceeds price; competitive price, long-term cost savings*
Empathy	*Understanding of customers/other stakeholders, partnership approach, communication of values to which market can relate, personal relationships, warmth/emotional bond, ease of working with, fun/enjoyable relationship, flexibility to changing market needs*
Enthusiasm	*Willingness to go the extra mile, fun to do business with, passion for customers' business, win-win mentality*
Humility	*Customer is king, ability to listen, recognition that others may know better, willingness to learn and improve, serving the customer is paramount*

Figure 8.2 Transforming generic themes into specific attributes

target audience. Indeed, much of the discussion in this book has shown how success in the marketplace is about the ability to engage with the emotions of customers, prospects and other stakeholders: to take a few examples, the importance of tapping into back-of-mind emotional needs; the recognition of loyalty as a *feeling* (to be distinguished from retention); and the value of understanding the different emotional, as well as rational, motivations of the different members of the DMU. The importance of emotion does, therefore, have a bearing on the way we communicate. This does not, however, mean that you focus on communicating the 'emotional' themes shown in Figure 8.2 without undertaking the action required to support what you have to say: banks that have been instrumental in precipitating the subprime mortgage crisis are hardly likely to be seen − by corporate and retail customers alike − as trustworthy, caring or humble!

On the face of it, emotion is particularly important in consumer markets, where spontaneous purchase decisions are more likely than in business-to-business markets. However, this is often a false assumption: the outward behaviour of business decision makers may well be rational (not least because they are hardly likely to admit to making irrational decisions), but this is quite likely to hide non-rational motivations; these may, for example, be linked to the bond which the principal contacts within the customer organisations have forged with their customer relationship managers.

How can the 10 generic themes be communicated so as to make the most powerful impact on your target audience? Well, the answer lies in realising that it is the qualities they embody, not the slogans, which need to be communicated; we can see this most obviously if we think of an attribute like humility: your target market is hardly likely to take kindly to your telling it 'look how humble we are'! Yet, when we think of some of the other attributes mentioned, this is precisely what many major brands are tempted to do; how often have we seen the word 'innovation' littering company literature without, apparently, a second thought being given to the possibility that, communicated as such, it can come across as a platitude? If every other mission statement goes on about how innovative or customer caring companies aim to be, in what way is the statement differentiating one organisation from another? This is a recipe for glazed eyes and suppressed yawns. Yet, this does not mean that innovation, if genuine, is not a real asset to the organisation; it simply means that it should not be communicated as such. In other words, the theme should be conveyed but the language should be translated into something meaningful to the target audience. This means looking at the more tangible attributes shown in the right-hand column of Figure 8.2, always making sure that the attributes are those that resonate with your customers and prospects and also with any other important stakeholders and influencers operating in your market.

How does all this work out in practice? Let us cite a few real examples of how generic themes, such as innovation and trust, can be given substance which is meaningful to the target market.

The first was the case of an international bank which found that, for part of its target market, 'innovation' was actually seen in a negative light. For these customers and prospects, the word had the connotation of being too quick to change, not being 'grounded', of being 'unpredictable' and 'flash in the pan'; this was a conservative market which valued steadiness, solidity and stability. This did *not* mean, however, that they did not appreciate the bank's forward looking approach or its desire to offer new and better ways of doing things; the message was that the language communicated had to be right, even though the fundamental benefits that the bank sought to convey were still desired. The bank shifted its message from simplistic declarations about being innovative to a more thoughtful approach which focused on how it developed new ways of doing things precisely in order to meet the requirement for security which was paramount in customers' minds; 'innovation', therefore, became a route to security and stability. The experience of the international bank in a way mirrors that of the consumer financial services brand mentioned earlier, which also found that innovation *per se* was not a draw for the consumers being targeted.

The second example illustrates how an overused word like 'innovation' can be seen as being a meaningless 'motherhood and apple pie' statement which, if anything, can dent the credibility of the organisation using the word in its communication. In this instance, an international manufacturing company found out that there were a number of underlying benefits which the term 'innovation' needed to convey: for some of the target audience, a genuinely innovative company would think of ingenious ways of 'doing things better'; the expectation was that this ingenuity would enable the organisation to achieve internal cost savings, some of which could then be passed on to its customers. In short, 'innovation' translated, in the target audience's view, to lower costs. The lesson for the manufacturing company was that if, indeed, it were able to apply innovative approaches to reduce its costs, the message to its audience would not be innovation *per se* – which was liable to mean different (and not always positive) things to different people; rather, it would be the application of ingenious solutions resulting in efficiencies that would offer customers cost benefits. *This* was what was meaningful to the audience.

The third example is of a UK financial institution, Prudential, which has developed a number of concrete measures, around the theme of ethics, designed to engender a feeling of trust. An important reason for initiating this was to counter the negative image attached to financial services companies in the wake of scandals associated with the mis-selling of products. A few examples of the measures taken by Prudential are the launch in 2001 of a senior management training programme, of which ethics was an integral part, and the development of employees' bonus schemes that have in part been linked to ethical conduct. Prudential also launched an international financial literacy programme, designed to encourage transparency by improving customers' understanding of financial issues. And in 2006 the company invested almost £5 million in community investment projects. Of course, Prudential is just one example of many organisations that have embarked on initiatives of this sort, often in response to the negative image associated with their industries.

In the last chapter we referred to the favourable press reporting enjoyed by British Airways at the time of its crash landing at Heathrow airport. The incident offered BA a (totally unplanned!) golden opportunity to show that it was a quality airline, amply demonstrated by its expertise, its professionalism and the fact that it was a safe pair of hands – three of the attributes associated in Figure 8.2 with the theme of quality. Unfortunately, the airline also gave conflicting messages when its baggage handling problems, culminating in the chaotic opening of Terminal 5, appeared to demonstrate a lack of competence – competence being a basic attribute linked with quality.

Implicit in the discussion about the generic themes and attributes shown in Figure 8.2 is the connection they have with the corporate values you may wish to convey to your target audience. It is useful to check each of the generic areas against your own values to see:

- which of these correspond with your core values
- which of them represent aspirational values.

According to P.M. Lencioni (Lencioni 2002), core values 'are inherent and sacrosanct – they can never be compromised. They are deeply ingrained principles that guide all of a company's actions.' Aspirational values, by contrast, 'are those that a company needs to succeed in the future but currently lacks'.

A consideration of corporate values is central to any discussion about communication since, ultimately, no communication is going to be successful if the values they represent are seen to jar with the values of your target audience. The earlier example of the international bank illustrated the point well: harping on about innovation fell on deaf ears because it was not seen to address the core values – of stability and predictability – of the bank's customers and prospects. Your core values should, therefore, correspond as far as possible with the core values of all those with whom you wish to communicate. Equally, your aspirational values should be well tested against the values and expectations of your marketplace; have you checked that what you are aspiring towards matches these market expectations, or have the aspirational values been arrived at because the board of directors went into a navel gazing huddle to discuss the future direction of the company?

Clearly, there will always be some core values which, as Lencioni states, 'can never be compromised'. These values need to be 'lived' at every level of your organisation. In practice, this means that they must be integrated into every employee-related process, including recruitment, performance management systems and criteria for promotion and rewards. Although there are many companies with vision and mission statements which their staff are not clearly aware of or cannot relate to, there are equally companies which seek to bring their values to life throughout their organisation. Ricoh, for example, seeks to instil its business values at every level by encouraging staff to act as role models for those reporting to them: the idea is that team leaders should take their example from department managers, who in turn should emulate divisional managers; the purpose is to empower people at every level of the organisation to be creative and innovative.

The core values which cannot be compromised often correspond with the business losers mentioned in Figure 3.8; for any bank, the highest ethical standards must always be a core value. However, these values will typically be relevant to any organisation operating in the same business – ethical standards being essential for *any* financial institution – so it is unlikely that such values will define what makes *your* organisation the way it is. This also means that focusing on a core value like ethics is unlikely to help you to differentiate your organisation from your competitors. The only situation in which ethics would be 'differentiating' would be if you or a competitor were seen to be less ethical than the rest of the suppliers in your market – in which case it would become a business loser (see Chapter 3).

We would, therefore, make a distinction between those core values which are immutable but not likely to be differentiating (as ethical standards are for financial institutions) from those which, though 'deeply ingrained' at any given point in time, should nonetheless be scrutinised for their relevance to a particular audience at a particular time. Innovation was a deeply ingrained value, on which the bank prided itself – but does that mean that, given market conditions and values, it was always the right one?

It is a useful exercise, therefore, to ask yourself a few basic questions:

- Have we identified and defined our core values?
- What are they?
- How were they developed – historically 'by accident', or as a consequence of a deliberate decision to position the organisation in a way believed to match the values of the marketplace?
- Is there a need to review or adjust these values?
- Which values need re-examination?
- How is the adjustment in values to be communicated to our stakeholders?

Clearly, any adjustments in the values you hold need to be made carefully and communicated so as to avoid confusing the market. However, without periodically modifying the values which have evolved over time, you can find yourself stuck in a time warp. The revival of fortunes experienced by Marks & Spencer did not result from any shift in the fundamental value of quality on which the company has prided itself, but there appears to have been a subtle shift away from the somewhat 'conservative' values with which it was historically associated to a greater focus on modernity, informality and stylishness. Skoda is an example of a brand which experienced a far more dramatic shift – from being a low cost car (which came with negative quality associations) to a brand which has been transformed with a far greater focus on the values of quality and performance. A shift in values can be seen at a more 'macro' level: products from China, associated traditionally with lower quality and lower cost, are now being seen as being of acceptable quality, and it is hard to imagine today that Japan and (more recently) Korea were at one time associated with shoddy quality. It would appear that Japanese industry made the conscious decision to transform its image by focusing on the value of quality. A long-lasting transformation of values must, however, be accompanied by real changes which support that transformation; Marks & Spencer and Skoda would not have succeeded in enhancing their standing if concrete improvements in service and product standards had not been made. Equally, care needs to be taken to ensure that quality standards are maintained if reputation is not to be set back: the recall in the US of toys made in China, on grounds of safety, cannot have helped that country's desire to position itself as an exporter of acceptable quality products.

COMBINING KNOWLEDGE WITH BRAND EQUITY

As we have been saying, the twin criteria of successful communication are that:

- your target audience should know enough about you, and
- whatever it knows makes it favourably disposed towards you.

Your aim should therefore be to maximise the visibility and knowledge of your brand as well as to enhance your brand equity. As mentioned in Chapter 4, brand equity is a measure of the strength of your brand, developed through the image/position you have occupied over time in the minds of customers, prospects, other stakeholders and even the public at large. Brand equity could also usefully be defined here to mean the strength of your brand based on positive associations with the generic themes and attributes shown in Figure 8.2.

Figure 8.3 shows that you can plot your position in terms of market knowledge and brand equity. As the diagram shows, the winning position to which we should normally aspire, represented by the circle in the top right-hand corner, is one in which our audience is highly knowledgeable about our brand *and* where that knowledge results in strong brand equity. An example of this position is the one occupied by the well-known cereal manufacturer who has succeeded in developing a strong image based on consumers' knowledge of the product's health-giving properties. The vulnerable position is, clearly, the circle in the bottom left-hand

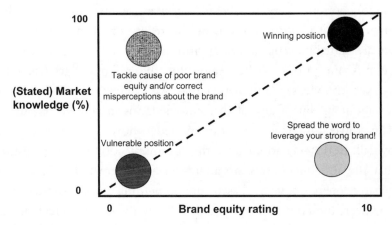

Figure 8.3   Ensure market knows you *and* has favourable perceptions about your brand

corner, where the opposite conditions prevail. The dotted line describes any position where knowledge and brand equity are broadly matched, and any position above or below that line would indicate that we are stronger on one dimension than on the other.

In reality, it is quite likely that we will not find ourselves at either the extreme winning position or the extreme vulnerable position but rather somewhere in between – or, quite possibly, on either side of the dotted line. If we find that we are somewhere in the area represented by the circle in the top left-hand corner, this position would indicate that, although a lot of people know what we stand for, what they know does not leave them with a positive impression. This would require us to investigate the reasons for the negative perception: what are we seen to stand for, how do we rate on the various generic themes which make up our overall market image, and why are we rated in this way?

The poor brand equity rating could well be based on substantive issues: to take an extreme example, if we are seen as being uncaring about the environment because we were indeed responsible for an environmental disaster, then the negative perception is hardly surprising. Conversely, the poor rating could be based on misconceptions: here the belief that we are uncaring about the environment is not borne out by the reality of all the good work we are actually doing on the environment. The fact that there can be misconceptions is the reason for the reference to '(stated)' market knowledge: our market may well believe that it knows a lot about us, but if any of that knowledge is inaccurate or out of date, those misconceptions can influence how we are perceived overall. In this scenario, part of the communication task is to ensure that the misconceptions are addressed and corrected. Where the negative perception is based on something more substantive, however, the communication task is likely to be more challenging because it can only be successfully achieved when the valid causes of the negative perception have been tackled.

It is possible that our position is the polar opposite of the area represented by the top left-hand corner of Figure 8.3. The circle in the bottom right-hand corner indicates a position where relatively few people know about us but those who do know us believe we have a powerful brand. It is a position akin to that described by the 'Weak marketing or niche operator' box of Figure 4.10 (although in that instance the contrast was between strong customer satisfaction and a weak brand). If we occupy this position, our task is to capitalise on the strength of our brand by communicating as strongly and widely as we can to ensure that the positive perceptions of the few are expanded to encompass the many whom we may wish to influence. It is, of course, possible that we are not interested in spreading the word to the many because we are content to focus on the specific segment of the market which already knows us well (again, a point made with reference to the niche operator scenario mentioned in the context of Figure 4.10), in which case the bottom right-hand corner in Figure 8.3 may well be a position that we wish to maintain.

PRODUCT/SERVICE COMMUNICATION

Just as the purpose of corporate communication is to provide information about your organisation and strengthen your corporate brand, so the purpose of product/service communication is:

- to provide information about the products/services you offer, and
- to encourage your target market to look favourably upon your products and services and thereby buy more from you.

As in the case of corporate communication, the provision of information and the strengthening of the profile of your products/ services should go hand in hand: there is not much point in a lot of people knowing about your product only to think that it doesn't perform; equally, there is a lost opportunity if very few people know about the product, however favourable the perceptions of those people might be.

Therefore, the overall objectives of corporate and product/ service communication run on parallel lines. There is another common purpose which is implicit in much of the discussion so far: the purpose of the communication is not merely to enhance the standing of your organisation, or of your products and services, but to do so to the extent of successfully differentiating what you have to offer from the competition's offerings (assuming that you are operating in a competitive environment). The earlier criticism of the easy recourse to 'motherhood and apple pie' declarations in mission statements is based precisely on the view that they fail to differentiate one organisation from the next. So the real question with product and service communication, as with corporate communication, is about how you can successfully convey to your audience not only that your offering is excellent but that what you have to offer is better than the competitor offering.

When we talk about communication, you may ask where 'brand' comes in the corporate → product/service spectrum. In some instances, the corporate and the product/service brands are so closely intertwined as to be indistinguishable, as in the case of Starbucks (coffee) or BMW (cars). Where they are different, however, you could be communicating your corporate brand (say, Procter & Gamble), your product/service brand (Tide washing powder, for instance), or both. 'Brand', therefore, does not exist independently of the organisation or the specific products and services being offered; for this reason, the discussion in the rest of this chapter will focus on the ways in which product/service communication is different from corporate communication.

Although they may seem obvious, the differences between product/service communication and corporate communication are worth summarising:

- Product/service communication operates at a 'micro' level compared with the 'macro' marketing and communication of the corporate entity; therefore, if you are Procter & Gamble, whereas you will be communicating the single Procter & Gamble corporate brand, you will be conveying messages about thousands of individual product brands.

- One implication of this is that the benefits conveyed to your target audience will tend to be 'high level' at the corporate level and more tangible at the product level. So, to continue with the Procter & Gamble example, the company's communications at a corporate level are about its global operations, its desire to 'improve the lives of the world's consumers', and its focus on the principles of 'personal integrity, respect for the individual, and doing what's right for the long term'. Communication about the Tide product will, however, focus more on the practical benefits of its use, for example, its 'high-powered, grease-cutting formula effective on tough, greasy food stains'.

- So far so obvious, one might say; there are, however, some important implications of the divide between corporate and product/service communication:

  - The communication may well be different, but it should at the very least not be incompatible; to take an obvious example, a company that claims to be environmentally concerned but at the same time makes products which pollute the atmosphere is going to find it hard to communicate the benefits of the product without being shot down for inconsistency and hypocrisy.

  - In some instances, it is not easy to retain consistency between the corporate and product/service positioning. If, for example, a company enjoying a premium corporate positioning needs to serve a particular sector which has more basic needs, the needs and values of that sector may well be incompatible with the premium stance adopted by the company.

○ The responsibility for corporate and product/service communication resides in different parts of the organisation, the former typically within the corporate marketing (or equivalent) department and the latter quite probably with the product marketing managers responsible for the specific product lines; in order that the communication emanating from these two sources should be compatible, it is critically important that there should be a clear and continuing line of communication between them. Here, the discussion about intra-organisational gaps of the type described in Figure 6.3 becomes highly relevant. Organisations must also be sensitive to how the pressures under which different parts of the organisation operate can encourage conflicting messages to be conveyed to the target audience: an organisation that positions itself as a premium brand can find its position undermined if, for example, sales staff, under the pressure of making their sales targets, succumb to the temptation to offer their prospects favourable price deals.

○ The audience to which the corporate communication is being directed is likely to be wider than the target audience for product/service communication: if you are seeking to communicate what you as an organisation stand for, you are likely to be addressing not only your immediate customers and prospects but also the media, shareholders, financial analysts, the public at large and all other potential stakeholders and influencers; if you are seeking to communicate the benefits of your product or service, it is quite probable that your primary audience will be those most immediately likely to be using, or influencing the use of, the product or service – the customers and prospects themselves, specifiers, consultants, and so on. Of course, these audiences overlap, and, even when they are quite different, they don't exist in isolation from one another;

the need for the corporate and product/service messages to be compatible remains, therefore, critical.

The point was made earlier in this chapter that the less your target audience is aware of your organisation the lower the likelihood of your potential customers to buy from you. The same point is clearly true if you fail to make your audience aware of the specific products/services you have to offer. As we saw in Chapter 6, the oil company which had embarked on a TQM programme had failed to communicate, *even to its own customers*, the extent of its achievement in improving delivery lead times. Because the improvement was made, it was taken as being axiomatic that at least the customers, who were after all benefiting from this improvement, would be aware of and appreciate it. Similarly, the chemicals company which prided itself on its HSE capability failed to communicate its pre-eminence in this service area, with the result that its customers believed the competition to perform better on HSE matters. On discovering this, the company embarked on a communications programme focusing on bulletins in its regular newsletter which provided information about its HSE capabilities; not long afterwards, the company found that its HSE rating had improved significantly.

The moral of these stories is two-fold: first, never to take for granted that your target audience knows what you are achieving; and, second, that it is far less costly and far more cost effective to communicate the benefits of the service you are offering than to continue to make product or service improvements in the absence of any evidence that these improvements are being noticed or appreciated.

One final point: in product/service communication, as in corporate communication, we should always question whether the message we wish to convey is the message being received, or sought, by the target audience. Earlier in this chapter we cited the case of the international manufacturing company that discovered that, for a part of its target audience, 'innovation' boiled down to lower costs. The point here is that the company started with the assumption that innovation was all about research and development, new product development, problem-solving solutions, and so on; whereas these assumptions were not in themselves incorrect, they blinded the company to the fact that, for its target audience, these attributes were the route to a more important underlying benefit – lower cost – which seemed initially counter-intuitive to the company.

The gap between the company's intentions, when it communicates, and the thought process of the target audience should, therefore, be considered carefully when embarking on any communications initiative. If, for example, you are a telephone salesperson representing a bank which has just launched a new service, you may think that you are communicating the benefits of an exciting new service to the customers you call; the customers may, however, react by wondering whether this is the latest cynical device employed by the bank to extract more money from them. Equally, if you are a vehicle manufacturer communicating the gadgetry of your latest car model, you may be missing a trick if it were to emerge that the target market's real interest was in the prestige gained through ownership of the car, not the gadgetry itself. It is important, therefore, that your communication should convey value propositions which resonate with your target market's (sometimes latent) feelings and desires. Here we come back to the importance of the intangible and back-of-mind issues mentioned in Chapter 3 which, we have suggested, help to explain the success of companies like Ikea and Starbucks: by surrounding the offer of the primary product (furnishings or coffee) with a warm, enjoyable experience, these companies are seeking not only to attract more visitors but also to establish more generally a corporate image based on the theme of empathy shown earlier in Figure 8.2 (warmth/emotional bond, fun/enjoyable relationship).

EFFECTIVE COMMUNICATION IS A TWO-WAY PROCESS

Chapter 3 focused on the need to penetrate the minds of customers and other stakeholders. In order to do this we need feedback from them which is detailed and accurate enough for us to take appropriate action. Figure 8.4 summarises the principal ways in which such information can be obtained. It is quite likely that no one method will be sufficient, that some will require a greater investment than others and that the effectiveness of the different methods will in part depend on the information you require and the business in which you are operating. You should, therefore, consider which approaches may best suit your requirements in any given situation.

1. *Feedback from market-facing staff*: Chapter 4 has already referred to the salesforce and other market-facing staff (like relationship managers) as potential sources of information about customers and other stakeholders. Whereas the value of those who are in constant touch with the marketplace should not be underestimated, we made the point that sole dependence on their

---

- **Feedback from market-facing staff**

- **Market research**

- **Commentary from consumers and other stakeholders/ influencers**

- **Observation and transactional behaviour**

Figure 8.4 Ways of getting feedback

feedback is liable to result in a one-sided view of the market. This is particularly true when seeking to understand market requirements and attitudes (as opposed to the more 'factual' information associated with, say, competitor intelligence). There is therefore the need to look at other sources of information as well.

2. *Market research*: Formal market research – commissioned to an outside professional agency – can be a powerful way of obtaining detailed and more objective information about market attitudes. This is because it involves information drawn directly from those whose opinions matter (the customers and other stakeholders), and because the research company obtaining the information is better placed to provide an unbiased interpretation of the market findings. Market research can also incorporate statistical and other analytical tools which enable us to apply many of the approaches suggested in this book for delving into the minds of customers and other stakeholders. Having said this, it can take time and effort to organise a market research project (for example, generating a sufficiently comprehensive and accurate database of customers to be interviewed); to integrate its results within the organisation; and (sometimes) to reconcile the market research results with one's own experience of the market and, as a result, to achieve buy-in. Above all, market research undertaken by a third party can be expensive. For this reason many organisations do not use it as an essential way of understanding their markets and identifying the courses of action they should take to improve their business – even though they may pay lip service to its value.

3. *Commentary from consumers and other stakeholders/influencers*: It is clearly valuable to keep tabs on what the media has to say about our market, about us and about our competitors, and the last chapter has already referred to the power of media commentary in shaping how we are regarded in the marketplace. This applies to commentary in both conventional media (print, in

particular) and the internet. What the internet has opened up, however, is the opportunity for consumers (who may be your customers, your prospects or the general public), as well as other stakeholders, to voice their opinions about you and your competitors with far greater impact than before: we live in a world of Web 2, social networking sites (including well-known sites such as MySpace and Facebook but also sites like orkut, popular in Brazil and India, and Habbo, which focuses on teenagers), virtual community sites of people with common interests, blogs, forums and chat rooms. The purpose here is not to describe these but rather to highlight some of the ways in which they have empowered consumers and other stakeholders to shape opinion in a way not previously possible:

○ First, and most obviously, it is possible, with a mouse click, to find out your stakeholders' opinions about a range of topics pertinent to your business – from consumer feedback about their needs and complaints to their views about your own organisation and your competitors.

○ The initiative for providing this information comes from the stakeholders themselves – unlike the feedback sought through conventional market research which depends on responses to questions you have formulated; as such, the information can more accurately reflect the spontaneous, strongly held views of some of the people you may be targeting. A note of caution here: the very fact that the opinions expressed come voluntarily from individuals who may feel strongly about a subject means that they may not be representative of the feelings of the market as a whole. The feedback obtained from internet sites should, therefore, be seen as providing useful additional insights, often of an anecdotal nature – but should not form the sole basis for the decisions you may need to make.

○ The internet has made word-of-mouth opinion, always important in shaping the views of your target market, a particularly powerful way of influencing how you are seen and what you decide to do: whereas previously word-of-mouth was generally spread between people who knew one another (family, friends, etc.), today's internet-based word-of-mouth is undertaken within much wider communities of strangers. Going back to one of the topics mentioned in the last chapter, if you are a retailer wishing to know what consumers or media opinion-leaders feel about battery and free-range chickens you could try finding out through the internet; equally, if you wish to know how people regard you as a retailer you could again find out through appropriate websites. Or you could find out what people feel about a product you or your competitors have introduced by clicking on the 'reviews' section of the relevant website. To take one example, in 2007 Renault reported that, according to research it had conducted, over 35% of people had decided not to buy a product after reading unfavourable online reviews about it. The Renault example illustrates an important point: as mentioned earlier, the views of people commenting online may not be genuinely representative of the market, and, as such, should not always be taken literally; however, your attention should certainly focus on the ways in which this vocal minority can shape the opinions of the silent majority.

o The internet, with its social networks, forums, chat rooms, and so on, has democratised the relationship between suppliers and their stakeholders: in the context of product development, for example, the traditional model was that of the supplier/provider proactively offering a product to the customer/recipient who reacted by accepting or rejecting the offering. The internet has encouraged the emergence of a more participatory model, described by some as 'co-creation' (a term popularised by C.K. Prahalad, among others), in which target stakeholders are actively engaged in the product development process. This can and has been done without the internet – most obviously, where industrial product manufacturers have involved their most important customers from the early stages of product development. The internet has facilitated the process, however, because it is easier to hold a dialogue with a wider range of stakeholders, from consumers to suppliers. One of the companies well known for having applied the co-creation model is Lego, whose MINDSTORMS product range enables potential customers to design and programme a range of robotic products. Another company, Philips Design, has established a presence in Second Life, the imaginary online community, in order to obtain feedback on new product concepts; here, 'residents' of the virtual community can participate in the design of products, providing feedback on product features, functionality, colours, and so on. Similarly, Boeing has, through the formation of its World Design Team, encouraged flyers and enthusiasts to participate in the design of the aircraft of the future. The benefit of increased stakeholder collaboration enabled by the internet is not just confined to the tangible one – the development of offerings which more closely fit the requirements of stakeholders; it also encompasses the more intangible advantage of engendering a closer relationship between the provider and all the other relevant stakeholders, and, consequently, the likelihood of greater loyalty and stronger word-of-mouth advocacy.

4. *Observation and transactional behaviour*: There are a number of ways of obtaining information about customers and other stakeholders which depend on observing their behaviour rather than on their conscious feedback. The point here is that by understanding what your target market *does* rather than depending solely on what it *says*, you can gain insights about how they make decisions in practice in a way which might not be

otherwise possible. The term 'ethnography' is often used in this context, to describe an information gathering approach based on observations of people in their natural environment rather than in a more artificially constructed set-up. To take a simple example, people may say that they are cutting down on fatty or sugary foods, but finding out what they actually buy in supermarkets may tell a different story. There is burgeoning literature on this subject, so the following summary provides just a few examples of how observation techniques may be applied:

- The in-store shopping behaviour of consumers – revealing, for instance, the shopper's decision-making process when going down the breakfast cereal aisle, or showing how many shoppers have noticed a new promotion.
- In-store transactional behaviour – it is common practice among large retailers to find out about shoppers' purchasing patterns.
- Website visiting behaviour – a study conducted by Forrester Research in 2007 is reported to have found two-thirds of business decision makers choosing supplier websites as among the most important ways of keeping themselves informed about suppliers.
- The shopping/transactional behaviour of online purchasers.
- Payment methods preferred by purchasers – useful, for example, for plastic card suppliers.
- Media viewing/listening habits – helpful for television/radio channels and advertisers.
- The ways in which people sit at their desks and use their computers – leading to improvements in ergonomic design (for example, the redesign of the mouse to make clicking a more hand-friendly process).
- Problems people may face in navigating through websites – resulting in website redesign to ease the navigation process.

We have discussed in this section some of the ways in which we can get information back from our customers and other stakeholders, so that we can make the overall communication process more effective. Although much of the discussion is clearly relevant to business-to-consumer (btoc) markets, it is also pertinent to those serving business-to-business (btob) or industrial markets: to take an example from the last chapter, an organisation building a new plant or involved in a construction project (whether it be a chemicals company or an airport authority building a new runway) may well need to confront vocal opposition from local consumer groups concerned about the project's environmental impact. Similarly, in the co-creation process, companies may involve outside designers, suppliers, engineers and other 'non-consumer' influencers, as well as the customers themselves. Again, in the context of observation and transactional behaviour, the same approach can be applied to business-to-business markets: observing the difficulties a machine operator has when using a piece of equipment may show whether there are ways in which the equipment can be better designed for greater ease of use; similarly, the problems faced when navigating through websites can apply to business users as well as consumers.

THE EXECUTIVE SELF-ASSESSMENT CHECKLIST: COMMUNICATION

Question	Yes, confident +3	Yes, tentative 0	No −3	NA
Do we believe that we communicate sufficiently with customers?				
Do we believe that we communicate sufficiently with our prospects?				
Do we believe that we communicate sufficiently with our staff?				

Question	Yes, confident +3	Yes, tentative 0	No −3	NA
Do we believe that we communicate sufficiently with other stakeholders and influencers?				
Are we good at listening to our customers?				
Are we good at listening to our prospects?				
Are we good at listening to our staff?				
Are we good at listening to our other stakeholders and influencers?				
Do we know what our customers think about us?				
Do our customers have a sufficiently good understanding of what we have to offer?				
Do we know the degree of awareness/knowledge prospects have of us?				
Are prospects sufficiently aware of us?				
Are prospects sufficiently knowledgeable about us?				
Has our communication succeeded in creating a favourable impact on prospects?				
Do our staff understand where our organisation is heading?				
Are our staff all focused on the same key objectives?				

Question	Yes, confident +3	Yes, tentative 0	No −3	NA
Do our staff communicate sufficiently with one another?				
Do we know the degree of awareness/knowledge other stakeholders and influencers have of us?				
Are other stakeholders/influencers sufficiently aware of us?				
Do our stakeholders/influencers understand what we stand for?				
Has our communication succeeded in creating a favourable impact on other stakeholders?				
Does our communication encompass both corporate and product/service issues?				
Does our communication succeed in both conveying information about our organisation and strengthening our corporate brand?				
If we are more successful in conveying information than in creating a favourable impression of our brand, do we have a plan of action to enhance our standing?				
If we are more successful in creating a favourable brand impression than in conveying information, do we have a plan of action to better inform our target audience?				

Question	Yes, confident +3	Yes, tentative 0	No −3	NA
Do we know what the components of a strong corporate brand are in our business?				
Do we fulfil the criteria of a strong brand in our business?				
In our corporate brand communication, have we identified the most important to our business of the 10 generic themes which are broadly relevant to all organisations?				
Have we succeeded in working on those areas?				
In our communication, have we succeeded in transforming the relevant generic themes into tangible attributes which are meaningful to our target audiences?				
Have we avoided the temptation to communicate 'motherhood and apple pie' platitudes in favour of more substantive benefits for our target audiences?				
Are we confident that, when we convey messages to our target audiences, what those audiences understand is what we intend to convey?				
Do we know what our core values are?				
Do all our relevant staff know what our core values are?				

Question	Yes, confident +3	Yes, tentative 0	No −3	NA

Do these members of staff 'live and breathe' the core values in everything they do?

Do we review our values to ensure that they remain relevant to the times and conditions in which we are operating?

Do the messages we seek to convey correspond with our core values?

Do we know what our aspirational values are?

Do our staff know what our aspirational values are?

Do we review our aspirational values to ensure that they should remain the ones to which we should aspire?

Do our values correspond with the values of our target audience?

Has our communications activity helped to differentiate us from the competition?

Are our corporate and product/ service communications conveying compatible messages?

Do those responsible for corporate communication and those responsible for product/service communication talk to one another?

Do we resist the temptation to take for granted that our customers are bound to know about our product/ service developments?

Question	Yes, confident +3	Yes, tentative 0	No −3	NA

Do we recognise that we need to constantly communicate, even to our customers, the successes we have had in our products and services?

Are we sufficiently aware of those instances when real product/service improvements are necessary and those when increased communication is more necessary than further improvements?

Are we satisfied that we obtain the right quality and quantity of feedback from our customers and other stakeholders?

If not, have we identified the gaps?

Are we taking action to fill those gaps?

Are we satisfied that we fully capitalise on the knowledge of our market-facing staff?

Do we undertake market research?

If not, do we have a good reason for not doing so?

Is our market research carried out systematically in a way designed to provide an input into our decision-making?

Have we found our market research has served its purpose?

If not, do we know why not?

Are we taking action to improve the way we do our market research?

Question	Yes, confident +3	Yes, tentative 0	No -3	NA
Do we systematically keep tabs on what the media has to say about us?				
Do we recognise the power of the internet in enabling us to understand consumers and other stakeholders?				
Do we systematically observe what consumers/other stakeholders have to say about us and/or our market?				
If so, are we acting on this information?				
If not, are we taking action to make better use of the internet as an information source?				
Do we actively use the internet as a vehicle for engaging in a dialogue with customers and other stakeholders?				
If not, is there a good reason for not doing so?				
If there is no good reason, do we have a plan of action to do so?				
Do we proactively utilise such engagement as a way of helping to improve/develop our business (e.g. in product development)?				
Do we use observation techniques to understand what our target market is doing?				
If not, do we have a good reason for not doing so?				
If there is no good reason, do we have a plan of action to do so?				

Question	Yes, confident +3	Yes, tentative 0	No −3	NA
GRAND TOTAL SCORE				
NET ABSOLUTE SCORE				
NET AVERAGE SCORE				

Now, taking each of the above questions, what in practice are we doing?

CHAPTER 9

CONSTANT RENEWAL – SEARCHING FOR WINNING NEW PRODUCT OR SERVICE PROPOSITIONS

INTRODUCTION: THE IMPETUS FOR NEW PRODUCT OR SERVICE DEVELOPMENT

The common reasons for seeking to develop and launch new products and services are two-fold:

- *To fulfil a market need*: There are many instances of products and services being offered in direct response to the expressed needs of the market.
- *To capitalise on a market opportunity*: For example, you may have the opportunity to diversify into new applications by applying existing capabilities to those applications so as to offer an enhancement over current offerings in those areas; a case in point is the application of the global positioning system (GPS) for civilian use – particularly as a way of enabling motorists to dispense with map reading – but developed from satellite

navigation system technology designed originally for military purposes.

However, the impetus for new product/service development does not – or at least should not – come solely as a response to market conditions. The market-sensitive organisation will recognise that, to be successful in a constantly shifting competitive environment, there is no room to stand still. This not only means the need to excel in the way it delivers its current products and services – by paying attention to the sorts of issues discussed in earlier chapters (particularly Chapters 3 and 4); it also means the need to *anticipate* future market requirements and preferences by developing new or enhanced offerings. The alert organisation will be constantly on the lookout for new product/service opportunities even when there is no apparent requirement for anything new – because if it ceases to be vigilant it will find itself in defensive and reactive mode when a competitor has stolen a march over it by being the first to come in with a product/service introduction. More positively, proactively anticipating future market requirements will enable the organisation to differentiate itself from the competition. The work on value innovation done by W. Chan Kim and Renée Mauborgne has shown that the most successful, high growth companies have been those who have made the leap by thinking outside the box which normally defines their marketplace. These companies will not be reactively looking over their shoulders to check what the competition is doing and will often think creatively about an entirely new way of doing things which is not necessarily defined by current market needs. They are the ultimate proactive marketeers.

This does not mean that the organisation must, as a matter of principle, *always* be the first to think about something new – sometimes it is better to be in a 'me-too' position which allows you to learn from the mistakes made by your competitors; but it does mean that you make the *conscious* decision as to whether you would rather be the innovative introducer or adopt a wait and see approach.

LOOKING AROUND US: UNDERLYING 'MACRO' TRENDS

When considering new product or service development, we must of course look at what our customers and prospects want, be aware of the competition, consider the impact of legislation/regulations, and so on. These are all factors which have a bearing on our market in particular. However, we should also take serious account of underlying 'macro' trends which are not specific to our business but which are liable nonetheless to have an impact on it. Figure 9.1 shows some of the key trends which we believe are likely to influence the shape of things to come in a number of business sectors.

Concerns about the environment

Since the 1950s we have seen an accelerating rush to develop new generations of products which are ever faster, better and

```
• Concerns about the environment

• Concerns about energy supplies and scarce
  resources

• Uncertain economic climate

• Changes in age profile

• Increasing power of BRIC economies

• Emergence of BRIC middle classes
```

Figure 9.1   Key macro trends

(sometimes) cheaper than their predecessors. And, at the same time, these products have become ever more disposable – hardly surprising when producing the 'next generation' which must supersede earlier product models has become the mantra of our technology-driven world. Planned obsolescence became part of the product development vocabulary. Now, however, we have entered – albeit often half-heartedly – the world of environmental consciousness. In practice, this has so far meant that, in the wealthier countries, it is no longer acceptable to throw away food, use plastic unnecessarily or leave our lights on.

Much of the discussion has focused on the consumer's need to behave in an environmentally responsible way. Curiously, the same pressure does not seem to have been felt by product manufacturers and even, in some instances, regulatory authorities: computer manufacturers continue to produce the latest, thinnest, lightest or most powerful laptop; white goods manufacturers continue to churn out their latest 'upgrades'; telephone manufacturers continue to encourage consumers to use not one but two or three cordless telephones; manufacturers of mobiles and iPods spew out their latest versions, resulting in millions of the older versions of these products lying unused or causing toxic emissions in landfills as a result of the mercury, lead and cadmium they contain. In some instances, the consumer is effectively forced to buy the latest product or at least invest in updating it, even though the older version works perfectly well, ostensibly on the grounds of better performance or increased enjoyment: the move to digital television, for example, means that people who have happily used an old analogue version – possibly for 20 years – will be obliged at the very least to invest in a digital box if they do not wish to discard the old television in favour of a new one (which will in all probability not last for half as long). Here, it is not just the manufacturers pushing for new products to be bought but also the regulatory environment which makes it impossible for consumers to keep their old products.

We would submit that this situation is unlikely to be tenable in the foreseeable future, and that planned obsolescence is quite likely to become a term of abuse. The canny manufacturer should, therefore, be seriously considering how the products of the future can be marketed as environmentally friendly *because they are long lasting*. This could mean a sea-change in the way of looking at new product and service opportunities. In the years to come, we expect the forward-looking, innovative company to be the one to introduce new products which last, not those which need to be churned out every few years. This should result in an interesting reversion to the 'old fashioned' values of solidity and long-lasting performance. 'Here to stay' will be the new buzz phrase, and 'the latest upgrade' could well become a badge of shame unless it is used sparingly and associated with 'built to last'; 'innovation' itself will become a dirty word if it is narrowly connected with the regurgitation of the latest offerings – although it will strengthen the brand if it is linked to new products or ways of doing things which are designed to last. The most immediate impact of this trend is likely to be felt in those areas where consumers have little emotional investment: it is not difficult to see consumers welcoming the introduction of washing machines and dishwashers which last longer. Conversely, the product areas where consumers are most likely to pride themselves on being the owners of the latest gadgetry – hi-fi equipment, for example – are the ones most likely to resist the trend, at least for the foreseeable future.

What opportunities would such a trend offer the manufacturer? Well, on the face of it, manufacturers would be faced with the prospect of making less money if they cannot persuade their customers to make frequent upgrades. However, if confronted with a trend which is going to be difficult to reverse, the imaginative company would seek to turn the situation to its advantage by seeking out opportunities which may give it a competitive edge. For example, whereas it is currently standard for white goods to come with a one-year guarantee (with extended guarantees paid for), what competitive advantage would the manufacturer gain by offering a free three-year guarantee? Clearly, a careful cost–benefit analysis would need to be undertaken before making such a change, and the manufacturer would need to factor in the possibility of competitors following suit. The point, however, is that the context of the new 'built to last' environment could well make something like a free extended guarantee a more interesting option than it may have been previously.

We are already seeing signs of consumer behaviour which is likely to encourage this new way of thinking: one example is the growing debate about the environmental merits of cloth nappies over disposable ones; although both have been found to have their environmental disadvantages (cloth using more water, energy and detergent, and disposable contributing more solid waste to landfill sites) the fact that there is a growing consumer consciousness about this issue is a sign of the increasingly questioning attitude that consumers are likely to take about the latest gizmos they are being offered.

Some authorities have already been encouraging the move away from wasteful purchasing behaviour by charging manufacturers and consumers to pay for recycling costs. In the US, for example, the states of Maine and Washington oblige manufacturers to contribute to the cost of recycling electronic waste.

Concerns about energy supplies and scarce resources

Closely linked to the worries about the environment are concerns about energy supplies and scarce resources. We are constantly bombarded with news items about the diminishing availability of oil and the impact of the increasing energy demands of countries like China and India. There is talk about the increasing scarcity of resources, including water and crops, linked to the demands made on the environment by human activity.

Actions taken to address concerns about the environment are often closely connected to the need to conserve resources; the advocates of greater use of nuclear energy, for example, support their argument on the ground of scarce resources – the need not to depend on depleting supplies of oil – as well as on the ground that nuclear energy is 'cleaner' than traditional fossil fuels.

Whereas the discussion on this topic has tended to focus, quite naturally, on general concerns about how we can cope in a world of increasing shortages, every organisation needs to think about the implications of this situation for its own business – in terms of the processes it uses and the goods and services it produces. To what extent does the scarcity of traditional resources also mean an opportunity to offer alternatives – an obvious consideration, for example, for oil companies looking at renewable energy – and equally what is the opportunity to offer new ways of doing things which reduce the consumption of resources? Examples of the latter are low energy light bulbs, low flow toilets requiring less water, and chargers designed to extend the life of disposable batteries 10-fold. But are there specific opportunities for us in our own businesses to develop products and services which can help to address the issue of shortages in energy and other resources?

Uncertain economic climate

At the time of writing, the newspapers are rife with scare stories about credit crunches, bank failures, falling house prices and global recession. The genuine concerns about the world economy cannot be belittled, but at the same time now is not the first occasion that financial markets have been seized by panic attacks. What is perhaps new is the conjunction of concerns about the environment and energy supplies, on the one hand, and fears about the world economy, on the other. All these factors, working in combination, are liable to result not only in greater consumer concerns about *how much* they spend but also on *how* they spend their money. This could well accelerate the move away from planned obsolescence to 'built to last', particularly when high value items are being considered. If you are selling low value items, especially if you are operating in 'essential' businesses – food products, for example – you are less likely to be vulnerable to tighter economic conditions, but if your products or services require a larger invest-ment, economic constraints, together with environmental con-cerns, are liable to push you into seriously considering how you should adjust your offering to suit the new climate in which you are operating.

Changes in the age profile of the population

Many suppliers of consumer products and services appear to live, ostrich-like, in a time warp: the signs of an ageing population in many west European countries have been around for decades, yet the focus of consumer goods marketing and advertising continues to be on the youth market. These suppliers seem to be behind the times in three ways:

- By not recognising the shift in the age profile of the population, they are apparently failing to see that there are simply going to be more old people around buying their goods and services.
- If low birth rates, particularly in countries like Spain and Italy, continue, the pool of younger people could well shrink (if immigration is excluded from the equation).
- The older people have more disposable income than the younger people; so, not only is there a growing number of them, but on average they spend more.

What all this amounts to quite simply is a lost opportunity for suppliers who remain obsessed with the youth market at the expense of the so-called baby boomers – a point well made by Dick Stroud in his book *The 50-plus Market* (Stroud 2007). When developing new products and services, therefore, we need to consider where the real opportunities lie in terms of age profile, and we should act accordingly. Some companies have done precisely that, with great success: in the UK, for example, the insurance company Saga has created a successful business by focusing on the over-50s market.

We should not only rethink who we target but also how we go about targeting them. This means looking at the media and other information sources most likely to be used by older people. In the last chapter, on communication, we referred to the development of social networking sites and other ways of developing a dialogue with customers and other stakeholders. In the consumer space, however, it is the younger people who are the most active users of these online sites. So perhaps, until such time as the use of the internet expands among older people, we should think carefully about what communication media we use for different sections of the population; whereas the web may be a powerful way of connecting with the young, we may need to consider more conventional ways of reaching older people.

Whereas west European populations are getting older, the proportion of young people in many other parts of the world remains very high. So, when we consider developing new products or services, who we target and how we target them will depend on the market we are aiming for.

Increasing economic power of BRIC economies

The world is seeing a shift in the balance of economic power, with the economies of Brazil, Russia, India and China (BRIC) becoming increasingly powerful. This is likely to require a corresponding shift in the way we look at business opportunities in general and new product/service opportunities in particular. For companies in western countries, the conventional thinking – based on looking at opportunities at home first, then considering the incremental business offered by overseas markets – may need to be modified. There may be a greater need to adopt the world view taken by small countries like the Netherlands and the Nordic countries where manufacturers and service providers have had to consider, from the start, the potential offered by the wider market-place, their own home market being too small to offer them a viable business.

At the same time, western companies will need increasingly to consider, from the start, that their major competitors may well come from BRIC. Whether making a general assessment of how they stand vis-à-vis the competition or looking more specifically at new product/service opportunities, western companies are increasingly likely to have to include in their competitor set companies from these countries. This is hardly surprising when one considers that India, for example, is today the world's second largest investor in the UK. We need only look at the recent history of global acquisitions made by Tata, the Indian multinational, to realise that there is emerging a significant shift in the global balance of economic power: in addition to owning Tetley, the UK tea company, and Corus, the Anglo-Dutch steel manufacturer, it made two further high profile acquisitions in the first quarter of 2008 – first, of the iconic British brands Jaguar and Land Rover, purchased from Ford, and, second, of General Chemical Industrial Products in the US, which, together with the 2005 acquisition of Brunner Mond in the UK, has made Tata the world's second largest manufacturer of soda ash.

At the same time, for enterprises based in the BRIC countries, the example set by Tata illustrates a corresponding set of product and service opportunities outside their traditional home or regional markets.

Emergence of middle classes in the BRIC economies

With the growth of the BRIC economies has come a burgeoning middle class which offers opportunities for local and overseas companies alike to sell new as well as existing products and services. In India, for example, the UK retailer Marks and Spencer held discussions in early 2008 with the Indian company Reliance Industries about selling its ready-made Indian food products in India. Within India itself Tata launched its $2500 Nano car, targeted at the Indian consumer wishing to graduate from a three-wheeler to a small, inexpensive car.

For foreign enterprises, investing in the BRIC countries is not without its problems – difficulties can arise from poor infrastructure, bureaucracy and corruption. However, the combination of growing wealth and an increasingly liberal investment environment in countries like India means that western companies, especially those who have not already made inroads in BRIC, will need to consider whether they can afford to neglect potential opportunities for them to develop new offerings which cater for these markets.

CRITICAL FACTORS FOR SUCCESS: INTRODUCTION

Clearly, you cannot rush into a new product or service launch without doing your homework. This section, therefore, discusses the factors that need to be taken into account if you are to make a success of your venture and avoid making hugely expensive mistakes.

One point to note before we discuss the factors for success in product/service launches: when we refer to 'new' products or services, we mean not only products/services which are quite innovative and unknown to the marketplace but also any which are intended to provide genuine enhancements over existing offerings. The research done by W. Chan Kim and Mauborgne (Chan Kim and Mauborgne 1997) has indicated that the true innovators generally make a larger profit than those taking a more gradual approach. However, in the real world, the number of brand new offers is far outweighed by adaptations or improvements on the products and services currently offered. The basic business considerations are nonetheless the same whether we are considering something quite innovative or planning on existing product enhancements: will there be a demand for the offer, will the returns be worth the investment, what makes the offer attractive (or not) to the target market, how best should we communicate the offer, and so on.

The factors determining the success of new product/service ventures can be internal or external to the organisation, and the failure to pay adequate attention to any one of these can result in your new product or service being shoved into the crowded dustbin of lost causes. Figure 9.2 summarises the key factors for

Figure 9.2 Determinants of success in new product/service development

success. These include a set of internal factors and another group of external factors. These are the factors which you should consider because they are likely to be directly relevant to your particular business. Figure 9.2 does not mention the underlying 'macro' trends already discussed in the last section because, although these trends could well be important influences on any new product/ service decisions you may take, they are general trends which can influence a wide range of organisations across different types of businesses.

INTERNAL SUCCESS FACTORS

- *Your own experience and knowledge*: Clearly, any new product or service must be built on your organisation's experience and knowledge – which may relate to your technical capabilities, your corporate culture and your understanding of the market for which the new offering is intended. Even when the new product/service capability is being bought in, rather than developed organically, the success of the new venture is likely to be influenced by the degree to which the bought capability can be understood and assimilated within the organisation – which means compatibility with the organisation's own way of doing things. Building on your experience and knowledge should not mean that you are constrained to do things in the way you have always done things. That would make it impossible to think outside the box. But it does mean that your idea, to become a realistic proposition, should have some connection with the way your organisation thinks and operates.

    Building on experience also means learning from past successes and failures: Joan Schneider (Schneider and Yocum 2004) reported the results of a survey of 98 business-to-business companies which had successfully launched a new product. The first factor for success identified was a documented launch process which identified clearly what did or did not work so that it was possible to improve with each new product launch.

- *Your ability to implement*: No matter how brilliant it is, no new idea is going to work if you don't have the wherewithal to make a success of it; it is true that you can buy the capabilities required, but here again compatibility with your own operations is likely to enhance the chances of success. In addition to your technical capabilities, you should have, or be able to generate, the financial resources necessary to carry through the idea.

- *Idea generation/brainstorming*: In order to stand out as an original or a better offering from your organisation, the idea for the product or service should be internally generated – or at least come across as being distinctly your own. It is true, of course, that no idea springs from a total vacuum and any 'new' concept is itself likely to result from a combination of experience, internal capabilities, current products/services already in the marketplace, ideas generated by others, developments in the marketplace, and so on. A successful process of idea generation must therefore learn from what is currently available and known – and, perhaps more to the point, a sensitivity and awareness about what is currently not available, known, or even conceived of – to produce propositions which will be seen to have distinctive benefits which distinguish what you have to offer from whatever is currently on offer.

  Notwithstanding the need for creativity, idea generation should involve a formal and disciplined process of discussion, questioning, challenging and testing – and this is where brainstorming is relevant. This is not to say that creativity should be stifled; indeed, your staff should be actively encouraged to suggest ideas, and the 'ideas box' is a device that organisations are increasingly adopting as a way of involving everyone in the initial generation of ideas. However, the brainstorming process is necessary to sift out those concepts which are the least feasible or attractive, so that the ideas which remain as potentially viable can be explored in greater detail.

The brainstorming process should involve all members of staff who are best placed to judge the viability of ideas and are likely to have a key role in further exploration and implementation of these ideas. The line of questioning below provides a broad basis for the types of issues to be discussed:

- Is what we are proposing in any way distinctive from what is already out there?
- Would this offer genuine incremental benefits?
- How are target customers and prospects likely to react?
- Can we do it?
- Will we need to charge more?
- How easily can we communicate the advantages of our offer? This is particularly relevant if there is something out there that looks similar (even if it isn't), or if the offer is likely to cost more.
- What investment will we need to make?
- Therefore what is the minimum we will need to sell and at what price?
- Is the market likely to pay a premium (especially if we need to charge more)?
- What do we need to do next to test the viability of the concept?

- *Leadership/drive for success*: No new idea, however attractive, will move much past the drawing board if it isn't championed by someone in a senior position who can make things happen. Once the brainstorming process is over, it is the role of this person to ensure that the necessary next steps are taken. Leadership, of course, does not mean that the CEO of the organisation should feel free to push through an idea he thought up while playing golf; the essence of the process of idea generation and brainstorming that we are describing is that it is democratic. The role of the leader is to ensure that the ideas, having been democratically scrutinised and assessed, move on to the next stage.

Returning to the survey reported by Joan Schneider, three of the other factors for success in the launch of a new product related to the establishment of a launch budget, agreement on that budget as early as possible, and commitment to retain the budget throughout the process. Commitment to a budget is not possible without the leadership and support of a senior champion prepared to see the process through to completion.

The internal process so far described is essentially about the development and partial testing of hypotheses – 'partial' because the hypotheses have so far only been tested by people within your organisation. The next stage is to complete the hypothesis testing process by examining the marketplace, and this is where the external factors shown in Figure 9.2 become relevant. In the real world, the process is not as neatly sequential as we are describing here – an input into some of the internal discussion could well be market information already in the possession of your staff. In practice, though, the internal factors are seldom sufficient to make the confident decisions necessary for a successful new product/service launch. In the end, the proposed product/service will stand or fall to the extent that it is attractive enough to induce the target market to buy it in the volumes and at the price necessary for it to be a commercial success.

EXTERNAL SUCCESS FACTORS

- *Market needs/opportunities*: We started this chapter by referring to the two common reasons for new product/service development – the better fulfilment of unmet needs and the drive to capitalise on market opportunities. The first step of the 'exter-

nal' investigation is the identification of gaps in current offerings and of likely future customer demands (unless this
information is already known to your organisation). Quite
obviously, if, on external investigation, you were to find that
there is no real need for the product/service you have in
mind, then the viability of the enterprise would be in jeopardy
– although your investigation might show, for example, that,
with some adaptation of your proposed offering, you would
be able to fulfil a genuine requirement. There will always be
stories of new product/service launches which successfully
took off even though preliminary investigations indicated that
they would fail. There are also, however, many stories about
product launches which failed because inadequate homework
was done in the marketplace. We would suggest that it is
always sensible to undertake an investigation of market needs
and opportunities; if, on assessing the results of the investigation, you decide, for other reasons, not to follow the conclusions drawn from the investigation, at least you will have made
your decision consciously rather than blundering into it without
real consideration of what the market appears to be saying.

- *Competitive environment*: When we talk about the need to consider the competitive environment, we are not referring to a
  process of constantly looking over your shoulder to see what
  the competition is doing; the value innovation approach
  espoused by W. Chan Kim and Mauborgne makes the point
  that ideas should be developed *without* worrying too much
  about the competition since that frees us to think truly creatively. Southwest Airlines appears to be a classic example of a
  company that has successfully forged ahead with innovations;
  it was the first airline to introduce plastic boarding cards and
  a no frills service.

  At the same time, however, it makes sense to double
  check that any idea produced for serious consideration has not
  already been generated by some other party! Clearly, if, say,

a competitor has just introduced an offer which is very similar to the one you are proposing, you would need to question whether your idea is as different as you thought it was. The key lies in the sequence of thinking: to move forward creatively, you should start the idea generation process without undue concerns about what the competition may or may not be doing. Having generated the idea (or ideas) it is then prudent to check whether there is, or is likely to be, anything in the competitive landscape which may colour whether and how you pursue your idea.

It is at this stage that questions about the competition become relevant: 'Are competitors developing products/services which may be seen to be similar to what we have in mind?' or 'How is the competition likely to respond to our new launch?' The last question gives rise to the need to anticipate as far as possible likely competitor reactions – which could range from the price cutting of their current products/services to the introduction of their own 'new' products/services as a counter-attack against your latest launch. There are many examples of competitor counter-offers being introduced which have in some instances, though by no means all, badly affected the original product: Baileys Irish Cream Liqueur, which is exported to 150 countries, is one example of a brand that has apparently remained impervious to the onslaught of the numerous imitations it has provoked, remaining a premier brand in the liqueur business; by contrast, Netscape, at one time dominant in the web browser market, found its market share reduced from 90% in the mid-1990s to less than 1% by the end of 2006 in the course of the first so-called browser war, losing most of its share to Internet Explorer which Microsoft offered free of charge; and Sony, which in 1979 created the portable music market with its Walkman, lost market share to Apple's iPod and has been struggling ever since to regain its once-dominant position.

As we will discuss later in this chapter, the pricing of your new offering is critical to its success, and market perceptions of what constitutes value for money will therefore be a key determinant of your success; competitors may already be offering – or may introduce in response to your launch – products/services which may not be as good or as innovative as yours but which are significantly less expensive: a competitor product which is 70% as good as yours but is offered at 50% of the price you would propose to charge may well be regarded as the better buy because the market can dispense with 'perfection'. The discussion we had earlier on what makes for value (surrounding Figure 3.4) becomes particularly relevant when considering the viability of a new or enhanced product or service.

- *External constraints*: An obvious piece of homework that needs to be done is an investigation of all legal, regulatory or technical constraints which may have a bearing on the viability of your new offer. These may relate, for example, to environmental considerations or, in the case of technical products, the specifications laid down by third parties. These constraints may come from private or public sector bodies residing at local, national, regional (for example, EU) or international level.

- *Attitudes of customers and prospects*: It should be obvious to any organisation that central to the success of any product/service launch is the likely reaction of customers and prospects to the new offering. Clearly, when assessing market attitudes, it is crucial to understand whether the improved product/service features offered are seen by prospective purchasers to be a real benefit. It is also important to identify those features that are particularly attractive so that resources are allocated appropriately. The market response may indicate that modifications to the proposed features are required if the new offering is to be seen to provide genuine added value, in which case you would need to consider whether or not you would be capable of making those alterations or whether it would be cost effective for you to do so.

Attitudes towards the new offering will also be influenced by the general factors which drive customer decision-making and the extent to which customers are already happy with their suppliers' current offerings. If customers are highly satisfied with the existing products/services on offer, they are likely to be in a less receptive frame of mind when presented with a new offering than if they have cause to be dissatisfied. The investigation of attitudes to the new offer cannot, therefore, be divorced from many of the issues discussed in Chapters 3 and 4 of this book (on market drivers and customer satisfaction/loyalty). The interlocking influences of the various areas of the 9 point plan have already been referred to in Chapter 1.

To be confident about your new venture it is critically important, therefore, that the proposed offering should be tested in the marketplace before it is formally launched. If the new product/service involves an entirely new concept, the testing process may commence with questions to find out whether the concept itself is appealing; if your target market sees flaws in the concept you may wish to go back to the drawing board to tackle those issues before seeking to give shape to the concept in terms of specific features.

This step-by-step approach, starting with concept testing before moving into the specifics of product features, is one adopted by many companies with a record of success in new product launches. To take one example from the automotive sector: BMW hypothesised that there was a gap in the market for a car which combined the functional aspects of certain types of cars with the more 'emotional' aspects associated with quite different cars. This was the concept that needed to be tested. Having tested the concept and found that it was attractive to target customers, the company was in a position to give shape to the concept by exploring in more detail the specific functional and style features which needed to be combined to have the strongest appeal to the target market.

When testing your product or service for its attractiveness, it is clear that this process will reveal which of the proposed features are really attractive and which are not. This is of obvious value in showing whether your new offering is seen to represent an improvement over the existing products/services in the marketplace. However, it is not enough to confine your enquiry to the features of your new offer if you wish to make a commercial success of your new venture: it is imperative that you also understand the price (or price range) which would make the launch a commercially viable proposition. There is not much point in offering a product or service which the target customer pronounces to be wonderful if he is not prepared to put his money where his mouth is. It is critically important, therefore, that product/service features and price should be considered side by side in the course of the testing process if you are to avoid errors which can be hugely damaging both in terms of wasted resources and, potentially, in terms of your reputation.

In addition to asking customers and prospects about the combination of features and price most likely to induce them to purchase the new offering, there is yet another factor which can influence your commercial success in undertaking the launch: the strength of your brand. We have already discussed earlier (in Chapter 3) how a strong brand can have a halo effect on customer satisfaction, and there is considerable evidence to suggest that the same halo effect can apply in a new product/service situation: if you offer a new product, the chances of that product being adopted are increased if your organisation already has a strong brand name. So, when testing market reactions to the product/service offered, it is important ultimately to address the extent to which your brand (compared with competitor brands) is likely to aid or hinder the successful launch of the new offering.

Implicit in much of the discussion so far on customer attitudes is the assumption that, for the commercial viability of the new venture to be properly assessed, the product/ service offering should be tested in the context of current offerings – your own as well as your competitors'. Unless you are operating in a monopolistic environment, customer attitudes towards your offer cannot be divorced from their attitudes towards the offers with which it would land up competing. The testing process should, therefore, include not only attitudes about how your new product/service compares with your existing offerings but also attitudes about how it compares with the offers currently available from the competition: your new offer may well be regarded as a significant improvement on what you have been providing so far, but if it is still seen to offer worse value than the offers of competitors you may yet fail to make the new launch a commercially viable proposition.

The suggestion that the new idea should be tested against current offerings seems to fly in the face of the point made earlier about not being obsessed with the competition. However, we need to return here to the issue of sequence in thinking: the idea generation process should take place without being hindered by competitive considerations, but it is only sensible that, once your ideas have been developed, they should be tested in a market context: however radical you may believe your idea to be, the marketplace may not place the same value on it as you think it deserves, simply because it still has the choice to remain with the conventional products.

Although we have frequently referred to the 'target market' as though it were a single, homogeneous grouping of customers and prospects, the reality is likely to be that your new offering will appeal to some more than to others. The concept of segmentation is, therefore, relevant in new product/service development. If we have segmented our overall market on the lines described in Chapter 2, we should be in a position to assess which segments are most receptive to the new offering; and if we know the approximate size of these segments, we can also estimate the likely demand for our new product/service within these segments.

Figure 9.3 summarises the key steps discussed so far about what we need to know from our customers and prospects if we are to maximise the chances of success in our new product/service launch.

- *Attitudes of other stakeholders/influencers*: The final influence on the success of your new product or service is the attitude of stakeholders/influencers other than prospective buyers. For example, financial analysts and shareholders may have views about the value added by the new offering – which may

---

What do you need to know?

- Establish whether **the concept has appeal**
- Establish **what you should put into your new product/service offering by finding out** …
    - o **Gaps/weaknesses in your current offering**, as perceived by customers
    - o Whether the proposed **product/service offering has greater appeal than your current offering**
    - o **Which product/service features will maximise the appeal** of your new product/service
    - o Whether it is **a feasible proposition** for you to meet customers' stated preferences
- Establish whether the **new offering will be a commercial success** by …
    - o Comparing market attitudes to the new offering **against your current and competitor offerings**
    - o Considering the impact of not only …
        - **Product/service features**
        But also …
        - **Price**
        - **Brand**

Figure 9.3 Assessing market attitudes to new products/services and pricing

influence your stock market performance if you are a publicly quoted company; environmental groups may be looking out for any enhancements in the 'green' performance of the product; and the extent to which media coverage is favourable could influence the buying decisions of the target market.

Although your current customers and prospects represent the key group whose attitudes will determine the success of your launch, the role of the other stakeholders/influencers cannot be ignored because at the very least they are liable to influence the speed of uptake of the proposed product or service. By uncovering the attitudes of these parties, you will be in a better position to know how to communicate with them and manage them in a way which encourages their endorsement of your new offering. To take an example from the financial sector, when looking at the potential for a new pension service, a credit rating agency had to consider the views of groups as diverse as pension fund sponsors, trustees, consultants, asset managers and scheme members.

HOW DO YOU GO ABOUT FINDING OUT WHETHER OR NOT YOUR NEW PRODUCT/ SERVICE IS LIKELY TO BE SUCCESSFUL?

Figure 9.4 provides a summary of the ways in which you may consider finding out information relevant to all the internal and external factors discussed in the last section.

Further thoughts about investigating attitudes of customers and prospects

Whereas the summary of 'How to go about it' in Figure 9.4 is self-explanatory in most cases, it is worth discussing in more detail

Critical factors for success	How to go about it
Internal factors	
Your own experience and knowledge	• Internal discussions • Review and collation of internal information • Brainstorming • Management/board decision about whether the new product/service idea fits with the organisation's goals • Management/board decision about whether the new product/service idea fits with the organisation's experience and knowledge • Learning from the experience of your previous attempts to launch products/services
Your ability to implement	• Internal discussions • Review of capabilities • Appointment of individual/task force to present and defend views about what is/is not possible • Management/board decision about what is feasible
Idea generation/ brainstorming	• Internal brainstorming sessions (which may involve an external facilitator) among all relevant staff in general management, marketing, product management, finance, technical departments, etc. • Individual (could be the facilitator)/task force to summarise and present results of brainstorming to management • Management/board decision about idea(s) to progress
Leadership/ drive for success	• Appointment of champion to ensure that the process is pursued to its ultimate outcome • Champion should be senior individual with decision-making authority
External factors	
Market needs/ opportunities	• Brainstorming of information already known about the market • Review and collation of in-house information about the market • Desk research to gather published market information • Initial discussions with knowledgeable sources/major operators in the market (key customers, intermediaries, consultants, trade press, suppliers of related products/services, etc.) • Potential requirement for a general investigation of market needs among customers, prospects and other stakeholders • Individual/task force to summarise and present results to management • Management/board decision about opportunities worth exploring further
Competitive environment	• Brainstorming of information already known about the competition • Review and collation of in-house information about the competition • Desk research to gather published information about recent competitor activities • Initial discussions with knowledgeable sources/major operators in the marketplace (key customers, intermediaries, consultants, trade press, suppliers of related products/services, etc.) • Potential requirement for a general investigation of attitudes of customers, prospects and other stakeholders with respect to competitors and their offerings (this investigation could be combined with the investigation of market needs/opportunities mentioned above) • Individual/task force to summarise and present results to management, together with other market information • Management/board decision to go ahead with the proposed idea(s) because they can be differentiated from the offerings of the competition
External constraints	• Review and collation of in-house information about legal, regulatory, technical constraints • Desk research to update information on these matters • Contacts with relevant bodies – trade, environmental, regulatory, government, etc. – at local, national and supra-national level • Individual/task force to include this information within the report to management • Management/board decision about how the new product/service opportunity needs to be assessed in the light of external constraints • Management consideration of whether any *new* opportunities may be found as a result of the introduction of rules and regulations
Attitudes of customers and prospects	• If not already known, market investigation to test reactions to concept, specific features, and the impact of price and brand (see below for further details); this could overlap with investigations of market needs and attitudes to competition mentioned above • Where appropriate/feasible, test marketing • Management/board 'go/no go' decision based on information obtained
Attitudes of other stakeholders/ influencers	• If not already known, investigation among relevant stakeholders/influencers (analysts, media, shareholders, pressure groups, etc.) • Enquiries among these groups should be discreet to ensure that information about your proposed new offer is not in the public domain before you are ready to disclose it • Management/board decision about how to manage and communicate to key stakeholders/influencers

Figure 9.4 Acting on the factors for success

how we can undertake market investigations to test reactions to the new offer we are proposing.

In the last chapter we have already referred to the ways in which the internet has offered opportunities to test market reactions in a way not possible (or at least not widespread) before – through product co-creation, social networking sites, online reviews, and so on. The rest of this section will focus instead on some of the approaches used in more conventional market research.

In all instances, it would be wise to have the investigations undertaken by independent market research firms, partly because they offer expertise in the line of questioning to be adopted, but also – at least as important – because of the bias which can result from any direct discussions between your organisation and the target market.

If we know very little about likely reactions to the new offer – for example, because it is based on a new concept, not just an adaptation of existing products – it could well be advisable to commence with an exploratory investigation. The purpose of this would be to probe in some depth into what the target market likes or dislikes about the concept. Typically, this sort of enquiry would be undertaken with a small sample of customers and/or prospects, either in the form of one-on-one interviews (more common with business than with consumer customers) or through a group activity (for example, conventional focus groups or online bulletin boards). Because it encourages interactive discussion, this type of group activity is particularly valuable when we wish to elicit reactions to new ideas.

If the exploratory investigation were to show that there was mileage in the concept being tested, the next stage would normally be a larger-scale survey, which may typically be carried out by telephone or online, to arrive at more robust information based on a statistically valid sample. The crucial point to make here is that, when carrying out any new product/service investigation, it is imperative that the line of questioning used minimises any bias which could result in misleading responses. Any market-sensitive organisation will recognise that, if you ask your customer: 'Would you buy this new product at this price?', the answer you receive is liable to be unreliable. This is because:

- the very act of drawing attention to the new product (and its purported features) could cause the respondent to overstate or underplay his preferences; the customer may exaggerate his interest in the product because he feels that a positive response is expected, or he may do the opposite because he wishes to put pressure on you to keep the price of the product as low as possible
- even if not particularly price-sensitive, he may be inclined to overstate his objection to the price proposed because it is in his interest to discourage you from charging a price premium
- his answer may not be realistic because you have presented your product 'in a vacuum' – that is, without reference to the competitive products already available; he may, therefore, express interest in the product you have presented to him, even though he intends to continue to buy another product.

Wherever feasible, therefore, any new product/service investigation should be designed so as to minimise the likelihood of bias arising from leading questions. It is not the objective of this book to offer a detailed explanation of how this can be done; you will no doubt find many excellent articles and books on the subject. However, in order to give you a flavour of the type of approach which may be suitable, we will provide an outline of the scenario-based trade-off analysis which is commonly used to minimise respondent bias.

There are a number of variants of scenario-based trade-off approaches, but the common characteristics they share are two-fold:

- Customers and prospects are asked to rank or select a favoured option from a range of scenarios presented to them.

- The ranking or selection is based on the trade-off they would make between the various elements which make up the different scenarios – to give a simple (if not simplistic) example: 'Would you rather have a basic option at £100, an advanced option at £150, or a middle option at £120?'

The advantage of this approach is that, by including a number of options (not just the one in which you are particularly interested), it minimises any potential skew in responses which could arise if the questioning focused solely on the option under consideration. In the simple example cited, it is not possible for the respondent to know, from the question alone, whether your interest lies in the basic, the middle or the advanced option.

Figure 9.5 shows an example, adapted from the private medical insurance business, of how the scenarios can be shown to your customers and prospects. It should be noted that the set of options

	Insurer A	Insurer B	Insurer C	Insurer D	None
Acute Surgery, including all hospital charges	Yes	Yes	Yes	Yes	
Day patient and in-patient diagnostic testing	Yes	No	Yes	Yes	
Outpatient tests and consultations	Yes	Yes	No	Yes	
Specialist cover for cancer and heart problems	Yes	Yes	Yes	Yes	
Complementary therapy (e.g. (physiotherapy)	No	No	Yes	No	
Dental and optical cover	Yes	No	No	No	
Excess	£0	£100	£200	£250	
Premium	£240	£220	£190	£230	

Figure 9.5   An example of trade-off scenarios

shown in the chart is just one of a number which each individual customer/prospect interviewed would be shown. The diagram represents, therefore, a simplified version of what your target market would be shown.

In the hypothetical example shown, let us say that you are Insurer A and that you normally offer a product similar to that offered by Insurer D. However, you have reason to believe that there could be demand for a package which also includes dental and optical cover and involves no payment of an excess since your experience indicates that the payment of excesses is unpopular. You feel that your target market would be prepared to pay a somewhat higher premium for a product on these lines, as described in the 'Insurer A' column in Figure 9.5.

In order to test the likely demand for your new product, respondents to your survey will be asked to select their favoured option from the ones presented to them. If they don't like any of them, they have the option to select the 'None' column. The example illustrates a number of the advantages of this scenario-based approach:

- The individual being shown such scenarios cannot automatically know that the product of interest is the one described in the Insurer A column.
- A trade-off can be made in the context of alternative options – in this instance the trade-off being between the provision of dental/optical cover and the removal of any excess charge, on the one hand, and the increase in the monthly premium, on the other.
- The commercial viability of the new offering can be made by taking into account brand and price as well as product/service features. In this instance, the brand is the name of the insurer, the price is the premium charged and the product features are all about the inclusion or exclusion of the various elements which make up the overall package being offered.

The diagram shows, in effect, a 'shopping scenario' which is far more likely to generate accurate responses than the answers obtained if we had simply asked: 'Would you be prepared to pay £240 for additional dental and optical cover and the removal of excess?' – a question which could well invite a negative response.

As should be evident by now, the indirect line of questioning shown here should represent good practice for any market-sensitive organisation; if you are treating your customers and prospects in an 'emotionally intelligent' way, you will realise that potentially leading questions – particularly surrounding the subject of price – can result in highly misleading responses. This can result in disastrously expensive mistakes, especially when the decision being made is about a new product/service which typically involves a considerable investment of resources.

So what is the output of the type of scenario-building exercise just described? By collecting all the responses of the people contacted in the course of the survey, it is possible, through statistical modelling, to arrive at:

- the likely demand for the proposed product or service
- how the product or service should best be configured in terms of its features and price
- which are likely to be the most important drivers in determining the target market's selection of the proposed offering; these may be some of the features of the product/service, price or, quite possibly, brand
- how best to communicate the value of the new offer, based on an understanding of the key selection drivers.

The conclusions drawn from this sort of information have provided many companies with a powerful basis for making important decisions influencing their future business. Trade-off approaches can also help companies to communicate a point or prove a case which may otherwise be difficult to validate: for example, a division of DuPont, the multinational chemicals company, which provides ingredients for the paint industry, has successfully used such trade-off approaches to demonstrate the incremental value offered by its ingredients and its brands. This incremental value was measured not only in terms of consumers' perceptions of enhanced paint performance but also in terms of their willingness to pay more for the product. When the time came for DuPont and one of its long-standing business partners to renew their contract, this evidence provided confirmation to the business partner of the value of its association with DuPont. The result was a renewal of the contract which may have otherwise proved difficult for both parties to justify.

One final point – about test marketing, to which we briefly referred earlier. Test marketing is a small-scale product/service launch which is sometimes undertaken to assess the likely acceptance of the product/service when it is introduced into the wider marketplace. It is a common practice, particularly in consumer markets, to note reactions to the new product or service, within a particular test area, before the final decision is made to launch it in the wider marketplace. However, even if you decide to test market your new offer, it would be wise to undertake as much preparatory investigation as is appropriate before the test marketing is undertaken. By the completion of the test marketing stage, a considerable investment of resources is likely to have already been made, so it is advisable to maximise the chances of the test marketing being successful. For this reason, we would suggest that investigations of customer/prospect attitudes, of the type described in this section and possibly through the internet-based approaches mentioned in the last chapter (co-creation, etc.), should always be undertaken if you wish to maximise the return on your investment and minimise wasted resources.

Having said all this, it may also be the case that your idea, especially if it is radically new, may not initially meet with a positive reaction in the course of your preparatory investigation even though it has long-term potential. In that situation, it is conceivable that, at the test marketing stage, when the target market has had the chance to try out the product or service, it may be possible to measure the true potential of the new offering more accurately. Test marketing, in so far as it simulates a product launch, will also enable you to communicate and promote to the target test market what makes the new idea exciting in a way that the 'laboratory' environment of a research investigation cannot (and arguably should not) do. To summarise, a market research exercise (based on a trade-off approach of the type described and possibly initial internet-based market feedback) can provide a cost-effective means of assessing, as objectively as possible, whether the demand for the product/service being considered is likely to be large enough to make it commercially viable. Test marketing, conversely, shows, in a 'real life' situation, how the market is reacting, not only to the product/service on offer, but also to the marketing and communications activity which is likely to accompany its launch.

EVALUATING YOUR OWN EXPERIENCE

Before concluding, it is worth taking a step back and asking ourselves what our own experience has been in the launching of new products/services, assessing why we have been successful (or not), and comparing how we went about the process with the approaches described in this chapter. Here are some of the basic questions that we should be considering:

- When did we last introduce a new product/service?
- Was the reception positive or negative?
- Why was it positive/negative?

- Did the new offer cannibalise any of our existing offerings?
- Was the net impact on our business positive – and in what way: for example, incremental revenue and profits, enhanced reputation, increased presence in new market segments or geographies?
- How did we arrive at the new offering: for example, top-down instruction (because the chairman thought it was a good idea!), bottom-up feedback (say, from market-facing staff), internal brainstorming, external market investigation?
- What lessons did we learn from the experience, and how, if at all, would we do things differently now?

THE EXECUTIVE SELF-ASSESSMENT CHECKLIST: NEW PRODUCTS/SERVICES

Question	Yes, confident +3	Yes, tentative 0	No −3	NA
Do we proactively seek new product/service opportunities?				
Do we encourage creativity at all levels of our organisation in an active and systematic way (e.g., through an 'ideas box')?				
Do we have a clear idea as to what we expect to gain from our new product/service launches?				
Do we have a clear plan of action to maximise the chances of our product/service launch being successful?				

Question	Yes, confident +3	Yes, tentative 0	No −3	NA
Do we take into account general 'macro' trends when we are considering a particular new product or service?				
Do we track 'macro' trends as a means of spotting new product/ service opportunities that we may not have otherwise considered?				
Do we seek to ensure that all the product/service ideas proposed are rigorously examined and tested through a systematic approach involving both internal and external enquiries and discussions?				
Do we ensure that any new product/service initiative builds on our own experience and knowledge?				
Do we have a systematic way of ensuring that, when considering new product/service initiatives, we have learnt from previous successes and failures?				
Are we confident that we have the ability to implement the new product/service development?				
Do we have a reasonably accurate idea of the scale of investment required for the development and commercialisation of the new product/service?				

Question	Yes, confident +3	Yes, tentative 0	No −3	NA
Do we undertake an idea generation and brainstorming process involving our relevant staff?				
Do we have sufficient budget, authorised by top management, to ensure that the idea and product/ service development process can be carried out properly and does not falter?				
Do we have top management championship to ensure that the impetus for the idea and product/ service development process is maintained throughout?				
Are we confident that the new product/service proposed fills a gap in the market by fulfilling a market need or capitalising on a market opportunity?				
Are we confident that the new product/service would offer us a clear competitive advantage?				
Do we check that the competition is not proposing or planning on something similar to our idea?				
Do we anticipate competitor reactions to our product/service launch and take pre-emptive action accordingly?				

Question	Yes, confident +3	Yes, tentative 0	No −3	NA
Do we take into account all the constraints which could limit what we can achieve when we seek to launch a new product/service?				
Do we always find out the attitudes of prospective purchasers to the new product/service before launching it?				
When assessing prospective purchasers' attitudes, do we recognise the need to take into account the impact of the new product/service features, price *and* brand?				
When assessing prospective purchasers' attitudes to our proposed offering, is this done in a competitive context − i.e. by seeing how our offer is seen to compare with existing offers (our own as well as our competitors')?				
Do we know which market segments offer the greatest opportunity for the new product/service (by seeking to identify, and quantify, those that are the most favourably disposed to it)?				
When finding out about prospective purchasers' attitudes towards our new proposition, do we employ an unbiased third party, rather than seeking to undertake the investigation ourselves?				

Question	Yes, confident +3	Yes, tentative 0	No −3	NA

When finding out about prospective purchasers' attitudes towards our new proposition, do we adopt, wherever possible, an indirect line of questioning to minimise biased responses?

Are we confident about the answers we get from our prospective purchasers?

Is our investigation of prospective purchaser attitudes systematic, if necessary starting with concept testing, followed by more detailed product/service testing and (where appropriate) test marketing?

Do we take into account the attitudes of other stakeholders?

Do we undertake a systematic cost–benefit analysis based on the investment required and the returns expected based on likely market reactions?

Are we confident about the way we price our new products/ services by taking into account not only our internal cost structures but also our target market's willingness to pay?

(Particularly if we have to charge a premium) are we confident that a sufficient number of our target purchasers will be willing to pay the premium?

Question	Yes, confident +3	Yes, tentative 0	No −3	NA
Do we know how we should communicate the new product/ service to our target audience – both customers/prospects and other stakeholders – before we undertake the launch?				
Are we confident that we can estimate the likely demand for our new product/service once we have investigated its potential?				
Are we confident about the net impact of our proposed product/ service on our business (taking into account possible cannibalisation, the investment required, etc.)?				
Are we confident about how the product/service should best be configured?				
Are we confident about the key drivers influencing demand for the proposed offering?				
Are we confident about how we can communicate a winning proposition to our target audience?				
GRAND TOTAL SCORE				
NET ABSOLUTE SCORE				
NET AVERAGE SCORE				

Now, taking each of the above questions, what in practice are we doing?

CHAPTER 10

AN ONGOING PROCESS – MONITORING YOUR PERFORMANCE

WHY MONITOR YOUR PERFORMANCE

We started this book by drawing an analogy between an organisation's financial statements and its stakeholder balance sheet. Just as you review your financial statements to assess the current health of your organisation, so you will, if you are a market-sensitive organisation, look at your stakeholder balance sheet. The stakeholder balance sheet is similar to the financial statement in providing you with a snapshot of how you are performing at a given point in time. However, the stakeholder balance sheet differs from the financial statement in the following ways:

• *Being far more focused on diagnostics, it is more relevant as a predictor of future performance*: The financial statement is strong in providing robust numbers reflecting the state of your organisation, and from the numbers it is possible to draw conclusions about where the financial strengths and weaknesses of your organisation lie; the stakeholder balance sheet, conversely, provides numbers which may be estimates (sometimes guesstimates) or may reflect market opinions. If you wish to know the size of a specific market segment, for example, it is quite probable that you will not have an exact number (as you would if you were looking at figures on sales, current assets or cash flow); similarly, if you find that you are given a customer satisfaction rating of, say, 8 out of 10, there is almost certainly a margin of error around such a number.

Having said this, the stakeholder balance sheet provides a wealth of information about *why* your performance is (seen to be) strong or weak, and from this it is possible to draw more direct conclusions about the course of action you need to take. Whereas the financial statement provides a strong account of your historic performance, the stakeholder balance sheet also addresses far more clearly what needs to be done in the future. For example, if your income statement shows a sales decline, you will need to look elsewhere to understand why sales have declined, and the reasons may not be obvious: the decline may result from a combination of tougher market conditions, poorer service performance on your part, the introduction of a new product by a competitor, or a host of other possible reasons; the weight to be attached to each of these factors is not always easy to estimate because there is no answer within the financial figures themselves. Conversely, if the stakeholder balance sheet shows that your customer satisfaction rating has declined from, say, 8 to 7.5, you should have a reasonable idea from the same set of results as to which were the critical drivers on which your performance fell and, therefore, what action you need to take to improve performance in the future.

It is the diagnostic power of the stakeholder balance sheet which, therefore, makes it particularly amenable to ongoing monitoring activity.

- *Your stakeholder balance sheet affects your financial performance*: While your market performance is ultimately liable to influence your financial performance, the reverse is not true: improved customer satisfaction, for example, should as a general rule result in increased customer purchases and improved financial performance, all else being equal; improved financial performance does not, however, result in improved customer satisfaction. This may seem like a platitude, but the point is relevant when we are talking about why it is important to monitor your performance in the marketplace: because it is your market performance which has a major impact in driving your financial performance, it would seem logical that you should be paying at least as much attention to monitoring the former as to the latter. Yet whereas every organisation will, as a matter of course, review its financial statements periodically, the same importance is not normally attached to the monitoring of market performance.

  Clearly, performance in your marketplace is by no means the only determinant of financial performance – how you control your costs would have an obvious impact on your bottom line. It is interesting, though, that the tracking of market performance is, again, not as common a practice as the tracking of costs. The truth is that market watchfulness is simply not in the DNA of some organisations; it is apparently quite acceptable for some organisations to state, 'we did a customer satisfaction survey three years ago and we are now thinking of doing one again', yet those same organisations would no doubt be horrified at the suggestion that they examine their financial statements every three years!

All organisations need to recognise that, if they have a reasonably high profile in their chosen marketplace, they are under the ongoing scrutiny of their customers (and, quite possibly, also other stakeholders) – and if they are under no such scrutiny, they would have a serious reason to worry because that would mean that they are fading away from the customer radar screen. As we have seen in this book, your customers' opinions about you are shaped all the time by a multitude of stimuli – your performance, your brand, what other stakeholders and influencers say about you, the way your staff behave, how you compare with competitors in providing proactive offers, how you communicate (or don't), and so on. If your market is watching you then it follows that you should, equally, be keeping tabs on it on an ongoing basis. But are you doing so? Does your stakeholder balance sheet show a consistent improvement in performance in the areas that matter, and what should be done if there are any shortfalls?

WHAT TO MONITOR

Your position in the marketplace

If you are a truly market-sensitive organisation you will most certainly have market watchfulness in your DNA. In practice this means not only the tracking of your own performance, as viewed by your customers, but also watching all the market and competitor trends against which your own performance should be assessed. So market watchfulness includes:

- *General 'macro' trends*: Examples of these have already been discussed in the last chapter on product/service development (the potential backlash against planned obsolescence, the changing age profile, etc.); these general trends are, however, relevant to you not only in the context of new product/service development but also more generally when you wish to assess the opportunities and threats that you are likely to face in your own business: if, for example, your behaviour flies in the face of a general trend away from the 'throw-away' society, your standing in the marketplace is likely to suffer in the long run.

- *The monitoring of market trends* which are specific to your own business: market growth/decline; price trends; emergence of new players; legislative, regulatory and technical trends; etc.
- *Ongoing competitor intelligence*, tracking the activities and plans of key competitors.
- *Staff training* to ensure employees have market-sensitive antennae.
- *Keeping a dialogue going with customers, prospects and other stakeholders*, and periodically interrogating them about:
  - what is important to them (which can change over time)
  - how well your organisation is regarded (which is certainly most likely to change over time) – vis-à-vis the competition
  - how they respond to any branding/communications and product/service initiatives coming from your organisation.
- *Looking at the effects of all this* on the way customers relate to your organisation (in terms of their loyalty and their purchase behaviour) and, ultimately, on your organisation's business performance.

Your marketing/sales effectiveness

Here the focus is on monitoring the impact of the marketing/sales activity you are engaged in when dealing with customers or other stakeholders. Examples include the activity of your sales staff, advertising, direct marketing, PR, promotions, the establishment of new distribution channels or outlets, participation in exhibitions or conferences/seminars, articles/editorials, sponsorships, and charitable/fund-raising activities.

HOW TO MONITOR

Your position in the marketplace

Figure 10.1 provides an example of how you can monitor your position in the marketplace with a view to achieving improvements in your business performance. In this example, we have looked specifically at customer satisfaction as the core issue being examined, but the logic of the diagram applies equally, albeit with some variations, to other subjects such as staff perceptions, attitudes of other stakeholders, branding and communication.

As the chart shows, in order to maximise the impact of the monitoring process, three elements are necessary:

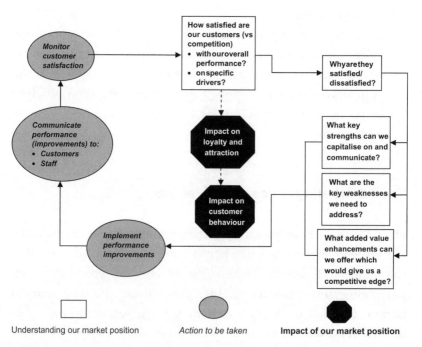

Figure 10.1 Monitoring performance among customers

- *An understanding of your position in the marketplace*: This is represented by all the rectangular boxes which describe the information you need to obtain and the analysis of that information for you to comprehend:
  - how you are regarded
  - why you are regarded in this way, and
  - what the information is telling you about the course of action you need to take.
- *The action you need to take*: The information collection/analysis stage must be followed by a plan of action if the knowledge you have gained is to be of any value; the action elements are described in the oval boxes and are concerned with:
  - performance improvements
  - the communication of your performance (where you are already strong or where you have made improvements), and
  - the monitoring of customer satisfaction, repeating the information collection and analysis already described.
- *The ultimate impact of your action*: This is represented by the octagons which show how improved satisfaction can have an impact on:
  - loyalty and attraction
  - customer behaviour (for example, increased purchase frequency or greater share of spend).

In order to provide themselves with a handy tool to review how well they have been performing, some companies have developed market 'dashboards' summarising the key information relating to their position in the marketplace. Rather like a summary overview of a company's financial data, the dashboard can include a snapshot of current performance as well as trend data. Figure 10.2 shows an example of a dashboard, adapted from one used by a major multinational in the petrochemicals industry.

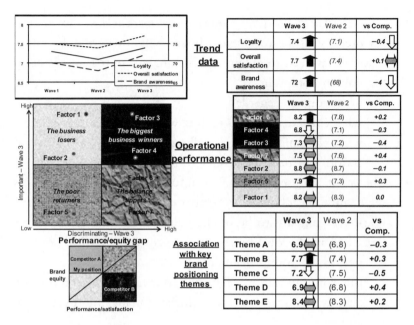

Figure 10.2 A market dashboard

In the illustration shown, the company has improved its overall performance in the most recent period (on the top line measures of loyalty, overall satisfaction and brand awareness), after having suffered a dip in performance in the previous period. However, it still remains behind or on a par with the competition. On specific operational factors, the performance in the most recent wave has been mixed, with improvements in Factors 5 and 6 and a decline in Factor 4, compared with the previous period. However, the fact that Factor 5 is a 'poor returner' means that the improvement on that factor is unlikely to yield great benefits and the company would be better off focusing more resources on Factor 4 which is one of the biggest business winners. Similarly, although performance on Factor 3 has remained consistent from Wave 2 to Wave 3, it lags behind that of the competition, a potentially serious matter given that it is the biggest business winner. On the brand positioning themes (the image factors the company would like to be associated with) the company has to pay particular attention to Theme C, where it has not only experienced a decline since the last wave but it has also fallen significantly behind the competition. And on the Performance/equity gap, the company's performance currently lags behind its own brand equity as well as behind the performance of Competitors A and B.

Your marketing/sales effectiveness

Since we are seeking to monitor the impact of our marketing/sales activity, the focus here should be on the success with which such activity has converted our current position to a better, new position.

Tracing success rate through the various steps of the marketing/sales process

We may wish to trace the success rate of converting to an improved position, going through the key steps through which the conversion takes place. If, for example, you are a professional services business (a management consultancy, a legal practice, a firm of chartered surveyors, etc.), you may wish to consider the following steps:

- How much the *activity* (say, a seminar or a direct marketing campaign) has generated *interest* in your service (measured perhaps in terms of requests for information about your business).
- To what extent that general interest has resulted in *concrete enquiries* (for example, in the form of discussions about a particular problem or opportunity which the prospective client faces).

- The extent to which those enquiries have resulted in *requests for proposal*.
- The success with which the proposals have resulted in *jobs*.

In Chapter 3, the point was made that it is not easy to draw a direct conclusion about the impact on your business of improvement activities you may embark on, and that an indirect, step-by-step approach is likely to be more realistic. The same is true when you wish to assess the impact of marketing/sales activity: the tracing process described above shows precisely how the activity has ultimately led to additional business, and the step-by-step approach also reveals whether there are any particular pinch points which you need to consider. For example, if your conversion rate from the general discussion stage to the proposal stage is relatively low, you may wish to examine exactly why those discussions are not as successful as they might be; conversely, if your greatest problem lies at the very earliest stage you may wonder whether the activity you have selected is the right one to go for or whether you could improve the way you are conducting that activity.

The steps shown above are just examples and their relevance may vary from one case to the next case: a marketing campaign may, for instance, lead directly to an enquiry or even a proposal, with the intermediate steps being skipped.

A critically important consideration that we have not so far mentioned is the quality/size of the enquiry. Whereas the rate of conversion is clearly important, this on its own does not provide us with the ultimate answer we need – the overall amount of incremental business gained as a result of the activity undertaken. So, from the proposal submission stage onwards we should have a dual set of figures: the rate of conversion in terms of the *number* of proposals and jobs won as well as the rate in terms of the *value* of proposals and jobs won. If we have a high rate of conversion, but that stems mostly from winning small jobs, that may not be as desirable as a lower rate of conversion related to higher value jobs (and therefore more revenue).

Monitoring how the success rate itself has changed from one period to the next

The step-by-step approach described above will tell us, for example, that 10% of those attending our seminar followed it up with an enquiry, 50% of those enquiring requested a proposal and 30% of the proposals submitted resulted in a job – resulting in a 'net' success rate of 1.5% (from seminar attendance to jobs). We may feel, however, that it is possible to increase the 1.5% rate and we decide therefore to examine exactly where improvements may be made (by talking to those who attended the seminar, establishing what can be done about the pinch points, etc.). After having made the improvements, we will probably wish to see whether those improvements have resulted in an increased success rate. So from one period to the next we can see whether and to what extent our last period's rate (in this example, 1.5%) has improved – and which steps have shown the greatest improvements in conversion: was our greatest improvement in the initial 10%, the subsequent 50% or the final 30%?

A final caveat

The tracing and monitoring activity described works best when the activity is relatively focused and easy to isolate. We can see, for example, exactly who attended a seminar and we can link that attendance to any subsequent steps which may have resulted (from interest/enquiries to sales). It is more difficult to measure the precise impact of, say, a general advertising campaign if the individuals viewing the advertising were simultaneously exposed to extraneous stimuli beyond the control of the advertiser (news coverage, for example) or they had at the same time an unhappy experience with their current suppliers, which caused them to look around for new suppliers. We have already mentioned the case of the international bank whose advertising messages were undermined by the unfavourable press reporting of its alleged association with an unsavoury regime.

Having said this, the challenges faced when seeking to measure the impact of the more general marketing activities should not deter us from making the best efforts we can to undertake such measurement. They do mean, however, that we should be very careful when interpreting the results and that we should always be mindful of all the external factors that can influence the outcome.

ACTING ON THE RESULTS

Having monitored our performance and drawn conclusions on what needs to be done, we still need to ensure that we act on the conclusions so that the improvements we wish to make are achieved. There are too many instances of companies that make substantial investments in finding out how they are seen in the marketplace but which fail to follow up these initiatives with appropriate and consistent action. Those who have been successful in carrying out the necessary follow-up will have typically set up a systematic process, starting with workshops to brainstorm what needs to be done, followed by a series of milestones to ensure that the momentum on the actions to be taken is not allowed to falter. Figure 10.3 offers one example of the steps to be taken in the course of this process.

The points made in Figure 10.3 are mostly self-explanatory. A few words of explanation, however:

- When we discuss the reasons for *favourable/unfavourable perceptions* of our performance, we need to be careful to consider whether these perceptions stem from real problems or poor communication on our part; as mentioned before, if we have problems in our product or service delivery we need to see how we can improve our performance, but if our market

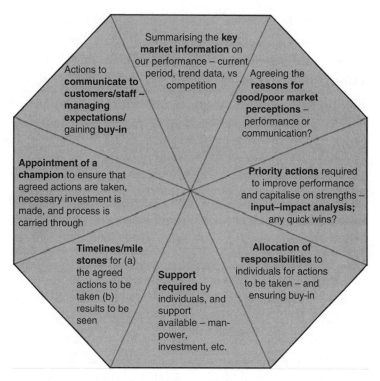

Figure 10.3 Acting on the results

views us unfavourably even though our actual performance is good, then the solution lies in improved communication to correct the market's misperceptions.

- When we consider the *priority actions* we need to take, we should undertake an input–impact analysis taking into account the costs, effort and time required for the actions as well as the benefits expected.

- Clear *allocation of responsibilities* for the actions to be taken ensures not only that there is no misunderstanding about where responsibilities lie and that nothing important slips between the cracks, but also that all the people involved are engaged and have bought into the process.

- One of the key obstacles in the way of implementation of an improvement programme is the belief of those allocated responsibility that they are not getting enough *support* from top management – be it moral, practical or budgetary; this issue needs to be addressed at the earliest stage if the process isn't to lose momentum.
- Similarly, clear *timelines* and *milestones* need to be agreed from the start, to ensure that all those involved have targets to work towards and that the process does not falter.
- In order to ensure that the required support is provided, the planned actions are carried out, and that milestones/timelines are taken seriously, a *champion* should be appointed to oversee the whole process – and this should be someone with the seniority and clout to keep the momentum going.
- Finally, decisions need to be made about what and when to *communicate* the actions agreed to staff and to customers/other stakeholders: in order that the actions are carried forward through all parts of the organisation affected by them, the appropriate staff should be told what is proposed and why it is proposed, so that they buy in to the process; at the same time, customers and other relevant stakeholders may need to be informed about the proposed actions at the appropriate time, care being taken to manage their expectations by ensuring that they are only promised results that are definitely achievable within a realistic time frame.

Figure 10.3 shows an example of what you may typically achieve through internal brainstorming workshops. However, another useful outcome of the monitoring process can be external discussions with key stakeholders: for example, some major companies operating in business-to-business markets make it part of their learning and action planning process to undertake follow-up sessions with their most important customers to review the results of the monitoring activity and to discuss in depth the issues which those customers may have with them. If, for example, you have conducted a market survey, this process helps you to fully understand precisely what customers may have meant when they made unfavourable comments about your performance on certain aspects and enables you, *with the customers' input*, to agree the most appropriate and effective courses of action to be taken.

IDENTIFYING AND ACTING ON THE BLOCKAGES

The process described so far will also help you to diagnose blockages which may be hindering progress: if you find, for example, that your customer satisfaction performance does not improve materially over time, is that because you have failed to carry out improvements sufficiently within the areas of key importance to customers – in which case you need to re-examine how you went about implementing the improvements; was it because you made clear improvements but they were not registering in the minds of customers, in which case your communication has not been sufficiently effective; or was it because you raised the expectations of customers who, being disappointed, could not feel satisfied – again, a communication issue, this time related to the management of customer expectations?

Blockages may also lie between the satisfaction results and the business performance results (in Figure 10.1, customer loyalty/ attraction and customer behaviour): if you find that even though your customers are more satisfied, this improvement in satisfaction does not result in improvements in business performance measures, you need to examine why this might be the case; as we have said before, there is clearly no point in improving customer satisfaction if this does not ultimately lead to business improvements. We have already seen (in the discussion surrounding Figure 4.9) how it is possible that there can be certain key trigger points at which

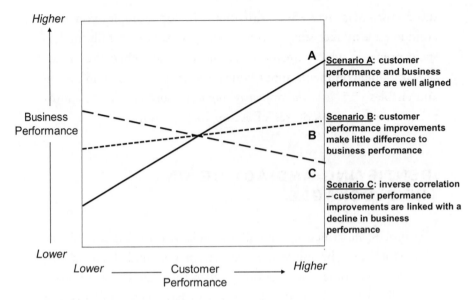

Figure 10.4   Monitoring performance

customer satisfaction performance improvements can have a particularly strong impact on customer loyalty, but outside those points, loyalty can appear static.

The disconnect between customer satisfaction and business performance can, however, also occur if your performance metrics are not appropriate. This point is illustrated in Figure 10.4.

Figure 10.4 shows three hypothetical scenarios. These are highly simplified (for example, in the real world the relationships are likely to be far less clean than those represented by the straight lines shown in the chart) and they are shown purely to illustrate strongly contrasting trends:

- Scenario A describes the desirable situation in which customer performance (that is, your performance as perceived by your customers) and business performance are closely aligned: as your customer performance improves, so does your business performance. So, for example, if the customer performance measure is customer satisfaction and the business performance metric is share of spend, we see that increasing customer satisfaction results in increasing share of wallet. Even though, as already mentioned, it is highly unlikely in reality that there will be a smooth straight line as shown in the illustration, as long as the trend is upwards we know that improvements in our customer performance seem to be having the desired effect on our business.

- In Scenario B, customer performance improvements make little difference to business performance; this may happen, of course, because the improvements you have made are irrelevant or relatively unimportant to customers, in which case you need seriously to consider reallocating your resources. But it may also happen because the performance measures are inappropriate: companies have, in the past, complained that the feedback they get from their customers does not seem to have any connection with their business; even when they have continued to invest in improvements which have increased customer satisfaction the profitability of their business has not improved in line with those customer performance improvements. This could be the case because profitability, as a measure of business performance, may not always be the appropriate metric to use against a customer performance measure, since profitability is a function of cost as well as sales revenue. If, therefore, you have more satisfied customers but your costs have increased, the net effect could well be that your profits do not increase materially. In a situation like this, it is clearly important to select a business performance measure which is more closely aligned to customer performance and less likely to be influenced by extraneous factors (in this case, cost). Even sales revenue may not always be the most appropriate business metric since sales can be affected by general market conditions (as well as customer satisfaction) – for example, if there is a downturn in the market which has resulted in the overall market size shrinking, which in turn has a knock-on effect on your sales. In this situation, we would do better to select a business metric like share of spend, because your share of spend can go up even if there is a market downturn.

The reference to share of spend does raise the need to examine not only the business performance metric but also the customer performance metric: it is possible that your customer satisfaction rating goes up but your share of spend goes down; this can happen when customers are even more satisfied with your competitors, in which case, even though your absolute levels of satisfaction have improved your *relative* customer performance has declined. This means that the X axis in Figure 10.4 should be a measure of *relative* customer performance; this can be easily done by, for instance, dividing your customer satisfaction score by the competition's score.

- Scenario C shows an inverse correlation between customer performance and business performance; here, customer performance improvements are apparently linked with a *decline* in business performance. This is an extreme version of the situation in Scenario B and, as such, is unlikely to occur often. An example of where this can occur is where you are operating in a business-to-business market dominated by a relatively small number of customers who each account for a significant share of your business. In your anxiety to offer the best possible service to such customers you lose track of the fact that the incremental cost to serve these large accounts may be outweighing the benefit of a good relationship with those accounts. The customers are delighted that you are bending over backwards to please them, but you are not making any money out of them. It is possible that even if they are giving you more of their business this incremental business is not compensating sufficiently for the incremental cost.

In the context of Scenario B we stated that profitability is not always a good business performance measure because costs can go up, often for reasons which are not connected with the customer. If, for example, your raw material costs go up and you cannot fully pass those costs on to your customers, your profitability may go down even though your customer performance has improved. In this situation, we would suggest reassessing profitability as the business measure to be used. However, if the costs which go up are directly related to your performance with customers then they should most certainly be part of the equation. The example cited about large accounts being overcostly to serve is a case in point: here it is quite relevant to look at the profitability of those customers because it will oblige you to consider whether you are overserving those customers and whether you could reduce some of the cost to serve without material impact on the volume of your business with those customers.

The discussion surrounding the different scenarios in Figure 10.4 points to the importance of ensuring that the metrics one uses are appropriate as measures of genuine performance improvements. It is tempting to conclude that, because there is no 'obvious' connection between your customer performance and your business performance, the focus on the customer can be diluted. This is perhaps one reason why so many organisations do not have the motivation to undertake regular customer surveys; such surveys are seen as 'nice to haves' which may be indulged in every few years, rather than essential barometers measuring their market performance. Because the results of these surveys appear to have little bearing on their business performance, organisations may conclude that they are ineffective. Whereas this may be true when surveys are poorly designed and executed, it may be equally true that the fault lies in the way the business metrics have been defined.

As we have sought to show throughout this book, a customer focus *does* pay enormous dividends, but – as we have equally sought to demonstrate – only if the way in which we assess our customers is rigorous and insightful. An accurate assessment, often delving beneath the surface response, empowers you with a genuine understanding of what makes the customer tick. An inaccurate assessment, based on superficial conclusions, can lead to mistaken assumptions and costly mistakes. This point applies equally to the discussion in connection with Figure 10.4: if we see insufficient connection between our efforts with customers and the rewards we would expect from such efforts, this could well mean that we are making the wrong connections or that our efforts have been misdirected. It does not mean that our customer sensitivity should in any way be diminished.

THE EXECUTIVE SELF-ASSESSMENT CHECKLIST: MONITORING YOUR PERFORMANCE

Question	Yes, confident +3	Yes, tentative 0	No −3	NA
Is market watchfulness part of our corporate DNA?				
Do we monitor our market performance as rigorously as we monitor our financial performance?				
Do we monitor and respond to general 'macro' trends which could affect our standing in the market?				
Do we monitor and respond to trends within our market?				
Do we monitor competitor activity?				
Do we ensure that our staff are alert to changes in the marketplace?				
Do we monitor how we are regarded by customers?				
Do we monitor how we are regarded by prospects?				

Question	Yes, confident +3	Yes, tentative 0	No −3	NA

Do we monitor how we are regarded by other stakeholders?

Does our monitoring activity include how we are regarded vis-à-vis our competitors?

Does our monitoring activity go beyond number crunching to include diagnostics as to *why* the changes we have spotted are taking place?

Does our monitoring activity show that our market performance is improving?

If not, do we know why not?

Do we assess and monitor the effectiveness of our marketing/sales activity?

Do we trace our success rate through the various steps of the marketing/sales process?

Is this success rate measured in terms of size/value of the desired outcome as well as number/frequency?

Do we monitor how our success rate has changed from one period to the next?

Do we use market dashboards to provide us with a quick overview of our performance?

Do we ensure that we act upon the results of this monitoring activity?

Do we have a systematic process in place to ensure that we act on our conclusions?

Question	Yes, confident +3	Yes, tentative 0	No −3	NA
Do we allocate clear responsibilities for the actions to be pursued?				
Do we set clear timelines and milestones?				
Is there a senior-level champion to ensure that the action plans are carried out?				
Does our action include effective communication with the market as well as product/service improvements?				
Are we careful to consider how we communicate to our staff – to ensure buy-in?				
Are we careful to consider how we communicate with customers and other stakeholders – to manage expectations?				
Do we actively engage our customers/other stakeholders in improvement programmes resulting from the monitoring process?				
If we find that our actions are not improving results, do we seek to identify and diagnose the blockages which are preventing the desired improvements?				
Do we use the right metrics when we are seeking to understand the impact of our actions over time?				
GRAND TOTAL SCORE				
NET ABSOLUTE SCORE				
NET AVERAGE SCORE				

Now, taking each of the above questions, what in practice are we doing?

CHAPTER 11

CONCLUSION: THE 9 POINT PLAN REVISITED

YOUR STAKEHOLDER BALANCE SHEET AT A GLANCE

Having gone through the nine areas for assessing your organisation's performance as a stakeholder-sensitive enterprise, you are now in a position to measure, through the self-assessment checklist, precisely how well it has done. In so far as you have responsibility, direct or indirect, in these areas, you are also able to evaluate your own performance as a manager. Your performance can be measured within the individual areas as well as on an aggregated basis across all the areas.

You can also measure the gap between your performance scores and the theoretical maximum (+3) which you could achieve if you gave yourself the top score (+3) on each of the questions in each checklist. In reality, of course, the gap will always be a negative one, and it is the extent of the gap which reveals how well or poorly you have performed.

What we are measuring	Net average scores	Net average score assessment	Theoretical maximum score	The gap against the maximum
Segmentation	−0.36	Watch it!	+3	(3.36)
Understanding the real stakeholder drivers	+1.23	Good	+3	(1.77)
From customer satisfaction/branding to loyalty/attraction	+0.45	So-so	+3	(2.55)
Decision-making dynamics	+0.78	So-so	+3	(2.22)
Staff motivation and perceptions	+0.95	So-so/Good	+3	(2.05)
Other external stakeholders and influencers	−0.88	Watch it!/Poor	+3	(3.88)
Communication	+0.15	So-so/Watch it!	+3	(2.85)
New product/service propositions	−1.36	Poor	+3	(4.36)
Monitoring performance	+0.37	So-so	+3	(2.63)
TOTAL OF NET AREA SCORES	+1.33		+27	(25.67)
AGGREGATE NET AVERAGE (TOTAL SCORE ÷ 9)	**+0.15**	**So-so/ Watch it!**	**+3**	**(2.85)**

Figure 11.1 The stakeholder balance sheet: our area and aggregate scores

Figure 11.1 shows a hypothetical example of what your performance could look like after you have completed scoring yourself on the self-assessment checklist, at the individual area level and in aggregate.

At the end of Chapter 2, we suggested the following way of assessing performance based on the scores achieved:

+3   +2   +1   0   −1   −2   −3

Excellent	Good	So-so	Watch it!	Poor	On the brink

Figure 11.1 applies this assessment system to the net average scores achieved. In our hypothetical example, you have a slightly positive aggregate net score (+0.15), which we see as near the borderline of 'So-so' and 'Watch it!'. This leaves you 2.85 points behind the theoretical maximum of +3. However, this hides a fair degree of variation in performance by area – from the most positive net score of +1.23 on 'Understanding the real stakeholder drivers' (Good) to the most negative net score of −1.36 on 'New product/service performance' (Poor).

With this information, you can decide what aggregate net score you should aim for next year and how you can achieve that score. If, for example, you wished to increase your current aggregate net score of +0.15 to +0.50 (still in the 'So-so' area but comfortably distant from 'Watch it!'), that would require the total of the net area scores to go up from +1.33 to 4.50 – an increase of 3.17 across the nine areas, or an average of 0.35 for each area. In practice, of course, you would not aim for an increase of 0.35 in each area but you would instead focus on those areas where improvements are likely to offer you the greatest benefits, including of course the areas of greatest concern (in this example, 'New product/service development' and 'Other external stakeholders/influencers'). You would also need to look at the individual questions within the self-assessment checklist in each of the areas to decide what specifically you need to work on to improve your scores. In doing so, you would do an input–impact analysis and look out for the actions most likely to yield improved results, including quick wins.

When we talk about what 'you' may need to do, we are referring not only to you individually but also to all the other people in your organisation who can contribute, directly or indirectly, to making your organisation a truly market-sensitive enterprise. This means that it is critically important for you to collaborate with all your key colleagues to ensure that the actions you propose to take are properly communicated and explained to relevant staff throughout the organisation so that they take them fully on board.

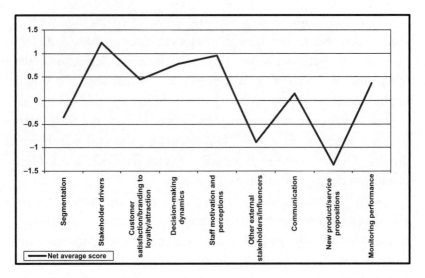

Figure 11.2   Net average scores by area

Figure 11.2, which illustrates the net average scores in graphical format, clearly shows that the areas of best performance are 'Stakeholder drivers' and 'Staff motivation and perceptions' and those representing the worst performance are 'New product/service propositions' and 'Other external stakeholders/influencers'.

AND FINALLY...A REMINDER ABOUT THE KEY ACTION AREAS

Finally, a reminder of the actions you may need to take on the 9 point plan: Figure 11.3 provides a schematic showing the 9 point plan, but this time with some examples of key action areas linked to each of the nine points. The purpose here is clearly not to replicate the comprehensive checklists shown at the end of each chapter, but rather to provide an aide mémoire of the topics covered within the chapters. Perhaps it could be used as a wall chart to remind you about what you need to keep tabs on if you wish to strengthen your organisation's stakeholder balance sheet!

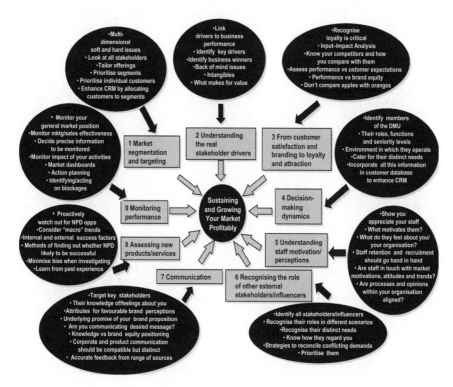

Figure 11.3 The 9 point plan – examples of key action areas

BIBLIOGRAPHY

Aaker, D.A. (1996) *Building Strong Brands*. New York: Free Press

Anderson, C. (2006) *The Long Tail: Why the Future of Business is Selling Less of More*. New York: Hyperion

Arkin, A. and Allen, R. (2002) Satisfaction guaranteed. *People Management*, Vol. 8, No. 21, 40–42

Ashby, F. and Pell, A. (2001) *Embracing Excellence*. Harlow, Essex: Prentice Hall

Ashkanasy, N.M. and Dasborough, M.T. (2003) Emotional awareness and emotional intelligence in leadership training. *Journal of Education for Business*, Vol. 79, No.1, 18–22

Ayuso, S., Rodríguez, M.Á. and Ricart, J.E. (2006) Using stakeholder dialogue as a source for new ideas: a dynamic capability underlying sustainable innovation. *Corporate Governance*, Vol. 6, Issue 4, 475–490

Bacon, F.R. with Butler, T.W. (1998) *Achieving Planned Innovation: A Proven System for Creating Successful New Products and Services*. New York: Free Press

Bardzil, P. and Slaski, M. (2003) Emotional intelligence: fundamental competencies for enhanced service provision. *Managing Service Quality*, Vol. 13, No. 2, 97–104

Briggs, R. and Stuart, G. (2006) *What Sticks: Why Most Advertising Fails and How to Guarantee Yours Succeeds*. Chicago: Dearborn Trade Publishing

Buttle, F. (2004) *Customer Relationship Management*. Oxford: Elsevier, Butterworth-Heinemann

Cann, C.W. (1998) Eight steps to building a business to business relationship. *Journal of Business and Industrial Marketing*, Vol. 13, Nos 4/5, 393–405

Carroll, A.B. and Buchholtz, A.K. (2008) *Business and Society: Ethics and Stakeholder Management*. Cincinnati: South-Western Pub

Cavallo, K. and Brienza, D. (2002) *Emotional Competence and Leadership Excellence at Johnson & Johnson*. New Brunswick, NJ: Consortium for Research on Emotional Intelligence in Organizations, Rutgers University

Chan Kim, W. and Mauborgne, R. (1997): Value innovation: the strategic logic of high growth. *Harvard Business Review*, January–February

Chun, R. (2003) *The Links between Employee Satisfaction and Customer Satisfaction*. Manchester, Manchester Business School

Clark, R. (2004) Flexibility adds to the bottom line. *People Management*, Vol. 10, No. 12, 49

Clarkson, M.B.E. (1995) A stakeholder framework for analyzing and evaluating corporate social performance. *Academy of Management Review*, Vol. 20, 92–117

Craven, R. (2002) *Customer is King: How to Exceed Their Expectations*. London: Virgin Books Ltd

Davies, G., Chun, R., da Silva, R. and Roper, S. (2003) *Corporate Reputation and Competitiveness*. London: Routledge

Denhardt, R.B. (1993) *The Pursuit of Significance: Strategies for Managerial Success in Public Organizations*. Belmont, CA: Wadsworth Publishing

Edmonds, J. (2003) How to turn technical innovation into commercial success. *Technical Textiles International*, July–August

Fortune Magazine The 100 best companies to work for 2008. New York

Freemantle, D. (2004) *The BIZ: Little Things that Make a Big Difference to Team Motivation and Leadership*. London: Nicholas Brearley

Freeston, R. (2004) *Questionnaire for the Development of a Common Customer Metrics Framework*. CMLG Customer Metrics Survey

Frei, R.L. and McDaniel, M.A. (1997) Validity of customer service measures in personnel selection: a review of criterion and construct evidence. *Human Performance*, Vol. 11, 1–27

Gale, B.T. (1994) *Managing Customer Value*. New York: The Free Press

Gerstner, L. (2002) *Who Says Elephants Can't Dance?* London: HarperCollins

Goleman, D. (1996) *Emotional Intelligence*. London: Bloomsbury

Grey, R. (2003) Brand benefits of loyalty initiatives. *Marketing UK*

Hansemark, O.C. and Albinsson, M. (2004) Customer satisfaction and retention: the experiences of individual employees. *Managing Service Quality*, Vol. 14, No. 1, 40–57

Harrison, J.S. and Freeman, R.E. (1999) Stakeholders, social responsibility, and performance: empirical evidence and theoretical perspectives. *The Academy of Management Journal*, Vol. 42, No. 5, Special Research Forum on Stakeholders, Social Responsibility, and Performance (Oct. 1999), 479–485

Heskett, J.L., Jones, T.O., Loveman, G.W., Sasser, W.E. and Schlesinger, L.A. (1994) Putting the service-profit chain to work. *Harvard Business Review*, March–April, 164–174

Hillman, A. and Keim, G. (2001) Shareholder value, stakeholder management, and social issues: what's the bottom line? *Strategic Management Journal*, Vol. 22, 125–139

Huber, M. and O'Gorman, S. (eds) (2008) *From Customer Retention to a Holistic Stakeholder Management System*. Berlin: Springer

Johnston, R. (2003) *Delivering Service Excellence: The View from the Front-line*. Institute of Customer Service, Warwick: Warwick Business School

Kaplan, R. and Norton, D. (1993) Putting the Balanced Scorecard to work. *Harvard Business Review*, September–October, 134–147

Kordupleski, R. with Simpson, J. (2003) *Mastering Customer Value Management: The Art and Science of Creating Competitive Advantage*. Cincinnati: Pinnaflex Educational Resources

Lencioni, P.M. (2002) Make your values mean something. *Harvard Business Review*, 1 July

Miller, R.B. and Heiman, S.E., with Tuleja, T. (2005) *The New Strategic Selling*. New York: Warner Business Books

Murphy, J.A. (2001) *The Lifebelt: The Definitive Guide to Managing Customer Retention*. Chichester: John Wiley & Sons Ltd

Murphy, J.A. and Burton, J. (2005) Listen to your frontline staff – they listen to your customers. *Customer Management*, Vol. 13, No. 1, 22–26

Murphy, J.A., Burton, J., Gleaves, R. and Kitshoff, J. (2006) *Converting Customer Value: From Retention to Profit*. Chichester: John Wiley & Sons Ltd

Osborne, D. and Gaebler T. (1992) *Reinventing Government*. Reading, MA: Addison-Wesley

Parasuraman, A., Zeithaml, V.A. and Berry, L.L. (1988), SERVQUAL: a multiple item scale for measuring consumer perceptions of service quality. *Journal of Retailing*, Vol. 64, No. 1, 12–40

Post, J.E., Preston, L.E. and Sachs, S. (2002) *Redefining the Corporation: Stakeholder Management and Organisational Wealth*. Palo Alto: Stanford University Press

Prahalad, C.K. and Ramaswamy, V. (2004) *The Future of Competition: Co-Creating Unique Value with Customers*. Boston: Harvard Business School Press

Reichheld, F.F. (1996) *The Loyalty Effect: The Hidden Force Behind Growth, Profits, and Lasting Value*. Boston: Harvard Business School Press

Rickards, T. and Moger, S. (1999) *Handbook for Creative Team Leaders*. Aldershot: Gower

Rucci, A.J., Kim, S.P. and Quinn, R.T. (1998) The Employee-Customer Profit Chain at Sears. *Harvard Business Review*, January/February, 82–97

Sandberg, J. (2000) Understanding human competence at work: an interpretative approach. *Academy of Management Journal*, 43, 9–25

Scharioth, J. and Huber, M. (eds) (2003) *Achieving Excellence in Stakeholder Management*. Berlin: Springer

Schneider, J. and Yocum, J. (2004) *New Product Launch: 10 Proven Strategies*. Stagnito Communications Inc

Schuppisser, S.W. (2002) *Stakeholder Management*. Bern: Haupt Verlag

Seltzer, J. and Bass, B.M. (1990) Transformational leadership: beyond initiation and consideration. *Journal of Management*, 16, 693–703

Sen, S. and Bhattacharya, C.B. (2001) Does doing good always lead to doing better? Consumer reactions to corporate social responsibility. *Journal of Marketing Research*, 38 (May), 225–243

Sergeant, A. and Frenkel, S. (2000) When do customer contact employees satisfy customers? *Journal of Service Research*, Vol. 3, No. 1, 18–34

Smethurst, S. (2004) The culture of care. *People Management*, Vol. 10, No. 11, 41–43

Sparrow, P.R. (2004) *Growing and Sustaining a Customer-based Culture*. Manchester: Manchester Business School, Literature Review

Sparrow, P.R. and Cooper, C.I. (2003) *The Employment Relationship: Key Challenges for HR*. London: Butterworth-Heinemann

Storbacka, K. (2000) Customer profitability, analysis and design issues. In J. Sheth and A. Parvatiyar (eds), *Handbook of Relationship Marketing*. London: Sage, pp. 565–584

Stroud, D. (2007) *The 50-plus Market*. Kogan Page

Stuart, G. (2007) Missing the mark. *Research World*, March

Sunday Times. The 100 best companies to work for 2007. London

Suntook, F., Gidney, D., Fredericks, J. and Rey, T. (2001) *Research for the Bottom Line: Converting What People Say to What People Do*. Paper at Esomar Congress in Rome

Suntook, F. and Murphy, J.A. (1998) Keeping the customer satisfied. *FT Mastering Management Review*

Suntook, F. and Murphy, J.A. (2000) Profiting through segmentation. *Customer Management*

Suntook, F. and Brooke, C. (2002) *From Customer Research to CRM: How Understanding the Customer is the Cornerstone of Effective CRM.* Paper at Esomar Customer Relationship Management Conference in Prague

Suntook, F., Ellinghaus U. and Strange, P. (2003) *Market Research for a New Car Concept.* Paper at Esomar Consumer Insights Conference in Madrid

Szwarc, P. (2005) *Researching Customer Satisfaction and Loyalty (Market Research in Practice).* London: Kogan Page

Turnbull, P.W. and Zolkiewski, J.M. (1997) Profitability in customer portfolio planning. In D. Ford (ed.), *Understanding Business Markets*, 2nd Edition. London: The Dryden Press

Vandermerwe, S. (1996) *The Eleventh Commandment.* Chichester: John Wiley & Sons Ltd

Whitely, P. (2002) *Motivation.* Minnesota: Capstone Publishing

Zenger, J.H. and Folkman, J. (2004) *The Handbook for Leaders: 24 Lessons for Extraordinary Leadership.* New York: McGraw-Hill

INDEX

Note: Page numbers in *italic* type refer to figures.

Index compiled by Lewis Derrick